Public Libraries in Malabar

Public Libraries in Malabar

Dr. Sudha Azhikodan

SERIALS PUBLICATIONS
NEW DELHI (INDIA)

First Published - 2010

ISBN: 978-81-8387-345-1

Published by

SERIALS PUBLICATIONS
4830/24, 1st Floor, Ansari Road
Darya Ganj, New Delhi-110002 (India)
Phone : 23245225. Fax : 91-11-23272135
E-mail: serials@satyam.net.in

In memory of

my beloved father

Com. Azhikodan Raghavan (Late)

CONTENTS

ACKNOWLEDGEMENTS

I record my sincere gratitude to **Dr. Rosamma Joesph,** Deputy Librarian (Retired), University of Calicut, my supervising teacher, for her valuable guidance, helpful criticism, and advice during the entire period of my investigation. I also owe deep debt to **Dr. G. Devarajan,** Professor and Head (Retired), Department of Library and Information Science, University of Kerala for his scholarly help and assistance.

I acknowledge with sincere gratitude and immense pleasure, the guidance and enthusiasm shown in my effort by **Sri. K. Balakrishnan,** Secretary, Kerala State Library Council, **Sri. I. V. Das,** its former Secretary and its staff by providing necessary records and valuable information relevant to my study. I also express my gratitude to **Sri. P. Appaukuttan,** Secretary, and **Sri. P. Ambu** Master, President, District Library Council, Kasaragod; **Sri. P. K. Narayanan,** former Secretary and **Sri. M. Padmanabhan,** President, District Library Council, Kannur; **Sri. V. K. Balan** Master, former Secretary, District Library Council, Kozhikode; **Sri. P.K. Sudheer,** Secretary, District Library Council, Wyanad; **Sri. Ahmad Ali Master** (late), former Secretary, District Library Council, Malappuram; **Sri. V.K. Jayaprakash,** President and **Sri V. Muthu Master,** Secretary, District Library Council, Plalakkad for giving permission to examine the records of the Councils and for providing adequate information for my research work.

I will be failing in my duty unless I express profusely my pleasure and acceptance to several persons who gave abundant information without which the present study would not have been materialized. It is also my privilege to acknowledge and appreciate, besides expressing heartfelt indebtness to **Dr. R. Ramasamy,** Assistant Field Officer (South zone), **Raja Rammohun Roy** (RRRLF) for providing important documents quite relevant for my study and also the help rendered by **Dr. Raju,** Reader, Department of Statistics, University of Calicut for helping me in the statistical analysis.

Finally I would like to state that this work is the outcome of collective, earnest, and effective endeavour of many personalities with rich experience and proven ability in the field of library organization and also I remember them with gratitude.

Dr. Sudha Azhikodan

1

INTRODUCTION

In the past, there was a system of recording and preserving human thoughts and ideas for future generations. This system or institution gradually came to be referred to by the term "library". There are different types of libraries such as public libraries, academic libraries, and special libraries. The essential functions of all libraries are the same, collection, preservation, and dissemination of knowledge. But the basic difference between public libraries and other types of libraries is in the concept that the former are open to all in the community. The term "public" (Latin: publice) means "so as to affect the whole people" (Oxford Latin dictionary).[1]

Public library is an integral part of the community. It has the social obligation to serve the whole community. It is a positive agent for change in the community. Ekbote (1987)[2] states the importance of the library in the community as "a library makes a substantial contribution to socioeconomic changes in a social milieu." Murison (1971)[3] highlighted the great role of public library in a community as "it is a social institution which converts a savage community into a state of civilization." The public libraries are a gateway to better life. They are capable of enriching the human personality and of helping the people to become responsible citizens.

The relationship between the library and the community it serves is of paramount importance. IFLA/UNESCO (1998)[4] declares: The public library service must be adapted to the different needs of communities in rural and urban areas."

Totterdell (1981)[5] stresses the importance of relationship between the public library and community as: "If the library is too responsive to community needs then its involvement with the community must be much greater."

ORIGIN AND DEVELOPMENT OF PUBLIC LIBRARIES IN THE WORLD

In order to understand the evolution of relationship between public libraries and the community, there is a need to understand the very origin and development of public libraries in the modern world. It may be noted that there were well known libraries in the ancient period including those of Alexandria, Mesopotamia, Greece, and Nalanda and Taxashila in India.

Traditional Public Libraries

The concept of libraries is very much related to the nature of society. Generally in a traditional society, knowledge has a very limited role in the life of majority of the population and the available knowledge is controlled by the priest and royal people who constituted an insignificant percentage of the society. Almost all earlier libraries were attached to royal palaces or temples. During this period, parish libraries and monastery libraries were established mainly based on Bible and other religious literary works (Kelly 1966).[6] In the strict sense, these libraries cannot be called public libraries.

Gradually feudal lords and wealthy merchants emerged as socially powerful groups who started to establish and support libraries as a symbol of power and prestige. This is the beginning of public libraries. Thus public libraries extended their service to limited elite of the society other than the priests and royal people (Kelly 1966).[7] During that time a majority of the population remained illiterate and as such public libraries had insignificant roles. With the spread of literacy and education, the society started to recognize the importance of books and public libraries. However, libraries remained very much traditional, limiting their services based on books to an elite class only. In the traditional society, books were the only channel for preserving and communicating knowledge and culture. Their role was passive and it remained static for a very long time without much change.

Modern Public Libraries

The concept of a modern public library originated in Europe in the mid-nineteenth century and later spread to other parts of the world. Great Britain is considered to be the pioneer in the modern library legislation and public library development. The study of modern public libraries can be made by tracing the origin, history and development of public libraries in Great Britain.

Public Libraries in the West

Since Great Britain is basically a Christian country, both monastery libraries and parish libraries played a very important role with regard to religious needs. However, these libraries also maintained a limited stock of secular books. Along with renaissance movement and mercantilism movement, several subscription libraries and guild libraries also emerged. With the improvement of general literacy there was a social demand for free public library movement in Great Britain. As a result, Great Britain emerged as a pioneer in library legislation and free public library movement. Public library movement of Great Britain can be considered as the model of the public library movement in the world. The British experiment influenced other Western countries such as U.S. to develop public library movements in their countries.

Modern Public Libraries emerged as the bye-product of industrial revolution and changing economic and political policies of Great Britain. During this period, guild libraries and commercial lending libraries emerged. Those libraries acted as a catalyst for industrial revolution in Great Britain. With the industrial revolution there was a need for equipping the workers of the factories with new technical knowledge and managerial skills. The industrial workers realized that by acquiring a new technical knowledge, they could shift to the upper strata from the present position. A good number of literate workers became the members of the guild libraries and they also started to make use of the commercial lending libraries. They are considered to be the initiators of the public library system (Kelly 1977).[8] Feather and Sturges (1997)[9] state: "For many years public libraries had a working class image, but in the 1930s this began to change as they increasingly attracted members of the middle class." Public library movement is one of the greatest organisational changes in human history.

RISE AND GROWTH OF PUBLIC LIBRARIES IN INDIA

The modern concept of free library service has come to India from the western countries. During the first half of the nineteenth century there were public libraries in three presidency towns of Bombay, Calcutta, and Madras and in other parts of the country under the active support and initiative of the Europeans in these towns (Jogesh Misra 1979).[10] Calcutta Public Library (1836); Andrews Library, Surat (1850); Gaya Public Library, Gaya (1855); Connemara Public Library, Mdaras (1860); and Adyar Library, Madras (1886) were some of the early established public libraries in India (Pandey 1985).[11]

The first three decades of the twentieth century is considered the golden period in the history of the public libraries in India. In 1903 the Calcutta Public Library was opened by the British for the common man. This library developed later as Imperial Library and still later as the National Library (Kesavan 1961).[12] Almost simultaneous with this development, subscription libraries were started in many cities of the country. Under the effort of Maharaja Sayaji Rao Gaekward III of Baroda, the father of library movement in India, a well structured library system was developed in Baroda (Panda 1993).[13] No such parallel development occurred elsewhere in India during that time.

With the advent of democratic governments in several provinces since 1937, another phase of the library movement started in India. Several village libraries and travelling libraries were established in Assam, Bihar, Punjab, Travancore, Cochin, and Malabar under government patronage between 1937 and 1942 (Ravindran 1990).[14] S.R. Ranganathan introduced the concept of establishing the public library system in India on the firm foundation of law. The involvement of Union government in the public library movement and enactment of public library laws contributed towards the improvement of public libraries after independence.

In the Five Year Plan projects, the government has included several schemes for the development of public libraries in the country. Important developments that occurred under these schemes are the establishment of the Delhi Public library in 1951; the enactment of Delivery of Books (Public Libraries) Act in 1954; appointment of an Advisory Committee for Libraries under the chairmanship of K.P. Sinha by Ministry of Education and Youth Services, Government of India in 1957 to investigate the state of libraries in India; the setting up of a Working Group on Development of Libraries in 1964; the setting up of the Raja Rammohun Roy Library Foundation (RRRLF) under the Department of Culture, Ministry of Education for the development of public libraries in the country in 1972; establishment of a library section in the Department of Culture under

Ministry of Education in 1979; appointment of a Working Group on Modernisation of Library Service and Informatics in 1983; appointment of a committee under the chairmanship of D. P. Chattopadhyaya, Chairman of the RRRLF, Calcutta to draft a National Policy on Information System in October 1985; the setting up of National Literacy Mission in 1986 which emphasized the establishment of rural libraries; and such other activities. During the Plan periods a large amount of financial assistance was made available for the development of public libraries in the country by the Central government (Jagnayak 1999).[15]

MAJOR ROLE OF MODERN PUBLIC LIBRARIES

On the basis of the services rendered by modern public libraries, the major role played by them can be brought under the following headings.

Educational

The role of modern public libraries is to educate every citizen by providing access to their collection in different formats and various services. It supplements formal education and supports the non-formal education and continuing self-education. It is also the best institution for eradication of illiteracy. In developing countries, the vital role of public libraries is to impart basic education to the common people.

Informational

Information is the basic resource for individual and national development. The public library has a key role in collecting, organising, and providing access to a wide range of information resources to meet the heterogeneous needs of the people. The public library has a particular responsibility to collect local information and make it readily available. Thus the public library can act as a community information centre.

Cultural

The public library has an important role in the cultural development of the society. A public library can collect and preserve the cultural heritage of the locality and this will enable the people to enrich their cultural awareness. Public libraries can promote the participation, enjoyment and appreciation of all art forms. The public library can foster culture by stimulating the creative talents and conducting cultural programmes.

Leisure

The public libraries can play a part in encouraging a positive use of leisure and providing materials for change as well as relaxation. Cultural and recreational activities enhance the social, physical and mental development of the people.

Social

The social role of public libraries is the provision of materials and services to the people which will help them to understand the different social conflicts, problems, and the different measures to control them. By eradicating the social evils in the community, the public libraries can establish order in the society. In addition to these, the public library has an important role as a public space and meeting place. Use of the library for various purposes brings people into informal contact with other members of the community and can be a positive social experience.

Developmental

The public library is the most effective instrument for the economic development by disseminating recent information in Agriculture, Industry and related fields.

Political

One of the modern roles of public library is to make contribution to democracy and citizenship through well informed people. The public library is the only agency which can provide a wide and varied range of knowledge, ideas, and opinion through the provision of resources and services in a variety of media to the people; which will enable them to know, defend, and enjoy their rights and realise and discharge their duties in a society.

Thus the public libraries play significant roles in the universal diffusion and enhancement of knowledge among the populace of a nation, in the moral and cultural enrichment, and in the economic, scientific, and industrial development of society.

PUBLIC LIBRARY: DEFINITIONS

The various definitions of public library stress on its crucial role in the society. An appropriate and universally acceptable definition of a public library stated by Mc Colvin (1956)[16] is that "it is provided by the local authority, the town, or county council, entirely or mostly at its own expense; governed and administered by the authority or a committee, wholly or largely appointed by itself; available free of any charge to all who live in its area; and offering a wide selection of materials chosen to embrace as completely as possible the varied interests of the individual and the community, free from bias or religion, political or other motives."

K. P. Sinha (India Ministry of Education and Youth Services 1959),[17] Chairman of the Government of India's Advisory Committee on Libraries describes the public library as "a library which is financed, for the most part, from public funds, and which is intended as an auxiliary educational institution providing a means of self-education, housing learning materials, giving reliable information freely and without partiality or prejudice on a wide variety of subjects as well as satisfying the interests of readers."

Viswanathan (1990)[18] defines it as "a centre of communal study, an information bureau, a continuation school and a training school for democracy."

Kalia, *et.al* (1991)[19] describe public library as "an institution, established and administered under a State law by a local government or an adhoc autonomous library authority or a government department maintained wholly out of public funds, open to all without distinction and free of charge."

The IFLA/UNESCO Public Library Manifesto (1994)[20] define public library as: "The local gateway to knowledge, provides a basic condition for life long learning, independent decision-making and cultural development of the individual and social groups;" and "a living force for education, culture and information, and as an essential agent for the fostering of peace and spiritual welfare through the minds of men and women;"

Feather and Sturges (1997)[21] state: "Libraries that are provided through public funding for public use and the public good are public libraries."

OBJECTIVES OF PUBLIC LIBRARIES

The basic objective of a public library is the circulation of books, which have values and can develop personality to its full potential. Johnson (1938)[22] describes it as "the people's university," capable of extending its services to all groups in the community, irrespective of age, race, colour, nationality, religion, language, states, sex, political conviction, or educational attainments.

The functions of a public library have been precisely stated in the Kenyon Committee Report: "The public library is no longer regarded as a means of providing casual recreation of an innocent but somewhat unimportant character, it is recognised as an engine of great potentialities for national welfare and as the essential foundation for the progress in education and culture without which no people can hold its own in the struggle for existence" (U.K. Board of Education 1927).[23]

The first seminar on "The Development of Public Libraries in Asia" which was held in Delhi under the auspices of UNESCO (1955)[24] concluded with the statement that "the public libraries should be an independent service for use according to the individual needs of the citizen. It can give special assistance in the advancement of technical knowledge and skills by distribution of literature at two levels, advanced and elementary."

According to ALA (1956)[25], the objectives of public libraries are:

1. To facilitate information for self-education of all people in the community;
2. To enrich and further develop the subjects on which individuals are undertaking formal education;
3. To meet the informational needs of all;
4. To support the educational, civic, and cultural activities of groups and organisation;
5. To encourage wholesome recreation and constructive use of leisure time.

The Library Association, London (1971)[26] has stated that the objective of a public library is "to contribute to sustaining the quality of life in all aspects, educational, economic, industrial, scientific, and cultural and promote the concept of a democratic society in which equal opportunity exists for all to develop into true citizens with whole and balanced personalities leading to an increase in the sum total of man's happiness and his environment."

Mc Colvin (1978),[27] carried out a survey of the public library service in Great Britain. He reported that the purpose of the public library is the development of the "whole personality."

The objectives of the public library as enunciated by Ranganathan (1988)[28] are as follows:

1. To help the life-long self-education;
2. To furnish up-to-date facts and information on all subjects;
3. To distribute in an unbiased and balanced way all shades of recorded views and thoughts so as to help in the discharge of political functions in respect of local, national, and international affairs;
4. To contribute to the productivity drive by informing top management of the latest trends in diverse enterprises by ploughing back, promptly, and pin-pointedly into the minds of researchers, designers, and technologists every piece of relevant new thought, promptly and pin-pointedly;
5. To provide a harmless and elevating use of leisure;
6. To preserve the literacy remains of humanity for posterity as vehicles of culture and as source material for antiquarian research; and
7. To work for continued social well being as the agency in charge of all socialised recorded thoughts.

Thus a library has educational, informational, political, economic, industrial, cultural, and antiquarian functions."

The IFLA/UNESCO (1994)[29] outlines four key missions which are at the core of public library services:

1. *Education:* Supporting both individual and self-conducted education as well as formal education at all levels;
2. *Information:* Ensuring access for citizens to all sorts of community information; providing adequate information to local enterprises, associations and interest groups;
3. *Culture:* Promoting awareness of cultural heritage, appreciation of the arts, scientific achievements and

innovations; providing access to cultural expressions of all performing arts; fostering inter-cultural dialogue and favouring cultural diversity; supporting the oral tradition;

4. *Literacy:* Supporting and participating in literacy activities and programmes for all age groups, and initiating such activities if necessary.

The Finnish Library Act (1998)[30] states: "The objective of the library and information services provided by public libraries is to promote equal opportunities among citizens for personal cultivation, for literary and cultural pursuits, for continuous development of knowledge, personal skills and civic skills, for internationalisation, and for life long learning."

The IFLA/UNESCO (2001)[31] states: "The primary purposes of the public library is to provide resources and services in a variety of media to meet the needs of individuals and groups for education, information and personal development including recreation and leisure."

U. K. Department of Culture (2004)[32] lists out the objectives of public libraries inherent in its standards for public libraries as follows:

- They underpin education, providing essential support for school children, students, and life long learners;
- They enhance public access to the world's storehouse of knowledge and information;
- They promote social inclusion, by helping to bridge the gap between those who can afford access to information and those who can't;
- They have a role to play in the modernisation and delivery of public services; and
- They provide information which underpins commercial and economic endeavour.

Various statements on the purpose of public libraries confirm that "the public library makes an essential contribution to democracy and citizenship. It is also vital to a nation's literacy and productivity" (Feather and Sturges 1997).[33]

In order to fulfil their objectives, public libraries should establish resource sharing networks, possess trained manpower, and build up strong need based collections. It must be based on certain standards and methods of evaluation. Co-operative bibliographic service and automation should be introduced. Public libraries have to change their concepts in order to meet the various issues and information needs of the society.

CHANGING CONCEPTS OF PUBLIC LIBRARIES

The very concept of public libraries has undergone drastic changes in the recent period, though it remained almost static for a very long time till the modern information technology revolution. Recent advances in information and communication technology, changing societal attitudes towards information and knowledge and increasing digitalization of libraries have brought about revolutionary changes in the very concept of libraries. Toffler (1980)[34] sees this present technological force as the "third wave" following the previous waves of agricultural and industrial civilizations.

The IFLA/UNESCO (2001)[35] states: "Public libraries have an exciting opportunity to help bring every one into this global conversation and to bridge what is often called 'the digital divide'. They can achieve this by providing information technology for public access, by teaching basic computer skills." The new concept of collection in the public libraries is the blending of traditional and electronic media. Potential users are attracted to the library by the introduction of new services based on new technology. In this new concept of public libraries, the traditional librarians are being replaced by the "knowledge workers" and they are going to be highly-skilled professionals. Public libraries are getting transformed as the open-gate to knowledge so as to exploit the digital resources to the fullest extent, they are championing e-literacy to the masses.

The traditional difference between public libraries, academic libraries, and research libraries has become obsolete. In other words, there is not much difference between all these libraries. The digital connectivity of various types of libraries and the new concept of management of knowledge paved the way for such kinds of revolutionary changes. Through this network, the public libraries enable all citizens to have access to their own resources and to those of other libraries through participation in electronic network at the local, national and increasingly international levels.

STATEMENT OF THE PROBLEM

"Organisation, Administration, Resources, Services, and Utilisation of the Public Libraries in Malabar: An Evaluative Study" is a topic of social value and academic interest in the context of the dynamic role of public libraries in the development of individual and society.

OPERATIONAL DEFINITION OF KEY TERMS

Organisation

Organisation means "the act or process of organizing"; organise means "to form as or into a whole consisting of interdependent or coordinated parts, especially for harmonious or united action" (Webster 1996).[36] Organisation in the public library context means to define the extent and scope of different sections in the public libraries and their activities, which are necessary to carry out the library's plan and purpose and put them into practice.

Administration

Administration means "the management of any office, employment, or organisation" (Webster 1996).[37] Administration in the public library context means the directive functions of administrative machinery at different levels through which the objectives of the libraries are fulfilled.

Resources

Resources mean "sources of supply, support or aid, especially one held in reserve" (Webster 1996).[38] Here the term refers to the information sources including book materials and non-book materials, finance, staff, physical facilities, and technological resources available in the public libraries of Malabar.

Services

Services mean "the act of helpful activity" (Webster 1996).[39] Here the term refers to the different services both in house services and community services offered by the public libraries of Malabar to the people of the area.

Utilisation

Utilisation means "to put to use" (Webster 1996).[40] Here the term refers to the use of various sources and services provided by the public libraries in Malabar to different categories of users.

Public Libraries

A public library is an organisation which provides access to knowledge, information, and works of imagination through a range of resources and services and is equally available to all members of the community regardless of race, nationality, age, gender, religion, language, disability, economic and employment status, and educational attainment' (IFLA/UNESCO 2001).[41] Here the term refers to all public libraries affiliated to the Kerala State Library Council and the public libraries under other governing bodies in the six districts of Malabar.

Malabar

The term "Malabar" denotes the geographical area covered by the northern part of the political map of Kerala comprised of six districts of Kasaragod, Kannur, Kozhikode, Wayanad, Malappuram, and Palakkad.

Evaluative Study

Evaluative means "pertaining to or tending to evaluation" and evaluate means "to determine or set the value or amount of, appraise" (Webster 1996).[42] Study means "application of the mind to the acquisition of knowledge, as by reading, investigation, or reflection" (Webster 1996).[43] Here the evaluative study means the acquisition of data by the investigation to determine how well the public libraries in Malabar/North Kerala are functioning, how good the resources in these libraries are, how appreciated a service is or how thoroughly the community is served to meet the objectives of the public library.

OBJECTIVES OF THE STUDY

The objectives of the present study are:

(1) To study the origin, development, organizational pattern, and present scenario of the public libraries in Malabar;

(2) To evaluate the role played by public libraries in the educational, cultural and socio-political development of Malabar;

(3) To assess the use behaviour of members and their evaluation of public library resources, services, and facilities; and

(4) To visualise the future of public libraries in Malabar by taking into account the emerging needs of the knowledge society and new technological developments.

HYPOTHESES

For the purpose of the present study, the following hypotheses were formulated:

(1) The development of public libraries in Malabar is in a slow pace.

(2) The existing condition of public libraries in Malabar with respect to library resources including staff, finance, physical facilities, and technology are inadequate and not satisfactory to meet the various requirements of the users.

(3) The various services provided by the public libraries are not effective and not efficient to meet the various needs of the users.

(4) The public libraries have contributed more in fulfilling the recreational or cultural needs rather than the informational or educational requirements of the society.

(5) The use of the public library resources and services by the different categories of community is very low.

SIGNIFICANCE OF THE STUDY

The need for this investigation arises from the fact that no comprehensive studies on the existing state of public libraries in Malabar have been conducted. In Malabar, the library movement was mainly a part of the nationalist movement. But in the erstwhile States of Travancore and Cochin, the government had their own role in the genesis and growth of public libraries. Considering the unique characteristics of the library movement in Malabar, and also its socio-economic backwardness in relation to Travancore and Cochin, the genesis and development of public libraries in Malabar together with the current status of public libraries in Malabar have been selected for the present study to find out their social objectives. In developed countries, the public libraries have been particularly active recently in trying to define, measure, and promote library effectiveness. But in India, no such comprehensive evaluative studies have been conducted on the effectiveness of the public libraries. Effectiveness is a major concern in the organisation of all sorts; so in addition to investigate the current status of the public libraries, an attempt is being made to find the effectiveness of this social institution.

The IFLA/UNESCO (1994),[44] recognising the significance of the public libraries through its *Public Library Manifesto* states that "freedom, prosperity, and the development of society and of individual are fundamental human values. They will only be attained through the ability of well-informed citizens to exercise their democratic rights and to plan an active role in society. Constructive participation and the development of democracy depend on satisfactory education as well as on free and unlimited access to knowledge, thought, culture and information. The public library, the local gateway of its knowledge, provides a basic condition for life long learning, independent decision making and cultural development of individual and social groups." The IFLA/UNESCO (1994)[45] also recognises its role as "a living force for education, culture and information, and as an essential agent for the fostering of peace and spiritual welfare through the minds of men and women." In the light of these roles of public libraries in a society, the significance of the present study is confirmed in terms of their dynamic part in the development of community life.

The present study is expected to help the library authorities to adopt the suitable strategies for improving their collection building and providing more efficient library services. It will assist librarians to assess whether the libraries fulfil their various objectives, and how far the libraries are lagging behind in providing satisfactory service to the community. It will remind the librarians of the expected role of public librarianship.

SCOPE AND LIMITATIONS OF THE STUDY

Kerala is the southern most State in India. Two erstwhile States of Travancore and Cochin and Malabar, a district of the erstwhile Madras presidency merged together and formed Kerala State in 1956. Malabar is the northern part of Kerala. The present study is confined to the public libraries in Malabar comprising six revenue districts-Kasaragod, Kannur, Kozhikode, Wayanad, Malappuram, and Palakkad.

The major emphasis of the present study is on public libraries that come under the purview of the State Library Council formed in accordance with the provision of Kerala Public Libraries Act, 1989. They belong to six grades, from A to F. However, there are some public libraries that are working under other governing bodies which do not come under the State Library Council. One well known public library of this type from each district is also included in the present study. However, the study has the following limitations.

There is no well known accepted criteria/standard for evaluating the public libraries at national level. Some guidelines given by the Raja Rammohun Roy Library Foundation (RRRLF), Kolkatta are not comprehensive. In the present study, the investigator makes use of the *IFLA/UNESCO*

Guidelines for Public Library Development, 2001 for assessing the present condition of public libraries in the area under study.

Performance indicators are valuable tools in monitoring the achievements of the library. As there is lack of reliable information, the following key performance indicators such as loans per capita; loans per item; total library visits per capita; unit costs for functions, services, and activities; and total costs per visitor could not be used to evaluate the library. This is also a limitation of the study.

The evaluation of the users on the library resources and services are not always reliable as these are based on their limited needs and views. A majority of the users are not aware of the various roles of public libraries in the community and these may reflect in their perceptions. It should be noted, however, that user evaluation of libraries are an often used tool in library survey.

SAMPLING

In the present study, survey population consists of all public libraries affiliated to the Kerala State Library Council and also the public libraries which come under other governing bodies in the six districts of Malabar and the registered users of these libraries. Purposive sampling was employed to select a sample of libraries and stratified random sampling was employed to take a sample of library members. All the public libraries in the area under study are stratified by grade, year of establishment, geographical location, and different managements and from each of the stratum, a sample of libraries is selected purposefully to attain better representation. The members of these samples of public libraries are stratified by gender, educational level, economic status, and occupational status and from each of the stratum, a sample of members is drawn randomly.

Size of the Sample

Libraries

In Malabar, there are a total of 1973 properly functioning grant-in-aid public libraries under the State Library Council under the period of consideration. Based on the number of books and periodicals including newspapers in the library and circulation of books, these libraries are categorised into six grades, from A to F. There are 179 A grade libraries, 310 B grade libraries, 330 C grade libraries, 389 D grade libraries, 425 E grade libraries, and 340 F grade libraries in the six districts under study. There are also some public libraries under the control of other governing bodies in the area under study. These libraries are not graded and do not get any grant-in-aid from the State Library Council.

A sample of 15% of libraries in A grade and 10% of libraries in each of B to F grade from each district under study representing different years of establishment, geographical location, and different managements were selected. Since A grade libraries are providing more services to the users than libraries in other grades, and since all these services have to be incorporated for the study, a larger sample from A grade libraries was selected for the survey. One well known public library under other governing bodies from each district was also taken as a sample. Altogether, a sample of 214 libraries was selected for the study. The break-up of the libraries selected as sample, grade-wise is given in Table 1.

Table 1
Break-up of Sample of Libraries (Grade-wise)

Grade	*Total No. of Libraries*	*Sample*	*Percentage*
Libraries under the State Library Council			
A	179	28	15.0
B	310	31	10.0
C	330	33	10.0
D	389	39	10.0
E	425	43	10.0
F	340	34	10.0
Total	1973	208	10.5
Libraries under Other Governing Bodies	-	6	-
Total Sample		214	

Members

According to the records of the District Library Councils, there are a total number of 5, 12, 316 members in the public libraries under the State Library Council in the six districts under study. There are 37, 229 members in Kasaragod; 1, 86, 518 in Kannur; 1, 26, 462 in Kozhikode; 32, 424 in Wayanad; 68, 499 in Malappuram; and 61, 184 in Palakkad. A sample of 0.5% of members of the libraries in each district representing both genders, different educational levels, economic status, and occupational status were taken for the study. A representative sample of 15 library members were also taken from each of the selected libraries under other governing bodies. Altogether, a sample of 2651 members was taken for the study. The break-up of the sample of library members, district-wise is furnished in Table 2.

Table 2
Break-up of Sample of Library Members (District-wise)

	Libraries under the State Library Council			*Libraries under Other Governing Bodies*			
District	*Total No. of Members*	*Sample*	*%*	*Total No. of Members*	*Sample*	*%*	*Total No. of Sample*
Kasaragod	37, 229	186	0.5	-	15	-	201
Kannur	1, 86, 518	933	0.5	-	15	-	948
Kozhikode	1, 26, 462	632	0.5	-	15	-	647
Wayanad	32, 424	162	0.5	-	15	-	177
Malappuram	68, 499	342	0.5	-	15	-	357
Palakkad	61, 184	306	0.5	-	15	-	321
Total	5,12,316	2,561	0.5	-	90	-	2651

METHODS OF DATA COLLECTION

In the present investigation, a survey was conducted for the collection of data regarding organisation, administration, resources, and services of public libraries in Malabar. This method was also employed to collect data regarding the use pattern of members and their evaluation of public libraries. In the survey, four different questionnaires in the regional language Malayalam were designed for collection of data. They are: (1) To the secretary/president of the six district library councils under study, to get a profile of public libraries affiliated to the council; (2) To the librarians of the selected libraries in Malabar, to collect data related to their functions and operations; and (3) To the adult members and (4) To the child members under 15 years old, to collect data regarding their use behaviour and for assessing the user evaluation of the library resources and services.

In addition, personal interview with librarians, field observation, and examination of library records were also used to collect the data and to examine the problems in their real and correct perspective. The researcher also incorporated documentary analysis and interview with personalities actively involved in the library movement to gather information regarding the history and development of public libraries in Kerala particularly in Malabar. The data collected is for the year 2003-04.

STATISTICAL ANALYSIS

The data collected for the study were analysed using the statistical package SPSS (Version 12). Statistical measures like mean, median, mode, variance, and standard deviation were calculated for all the study variables. Testing problems were solved using chi-square tests.

APPROACHES TO EVALUATION

According to Lynch and Yang (2001),[46] the most comprehensive definition of evaluation is given by Hernone and McClure in *Evaluation and Library Decision Making,* which states that "the process of identifying and collecting data about specific services or activities, establishing criteria by which their success can be assessed, and determining both the quality of the service or activity and the degree to which the service or activity accomplishes stated goals and objectives." In times of rapid and profound societal and technological change, evaluation is essential to preserving the viability and visibility of libraries. Evaluation of the library resources and services is essential to the survival of the library itself which leads to better quality and enhanced efficiency. Study of information needs and satisfaction surveys, and performance indicators are valuable tools for evaluation of libraries. The performance indicators such as total stock per capita, average cost of books, per capita income of the libraries, per capita expenditure for reading materials on literate population, per capita expenditure for reading materials on members, per capita expenditure on staff, and percentage of members in the total literate population are used for the evaluation of public libraries in the area under study.

Two approaches to the evaluation of public libraries were applied for this study. They are (1) the expertise-oriented approach in which judgments were made based on a standard and (2) the objective-oriented approach in which objectives of public libraries are specified and the extent to which they have been achieved are determined (Lynch 1998)[4]. The *IFLA/ UNESCO Guidelines for Public Library Development, 2001* which embrace *UNESCO Public Library Manifesto,* is used for expertise-oriented approach. IFLA/UNESCO (2001)[5] states in the introductory part: "The introduction to the 1973 Standard stated that separate standards were not considered desirable, since the general objectives in all countries were the same, the modifying factor being the pace at which development could take place." In accordance with this statement, the *IFLA/ UNESCO Guidelines for Public Library Development, 2001* which is an internationally useful tool to make judgments about value or worth of public library services are employed in this study. These international standards assume that national and local variations will lead to local difference in the resource criteria. So no specific numbers of resources are included in this standard except on collection development, where specific quantitative standards for collections are presented.

In objective-oriented approach, the evaluator gathers evidence of programme outcomes and compares the actual performance against the programme objectives. The IFLA/ UNESCO (1998)[6] outlines four key missions which should be at the core of the public library services are: (1) Education,

(2) Information, (3) Cultural and (4) Literacy. These four basic objectives are specified for evaluation in the objective-oriented approach in this study. This is a relatively straight forward assessment of the success or failure in achieving the objectives of public libraries.

ANALYSIS OF THE DATA

The data collected through various methods discussed above are analysed using suitable statistical tools and the report of the study is presented in chapters 3, 4, 5, 6, and 7.

ORGANISATION OF THE STUDY

The present study has been organised under eight chapters.

Chapter 1 of the present study is an introduction that presents the general background to public libraries which also includes the origin and development of public libraries in the world, rise and growth of public libraries in India, major role of modern public libraries, public library-its various definitions and objectives, and the exploration of the changing concepts of public libraries. It also presents statement of the problem, operational definition of key terms, the objectives of the study, the hypotheses formulated, the significance of the study, the scope and limitations, sampling procedure employed in the study, size of the sample, methods used to collect the data, statistical tools used for the analysis of the data collected, and the two approaches to evaluation applied for the study, and organisation of the study.

Chapter 2 furnishes a review of literature related to the research area.

Chapter 3 traces the genesis and development of public libraries in Kerala and focuses on Malabar.

Chapter 4 presents the general characteristics of the sampled libraries. It also evaluates the current status of the libraries in terms of organisation; resources such as collection, finance, manpower, technology, and physical facilities; visitors and members; and administration.

Chapter 5 examines the various activities and services provided in the public libraries such as lending service;

reference service; referral service; educational services; information services; services for different sections of the society such as children and women; mobile library service; literacy activities; services to disadvantaged and ethnic groups; various cultural programmes; and other activities such as user education, co-operation with other organisations, resource sharing, and literary activities. The working days and opening hours of the libraries are also analysed in this chapter. The main problems faced by the librarians in the proper functioning of the libraries are listed out at the end of this chapter. These services offered by the public libraries are evaluated to find out whether they play significant roles in educational, cultural and socio-political development of the society.

Chapter 6 analyses the individual characteristics of library members, their use behaviour and the perceptions of them on resources and services of the public libraries.

Chapter 7 presents the findings of the study, analyses and interprets the data collected to test the hypotheses formulated for the study. The suggestions for the improvement of the existing library system in Malabar are also incorporated in this chapter. The future of public libraries is also outlined in this chapter. Areas of further study are also given at the end to guide the future researchers.

Notes and References

(*Note:* The Chicago Manual of Style, 15th Ed. has been followed in compiling the reference list in all chapters).

1. *Oxford Latin Dictionary*, 1512.
2. Ekbote, Gopal Rao (1987), *Public Libraries System*. Hyderabad: Ekbote Brothers, 24.
3. Murison, W. J. (1971), *The Public Library: Its Origin, Purpose and Significance*. 2nd rev. ed London: George G. Harrap, 11.
4. IFLA/UNESCO (1998), *Public Library Manifesto, 1994,* rev. version. The Hague: IFLA. *http://www.unesco.org.,* para 5.
5. Totterdell, Barry (1981), Public Libraries in a Changing Society. In *Public library policy*. Ed. K. C. Harrison, 37- 42. New York: K.G. Saur, 40.

6. Kelly, Thomas (1966), *Early Public Libraries*. London: The Library Association, 17.
7. *Ibid.*, 127-129.
8. Kelly, Thomas (1977), *Books for the People: An Illustrated History of the British Public Library*. London: Andre Deutsh.
9. Feather, John and Paul Sturges (1997), *International Encyclopedia of Information and Library Science*. London: Routledge, 380.
10. Jogesh Misra (1979), *History of Libraries and Librarianship in Modern India since, 1850*. Delhi, Atma Ram, 19.
11. Pandey, S. K. Sharma (1985), *Public Libraries in India*. New Delhi, Ess Ess Publications, 9.
12. Kesavan, B. S. (1961), *Indian National Library*. Calcutta: National Library, 13.
13. Panda, B. D. (1993), *Handbook of Public Library System*. New Delhi, Anmol, 23.
14. Ravindran, K. (1990), Public Libraries in India. In *Public Library System*. Ed. C.A. Augustin and G. Devarajan, 1-7. New Delhi, Ess Ess Publications, 3.
15. Jagnayak, S. S. (1999), Public Library Development in India: An Historical Perspective since 1947. In *Fifty Years of Indian Librarianship*. Ed. G. Devarajan, 41-74. N. Delhi, Ess Ess Publications.
16. Mc Colvin, Lionel R. (1956), *The Chance to Read*. London: Phoenix House, 12.
17. India. Ministry of Education and Youth Services (1959), *Report* of the Advisory Committee for Libraries. New Delhi, Ministry of Education, 32.
18. Viswanathan, C. G. (1990), *Public Library Organisation*. 4th ed. New Delhi, Ess Ess Publications, 6.
19. Kalia, D. R., *et. al.* (1991), Guidelines for Public Library Systems and Services. *Granthana* 2, No.1 (January), 31-84.
20. IFLA/UNESCO, *op. cit.*, 4, para 1.
21. Feather, John and Paul Sturges, *op. cit.*, 9.
22. Johnson, Alvin. 1938. *The public library: A people's university*. New York: American Association for Adults, 61.
23. U.K. Board of Education. Public Libraries Committee. 1927. *Report on Public Libraries in England and Wales*. London: H.M. Stationery Office, 37.

24. UNESCO (1955), *Proceedings of the International Seminar on Development of Public Libraries in Asia,* 6-26 October, Delhi, 23.
25. ALA (1956), Public Library Division. Co-ordinating Committee on Revision of Public Library Standards. *Public Library Service: A Guide to Evaluation with Minimum Standards.* Chicago: ALA, 4.
26. Library Association, London. Public Libraries Research Group. (1971), Public Library Aims and Objectives. *Library Association Record* 73, No. 12 (December).
27. Mc Colvin, Lionel R. (1978), The Purpose and Values of Library Service. In *Public Library Purpose: A Reader.* Ed. Barry Totterdell, 33-37. London: Clive Blingley, 36.
28. Ranganathan, S. R. (1988), *Library Manual.* 2nd ed. New Delhi, UBSPD, 21.
29. IFLA/UNESCO, *op. cit.,* 4, para 3.
30. Finnish Library Act, 1998. In *Public Library Service: IFLA/UNESCO Guidelines for Development,* 89-99. Munchen: K. G. Saur, 2001, c., 1.
31. IFLA/UNESCO (2001), Section of Public Libraries. *Public Library Service: IFLA/UNESCO Guidelines for Development.* Munchen, K.G. Saur, Sec. 1.3.
32. U. K. Department of Culture. Media and Sports. Libraries, Information and Archives Division. 2004. *Library Standards. http://www.culture.gov.uk/NR/ rdonlyres/.../o/ Librarystandardscons.pdf,* 4.
33. Feather, John and Paul Sturges, *op. cit.,* 9, 381.
34. Toffler, Alvin (1980), *The Third Wave.* New York: William Morris, 361.
35. IFLA/UNESCO, *op. cit.,* 31, xiv.
36. Webster's Encyclopedic Unabridged Dictionary of the English Language, 1996, 1014.
37. *Ibid.,* 19.
38. *Ibid.,* 1221.
39. *Ibid.,* 1304.
40. *Ibid.,* 1575.
41. IFLA/UNESCO, *op. cit.,* 31, Sec. 1.2.
42. Webster, *op. cit.,* 36, 493.

43. *Ibid.,* 1411.
44. IFLA/UNESCO, *op. cit.,* 4, para.1.
45. *Ibid.*
46. Lynch, Beverly P. and Wenxiang Yang (2001), Evaluation of Public Libraries: The 2001 IFLA Standards and the 2003 Standards for Provincial Libraries in China. *Libri.,* 54: 179-189.

2

REVIEW OF RELATED STUDIES

INTRODUCTION

Review of related studies helps to bring clarity and broaden the knowledge base in the subject area. The review shows that many studies were conducted in India and abroad to examine the different aspects of public libraries. The review of these studies were made under different headings such as public library movement, library development, library collections, library finance, library services, public library special services, use and user study, computerisation of public libraries, role of public libraries, collaborations with other institutions, evaluation of public library effectiveness, and public libraries Acts.

PUBLIC LIBRARY MOVEMENT

Ramanujan Nair (1974)[1] has traced the history of library movement in Kerala. He describes its beginning, organisational movement, the objectives and programmes of the Kerala Granthasala Sanghom, and its administrative set up. He has also examined the several attempts at public library legislation. His study revealed that the Trivandrum Public Library, established in 1829 is the first public library in Kerala. The organised movement arose in Kerala with the establishment of Malabar Vayanasala Sanghom in Malabar in 1937. Travancore Granthasala Sanghom, which was established in 1945, was converted into Kerala Granthasala Sanghom and its services were extended in Kerala. It stressed the need for library legislation as it would facilitate collection of finance, standard and adequate library service, and also administrative efficiency.

Menon (1974)[2] has traced the early history of Trivandrum Public library. He gives an account of the different opinions about the year of its establishment, its founders, its different locations, recognition of it by the State, conversion of it into people's library before 1878, transfer of it to the government in 1898, and construction of the new building in 1902 in commemoration of diamond jubilee of Queen Victoria in 1897. It has been reported that the most important event in the early history of Trivandrum Public Library is the take over of the library by the government in 1898 and the opening of its membership to the public.

Hamsath (1979)[3] sketches out the public library movement in the union territory of Lakshadweep and the important events highlighted by the author are: (1) At first Lakshadweep Central Library was located in Calicut, where the Lakshadweep secretariat was situated initially; (2) At present, besides the State Central Library, there is one rural library in each island; (3) All the libraries have trained librarians; (4) Libraries are administrated by the Social Welfare Wing, and the Social Welfare Officer, Lakshadweep; and 5) Sole source of income of the public libraries is the government grant.

John and V. K. G. Nair (1979)[4] have given an account of public library movement in Kerala and their study has documented the following events: (1) Public library movement in Kerala started in 1829 with the establishment of Trivandrum public library, (2) The establishment of Malabar Vayanasala Sanghom (1937) and Granthasala Sanghom (1945) has contributed much to the growth of public libraries, (3) Under local library authorities several libraries were established in Malabar, and (4) In 1979 there were nearly 4000 libraries in Kerala.

Ramachandra Rao (1981)[5] has mentioned that the national factors such as the advent of English education, emergence of the educated elite, the Swadeshi movement and the spread of liberal and democratic ideas were the roots of the library movement in Andhra. The events such as the passing of Madras Public Libraries Act, 1948; the role of Hyderabad Library Association led to the enactment of Hyderabad Public Libraries Act, 1955 and Andhra Pradesh Public Libraries Act, 1960.

Shantaram (1985)[6], in the historical study of public libraries in Western Mahasrashtra, from 1805 to 1921 has highlighted that: (1) All the libraries established up to 1805 were manuscript libraries mostly in Sanskrit and Marathi language; (2) In 1830, Bombay General Library was established; in 1838, Ahmednagar Native Library and in 1845, Bombay Native General Library were established; (3) By the end of 1880, about 100 libraries were established in 78 towns, with the encouragement of Government of Bombay; and (4) By 1921 the number of libraries was increased to 227.

Job (1990)[7] has surveyed the historical development of public libraries in Ethiopia. The survey states that the libraries in the modern sense started to appear in Ethiopia only in 1930. The study describes the activities of National Library, branch libraries, City Council Library, and British Council Library and says that 16 branch libraries were established between 1967 and 1986. It outlines the Addis Ababa Municipality Plan for the development of public libraries in municipal area which visualises to establish one central library and five zonal libraries with in a period of three years, and to establish 25 libraries within a period of 10 years. It also states that 9, 457 reading rooms were established mainly intended for the benefit of neo literates in the locality. The general set up of and the role played by the Ethiopian Library Association in bringing the various aspects pertaining to the libraries to the notice of the authorities concerned has also been described.

Sewa Singh (1991)[8] has traced the historical development of libraries in Punjab during the 19th century and early 20th century. There is also an attempt to analyse the role of libraries in the society. The study critically looked at the facilities such as building, collection, services and finance. It mentioned the role played by the voluntary organisations and the Punjab

Library Association in the library development. It revealed that the development of library services was lop-sided because of its greater emphasis on cities and towns than on villages. The study offered various suggestions for improvement of the library services in Punjab.

Wiele (1991)[9] has described the historical development of public libraries in France since 1789. The study states that the land mark in the public library development after the Second World War was the creation of the Directorate for Libraries and the setting up of reading club in the public libraries from the fifties onwards. Different types of public libraries such as city libraries, rural public libraries are mentioned and their collection, user services, finance, and membership have been discussed in detail. It is pointed out that the libraries in urban and rural libraries are very modest and there exists an effective structured network.

Pasilithil (1992)[10] has evaluated the history of public libraries in Kerala during the pre and post Granthasala Sanghom period. He has traced out the origin and development of the mass movement and assessed its contribution in the socio-cultural fields. In order to study the socio-cultural relations of the libraries with the society, a survey has been conducted. The study indicated that Sanghom enabled rural populace to form their opinions on the social, political, and economic problems of the society and it contributed much to the elegance of the social fabric of Kerala.

Anis Khurshid (1998)[11] has traced the history of the library movement in the city of Karachi (Pakistan) with emphasis on Karachi Library Board whicn designed the library system in the city. The salient features of the Education Policy (1972-80) and its impact on public libraries have been described. He draws attention to the findings of the survey in the seven public libraries in Karachi in 1975 which revealed that the status of all the public libraries in respect of their resources, services, and physical facilities were poor and the use of the public libraries was diminishing. The study traces the three phases of Karachi municipal libraries development, the first phase from 1947-1970, the second phase from 1970-78, and the third phase from 1979-87; and also examines the position of municipal libraries in Karachi in 1994.

Kalia (1998)[12] has enlisted seven different public library systems in India. The first system is the Local Bodies System, under which the British government in India entrusted public libraries to the local bodies with the expenditure on public libraries being met from the consolidated fund of the local body concerned. The second system is termed the Library Cess System with Local Library Authorities. In this system, library cess is levied on property tax which has to be collected by the local bodies in their areas and then passed on to the Local Library Authorities (LLAs). LLAs are the provision of Madras Public Libraries Act (1948). The third system is called the system of State Library Autonomous Board with, in which statutory State councils are empowered to select and buy books. The Andra Pradesh Public Libraries Act belongs to this system. In the fourth system, there are subscription libraries in which an annual subscription and a deposit to finance are charged. Employees of the subscription libraries are paid by the government. Public libraries of Maharashtra and West Bengal belong to this system. In the fifth system, public libraries are entrusted to the local bodies by authorising each one of them to levy library cess with the approval of government, collect the same and disburse it. Public libraries of Haryana belong to this system. The Kerala Public Libraries Act belongs to the sixth system. This Act creates a three-tier system namely State Library Council, District Library Council for each district and a Taluk Library Union for each taluk. All grants to individual libraries are routed through the council at a pre-determined rate. Public libraries run as governmental institutions belong to the seventh system. A majority of them has directorates of public libraries under a director or a superintendent as in Bihar. The entire expenditure is met by the governments. It is suggested that a model bill, which can offer one system which should have constitutional and legal support might be adopted by the State governments.

Jones (2005)[13] has traced the genesis and growth of public library movement in New South Wales (Australia). The study pointed out that the first move into free public library services was made with the opening of the Melbourne Public Library. He has also highlighted the impact of the Public Library Act in the development of public libraries in New South Wales. By the end of 1946, a quarter of the three million inhabitants of New South Wales were being served by free public library. In 1950s and 1960s more and more local authorities adopted the Library Act and set up free library services.

PUBLIC LIBRARY DEVELOPMENT

Odini (1990)[14] has pointed out the need for and the role of the public libraries, and the planning cycle that could be applied in the management of public library development. He has stressed the importance of assessment of the needs of library users and the evaluation of current library services and resources in the planning process.

Singh (1991)[15] has assessed the current status of public libraries in Bihar. He discusses in detail the position of public libraries in different levels of State, divisional, district, sub-divisional, block, and village. He also deals briefly with the activities of library associations in Bihar, training in librarianship, the library services, and the administrative structure of the libraries. This analytical report states that the reason for poor performance in this sector seems to be the low literacy rate and dearth of fund.

Bouri (1994)[16] has described the development and current decline of public libraries in Egypt. Egyptian public libraries have been in decline since the late 1960s because of an overall policy which directed the Egyptian government to shift the developmental priorities from education for development towards a new development priority referred to as "information for development". The new priority has subsequently oriented the Egyptian government towards building national information infrastructures for decision-making, overshadowing the earlier assumption that public libraries were central to development.

Sahib Singh Verma (2002), [17] in his survey of the existing conditions of public libraries in Delhi, Haryana, and Rajasthan examines the effect of the library legislation in the development of public libraries and the role of public libraries in literacy movement. The study revealed that: (1) The role of public libraries has not been realised much in the rural areas as compared to the urban areas, (2) Public libraries have contributed more in fulfilling the recreational/cultural rather than the information/educational requirements of the society, (3) A majority of the public libraries are not associated with literacy programmes, (4) Only big libraries have their own buildings, and 5) Public library reading materials and services are not based on the needs of the community.

Jones (2004)[18] has outlined in detail the critical issues in public library building planning in New South Wales. The study recommends that (1) the variety of user needs should be taken into account while planning the library buildings and (2) growth areas of the public library building should include group study, training, volunteers, meetings and seminars, exhibitions and other public programmes. The study revealed that 1) there are 392 public library building in New South Wales ranging in size from under a hundred square meters to over 5500 square meters, and 2) funding new library building has never been easy in New South Wales.

Hennen's (2005)[19] survey report on American public libraries has indicated that (1) in the State Plains there were 1655 public libraries, the highest in U.S. and in Far West there were only 476 public libraries, the lowest in the country; and totally there were 9211 public libraries in U.S. (2) an average of 1.2 square footage per capita buildings was constructed in U.S. for public libraries; (3) 95% of the libraries spent less than $ 10.52 per item circulated; (4) on an average, libraries spent per capita of $0.66 on electronic materials, while the spending per print item use averaged per capita of $0.81; and (5) an average of six computer terminals for every 10,000 residents was provided.

LIBRARY COLLECTIONS

Doll's (1984)[20] study of overlap and duplication among children's collections in selected public and elementary school libraries was conducted in four Illinois communities with populations between 25,000 and 40,000. One public library and two elementary school libraries have been surveyed in each community. Two hundred book titles have randomly been selected from the shelf lists of the libraries and the lists were compiled of magazines, science filmstrips, and fiction sound recordings. Analysis of the data indicated that overlap is linear and positively correlated to collection size, but there is no apparent relationship between collection size and duplicate titles. The demand is the criterion used to purchase duplicate copies. No library subscribed to duplicate copies of magazines. The study indicated that co-operation would be more practical than merging the libraries.

Serebnick and Quinn (1995)[21] have conducted a study to develop a method for measuring diversity of opinion in public library collections in OCLC (Online Computer Library Centre). For this purpose four potentially controversial subject areas were investigated viz. abortion, capital punishment, disarmament or arms control, and euthanasia. Testing the method included analysing the questionnaires, the library holdings of books and the audiovisual materials, publishing and reviewing patterns, and the checklists from Special Interest Groups (SIGs). The important findings of this study are: (1) 78.3% of respondents considered diversity of public library collections as "very important", (2) Librarians have difficulties in selecting and acquiring diverse materials on certain subjects, and (3) The librarians were much more willing than the general public to include potentially controversial materials in subjects. According to this study, Special Interest Groups (SIG) serve as useful resources of selection aids for potentially controversial titles and it was broad in scope and not subject to investigator bias.

Cole (2000)[22] has examined the influence of librarians and the attitudes of elected members and library users on the availability of materials in public libraries in United Kingdom. The study was carried out in six British Library Authorities. The primary method of data collection was in-depth interview with 76 persons including 24 librarians, 10 elected council members and 42 library users. The interview data were supplemented by data generated by a questionnaire. The important findings of the study are: c1) A majority of the respondents agreed that stock management should be conducted according to a philosophy of intellectual freedom; (2) A majority of the respondents stated that stock management decisions should relate to local council policy; (3) In all six library authorities, librarians restrict access to materials that they believe, it might stimulates negative or unfavourable actions or attitudes; (4) Seventeen librarians working in all authorities surveyed said that they had restricted access to materials if their presence on the open shelves caused problems for them, or if materials of similar type had previously been problematic; (5) Five librarians observed that their stock management decision was influenced by their desire to avoid potentially negative media coverage; and (6) Twelve librarians cited lack of money as a barrier to conducting stock management in accordance with the principle of intellectual freedom.

LIBRARY FINANCE

Goudy (1982)[23] has provided an overview of the history of General Revenue Sharing (GRS) and focused on the contribution of the funds to public libraries in U.S.A. The first objective of the study was to determine the allocation of GRS fund to public libraries during the fiscal years 1973 through 1977. The second objective was to estimate the fiscal impact of these funds on public libraries. The study revealed that (1) the libraries received $ 374.55 million during the five year period under consideration, (2) the libraries acquired a greater proportion of revenue sharing funds relative to their normal share of total government expenditures, and (3) nearly two-thirds of the GRS funds were used for development, maintenance of programmes and services.

Guruswamy Naidu (1990)[24] has critically analysed the trend and pattern of financing of public libraries in Andra Pradesh. The study indicated that (1) no district in the State spends optimum on reading materials; (2) the expenditure on the staff is not optimum; (3) though cess is a major source of revenue, the yield has been unsatisfactory; and (4) the per-capita revenue does not provide an encouraging picture.

Ramaiah's (1993)[25] critical perspective on public library finance in India has stressed that public libraries required mandate of law and adequate finance for their efficient functioning, growth, and sustenance. Various aspects of the financial provisions were discussed. It was suggested that a proportional method of providing a certain percentage either of the education budget or the regular State budget for the public library development is advisable.

Merrifield (1995)[26] has discussed two funding sources for the rural libraries in USA which are Federal and State. It discussed the first federal public library grant-in-aid programme, the Library Services Act and its amended act called the Library Services and Construction Act (LSCA) and their funding levels to the rural libraries in USA from fiscal year 1964 to fiscal year 1992. It discussed three types of State aid to meet required standards, to support the operation of multi type library systems or networks, and to assist in the construction of public library buildings. The comparison of State funding shows that in 1989, per capita State funding for the large urban libraries is nearly five times than for the smallest libraries. It also traced the historical background of State role in aiding public libraries in U.S. which goes back to 1835, in which year New York adopted a law authority for each district to levy tax for the establishment of a public library collection. It revealed that all funding sources are critical to the survival of rural libraries.

LIBRARY SERVICES

Sarada (1986)[27] has conducted an intensive study of Branch Library in Pendurthi village in Visakhapatnam taluk and district (Andhrapradesh). This study also analysed the information needs of the village community and examined the nature of the policy of the government towards the public library. For this purpose three sets of structured questionnaires were distributed, one for the deposit holders of the library, the other for the visitors-cum-readers of the library, and yet another for the non-users of the library. The findings of this study are: (1) Telugu fiction occupies a large portion of the collections; (2) 80% of the loaned books are novels, short stories and other forms of fiction; (3) A stationary group uses the library frequently for reading newspapers and magazines; (4) A large percentage of the people (79.79%) who belong to the middle class in term of social and economic status use the library; (5) The educational, social, informational and cultural functions of the library have been almost completely neglected; and (6) Since the library functions as a government agency, it provides information about citizens and the programmes of the government.

Richardson (1987)[28] has surveyed children's services of public libraries in Illinois in 1977 and 1987 and found that (1) the children's room is open on an average of 41 hours per week, (2) expenditure for children's books and magazines represents an average of 28% of the total expenditure for books and magazines of the libraries, (3) children's books represent 33% of the total book collection of the libraries, (4) the average number of children's books in the collection is about 10000, (5) children's materials account for 37% of the total circulation of the libraries, and 6) 85% of the libraries in the State have at least one story hour for children. The study indicated the ranges in the extent and quality of public library services in U.S.

Saiful Islam (1990)[29] has carried out a research on the current status and structure of public library systems and services in Great Britain and Bangladesh. It evaluates the British public library systems, passage of various Acts, various library authorities, total number of public libraries, constituent libraries, computerised acquisition, cataloguing, classification, literature search, and library finance. Major differences in library services between the two countries were brought out and recommendations for developing an effective public library service in Bangladesh were made.

Ottensmann, *et al.* (1995)[30] have examined the patterns of circulation of adult books in the public library branches and the distribution of circulation across subject categories for the Indianapolis Marion County Public Library. The analysis of the data revealed that the distribution and circulation across various categories of adult books were very similar among the various branches, and were weakly related to the social and economic characteristics of the populations served by the branches. Adult fiction accounted for the largest share of the circulation over one quarter of the total. The findings also indicated that at least some of the differences in circulation patterns between branch libraries might be due to the variations in the interests of individual patrons of those branches rather than to systematic variations in the broader interests of the community using the branches. The study led to the conclusion that people who read and borrow books from the public libraries seem to share a broad common set of interests. This study had important implications for materials selection and materials acquisition budgeting.

Wigg (1995)[31] has examined rural library services to young people in New York State. These services include collection of quality materials, providing culturally diverse materials, working with preschoolers, assisting students, conducting summer reading clubs, and giving computer literacy. The study concludes with the suggestion that a rural library action plan is needed to overcome the barriers which prevent rural librarian from making use of existing resources.

Aslam (1998)[32] recognised the importance of rural libraries to be reshaped as Community Information Centres. A retrospect of rural libraries in India is traced back from 1910 when free public libraries were established in Baroda; discusses the present scenario in selected States such as Karnataka and Kerala; emphasises the need for strengthening the rural libraries to shoulder new responsibilities for the socio-economic development. It identifies the following main objectives of Community Information Centres (CIS): (1) Provide easy access to necessary information to enable rural people to effectively participate in the process of development, (2) Serve as centre for educational and cultural activities, (3) Provide access to non-print media such as radio,

TV, audio-video tapes particularly for those who lack study skill, and (4) Develop the effective communication strategy with appropriate media mix such as print material, charts and graphics, posters, non-print media to educate the rural populace.

Padmamma *et al.* (2001)[33] have conducted a study of the public library service for women in the Chickmangalore City Central library, Karnataka. The necessary data for this study were collected through interviews of and questionnaires to the women users of Chickmangalore City Central Library. The results of the study pointed out that (1) almost all respondents were satisfied with the collection of books, magazines, and newspapers and 58.33% were satisfied with the borrowing facility and (2) the library did not provide the user services such as new arrivals display, inter library loan, paper clipping service, reference service, over night issue, and book exhibition.

Vijayakumar and Kumar (2001)[34] have made quantitative study on the different aspects of rural libraries such as functions, staff, finance, collections, services and facilities in Shimoga district of Karnataka. The important findings of the study are: (1) None of the rural libraries under study had any permanent, professional or semi professional library staff; (2) Four libraries had a library committee and other 11 rural libraries did not have library committee; (3) All rural libraries under the study got financial support from the district central library, 5 libraries received fund through Raja Rammohun Roy Library Foundation and only one rural library enjoyed financial source from the grama panchayath; (4) Maximum collection was of novels, and maximum reference collection of biographies; (5) All the rural libraries had adopted their own system of classification, no library maintained any library catalogue; (6) None of the rural libraries had mass media like Radio, TV, Projectors or computers; and (7) None of the libraries had its own building and was in good condition. The investigators have suggested that the Department of Public Libraries should have more concern for upgrading the rural libraries.

Malarvele and Higgins (2003)[35] have explored the provision of public library services to the Tamil community through the

National Library Board of Singapore's system of public libraries. The methodology employed in this study was the focus group interview technique comprising of 12 participants aged between 14 and 65. The important findings of the study are: (1) All twelve participants visited the library at least once a month, (2) Eight participants proposed that all magazines should be placed in the lending section, (3) Four participants felt that library could develop non-print materials for children in Tamil, (4) Eight participants said that the reference collection in Tamil did not meet their intellectual needs, and (5) All participants were not satisfied with the collection as a whole including the classification and location of these materials in the library. They all suggested that home delivery services for Tamil books, internet services in Tamil, one regional centre for Tamil studies should be provided to the Tamil community

Sule (2003)[36] has discussed the functions, problems, and prospects of rural library services and examined their role in the development of literacy in Nigeria. The study revealed that major problems faced by the libraries are: (1) Lack of qualified library staff, (2) Financial constraints, (3) Scarcity of reading materials, (4) Scattered settlement pattern, and (5) Attitudinal problems of government. The prospects of the libraries are listed as follows: (1) Rural libraries can sustain the level of literacy of the rural populace; (2) They can check rural-urban migration, which has negative consequences on development; (3) They can be the centres of independent study; and (4) They can serve as centres of recreation and culture.

Brown (2004)[37] has studied the reference service for children in public libraries in Australia. The study revealed that (1) the reference needs of children are primarily the requirement of information to enable them to complete a given school assignment; (2) for the successful reference transaction, the librarian needs to be conscious of children's wants and needs; (3) it is important to create an environment in which children and their questions are taken seriously; (4) to facilitate the delivery of quality reference and information services to children, it is important to have accepted guidelines or standards; and (5) the need for specific evaluation methods for children's reference services will increase the quality of the reference service.

Ranjith (2004)[38] has conducted a study on the rural libraries in Kerala. Data were collected on books and periodicals collection, membership, working hours, circulation of books, daily average attendance of members, grade, yearly grant, other assistance received, and reading habits of public. The important findings of the study are: (1) A majority of the libraries (60%) have book strength in the range of 1001-5000; (2) 90% of the libraries have own land and building; (3) A majority of the libraries (75%) have women membership of less than 30%; (4) 45% of the libraries work 9 hours or more, 30% of the libraries work 4 to 9 hours, and 25% work less than 4hours; (5) A majority of the libraries (62%) have the membership 500 or below; (6) 45% of the libraries have a distribution of 500–1000 books on an average per month, 40% unto 500, and 15% 1000 and above; (7) The average daily reading time was the highest among the youngest age groups of 15-30 years of both male and female; the highest in degree holders; and (8) 60% of the members are satisfied with the collection of the libraries.

PUBLIC LIBRARY SPECIAL SERVICES

Griebel (1995)[39] has discussed the development and implementation of an innovative, cooperative model of library service for blind and print disabled Canadians through the 'Visunet: Canada'. As it is described, it is the partnership between the Canadian National Institute for the Blind (CNIB) Library, a private, charitably funded organisation; and the local libraries. The study revealed that technology and library consortia are essential for the successful implementation of this service. The partnership is expressed in terms of the programmes such as virtual library; online catalogue; delivery of full-text newspapers, magazines, and publications through computer or telephone.

Mcharazo's (2000)[40] research report has highlighted the issues and dilemmas facing public libraries and distance learners in Tanzania. The author used a case study approach.

A total of 56 students of OUT (Open University of Tanzania) and librarians of 6 distance learning institutions were interviewed. Both participatory observation and direct observation methods were also used to ascertain the students' usage behaviours. The study revealed that (1) the main issue of public libraries in the provision of effective distance education service is the inadequacy of reading materials to the students; (2) to 50% of the participants, the reading space in the public libraries is enough while to another 50%, the space for reading was inadequate; (3) reference and readers' advisory desk was being staffed by library attendants and untrained library assistants and they failed to satisfy the users' needs; and (4) students are not in favour of being charged by the public libraries for the service. The study recognised the need to embark on new approaches in public libraries to support the distant learners.

Leong and Higgins (2002)[41] have conducted an exploratory study of public library services in Singapore for young people between thirteen and nineteen years of age who are wheelchair bound. Three main research questions explored in the study are: (1) What are the information needs of wheelchair- bound young people? (2) What are their perceptions of libraries and library services? (3) What are the problem they face in using library facilities and services? The findings indicate that: (1) Most participants enjoyed reading books but did not read newspapers, (2) The computer was used primarily as a recreational tool and the convenience of the internet appealed to them, (3) Their use of public libraries was infrequent (4) They were unaware of the full range of library facilities and services, (5) Current library promotions were inadequate in stimulating or sustaining their awareness and interest, and (6) The problems faced in using libraries were mainly related to architectural and physical access to library facilities and services.

Myhill (2002)[42] has made a case study on the different information services offered by the Gateshead Library (UK) to the disabled and has highlighted them as: (1) Provision of national and regional talking newspaper service;

(2) Transcription service; (3) Offering Braille; (4) Provision of large print, audio tape and digital formats to organisations and individuals; (5) Products of CD-i (Compact Disc interactive) (6) Provision of cable television information services; (7) Networked Internet access, and (8) Gateshead grid for learning through online educational programme.

Ng'ang'a (2004)[43] has presented in detail the different services offered to the visually impaired through public libraries in Kenya, their impact, challenges faced by them, and has suggested a way forward. The KNLS (Kenya National Library Service) established library and information service to the visually impaired in Kenya in 1996. The services offered in all 34 KNLS branches countrywide are lending of books; reading of stories and newspapers to the blind; document delivery to the homebound, elderly and such others; production of Braille materials; provision of talking books; inter library lending; and transcription of popular local information materials.

The objectives of the services are: (1) Integrate the visually impaired persons among the sighted population, (2) Sustain Braille literacy and support continuing education, (3) Empower the visually impaired persons with information and knowledge, and (4) Inculcate a reading culture among the visually impaired. The main challenges faced by KNLS are: (1) Society's perception of the visually impaired, who are viewed as people who require sympathy and alms rather than being empowered; (2) Inadequate information materials in Braille and equipment for providing services; and (3) Limited mobility of visually impaired persons. The way forward suggested by the author to meet the challenges mentioned above are (1) Awareness creation through sensitisation of society to visual impairment and through the acceptance and appreciation of their role in national development, (2) Seeding more copy right agreements from publishers and authors for transcription of their tittles into Braille, (3) Acquiring vans for transporting visually impaired persons to the library, and (4) Construction of a purposely-built national resource centre for visually impaired persons.

Vang (2005)[44] has provided an insight into the public service to Hmong-American community. Hmong are the immigrants to U.S. and many of them still remain illiterate. The observations made by the author are: (1) Even though majority of Hmong students and Hmong adults do not read or write in their native tongue, some major public libraries in the United States where there is a large community of Hmong, collect Hmong language materials; (2) Often the public libraries provided services like story time for children, literacy programmes, and computer classes but they are never publicised among the Hmong community; and (3) 90% of Hmong people never go to the libraries to meet their information needs; they either rely on family or friends for necessary information or they go to the agencies, organisations, and centres in their community. The author opines that the public libraries should take a proactive role in providing services to the Hmong and he also adds that the library's story time programme would be a great catalyst for librarians to introduce the library and literacy to Hmong people.

USE AND USER STUDY

D' Elia (1980)[45] conducted a study with the primary objective of the development and testing of a conceptual model for adult use of the public library. This study proposed a definition of library use, which recognises three distinct dimensions of use: (1) Non use and use, (2) Frequency of use, and (3) Intensity of use. The study was based on variables such as library use, characteristics and behaviour of individuals, and individuals' relationship to the library. In order to test this model, data were collected from 202 residents of the Syracuse metropolitan area (U.S.A.) by means of a telephone interview survey. Results indicated that (1) individuals' characteristics have association with library use, (2) users of the public library found the library more accessible than did non-users, (3) there was no difference between non users and users in their degree of awareness of library services, and (4) frequency and intensity of use was related to awareness of special library programmes.

Spiller (1980)[46] has studied the provision of fiction for public libraries. For this purpose a survey was conducted at four service points in British public libraries. The major findings are: (1) Readers like to read recreational novels rather than serious novels; (2) Most of the borrowers borrow novels for self use and a very few of them borrow novels for others; (3) 54 % of the novels had been chosen on an author basis, 46% by browsing; (4) Most of the respondents found booklists of the library useful in choosing the novels; (5) A majority of the respondents do not reserve novels; and (6) A majority of the readers borrow from 1-2 to16-20 novels a month. The study was intended to provide information of practical value to librarians in the selection and promotion of fiction in public libraries.

Ramaraj Urs (1984)[47] has surveyed the reading habits of clientele of the public libraries in the rural district of Bangalore. The distribution of population, occupations, membership pattern, extent of utilisation of library services, and reading habits of users in terms of subjects and type of books read were discussed. The survey revealed that the development of infrastructures for library and information system for Bangalore rural district indicated a steady growth. It also indicated that there was a steady increase in membership during the five years.

Khaiser and Ramesh (1991)[48] have assessed the reading interest; factors inimical to the use of City Central Library, Mysore; and the necessary improvements suggested by the users to the existing condition of this library. The major finding of the survey is lack of books, noisy environment, inadequate seating arrangements, distance, and improper location are the key factors affecting the use. The desired improvements indicated by the respondents are: (1) More books in different subject areas, 2) Additional space with chairs and tables, (3) Modern photocopying units, (4) More reference books, and (5) Provision of carrels and computerisation.

Chandraiah (1993)[49] has conducted a survey of the circulation libraries in Thirupathi, Andrapradesh and made an attempt to understand their nature, utility, the kind of users and their profitability. His major findings under the heading the "libraries" are: (1) The libraries were generally kept open from 8am to 8 pm with break of two hours in the noon; (2) The average stock of circulation libraries ranged between 120 and 800 titles; (3) Books were arranged by author; (4) Collection of security deposit was compulsory; and (5) The demand for novels of romance, sex, suspense, and adventure was observed to be overwhelming. Under the heading "users" are: (1) The readers in the age group of 21-25 constituted the highest stratum, (2) The customers with family income between Rs. 15,001–20,000 constituted the largest user group, (3) Users with educational background of intermediates figured as the highest stratum, (4) 42% users borrowed books once a week and 32% twice a week, (5) 34% of readers spent two hours per day and 26% an hour a day, and (6) Two reasons for the non-use of the public libraries are they were not accessible (64%) and books of their choice were not available (20%).

Kar (1996)[50] has analysed the reading habit and satisfaction of the users in public libraries. This study was conducted in nine public libraries of Cuttack, Balasore, and Bhadrak. The findings of the study revealed that: (1) Most of the users of the public library are from poor or middle class families and (2) Most of the users belong to unemployed or under employed category, followed by the student category.

Sathyanarayana (1996)[51] conducted a survey to identify the usage pattern, reading behaviour and other characteristics of deposit holders of the District Central Library of Visakhapatnam, Andhrapradesh. The analysis of the data showed that there is an active participation of youth in using the library and persons with advanced academic education constitute the core users among the deposit-holders. It is observed that the majority of deposit holders visited the library once a week and they did not prefer to spend more time in the library.

Kumbar and Biradar (1997)[52] have studied the use pattern and extent of utilisation of mass media particularly the newspaper, radio, television and public library by the people of Singanamane Grama panchayath area of Shimoga district in Karnataka. The findings related to the public libraries are: A majority of the respondents (73.57%) felt the need of a public library, 82.69% visited the public library for reading newspapers and magazines, 44.23% respondents visited library daily, and 36.45% of them spent less than 30 minutes for reading in the library. 24.29% opined that library collection was adequate, whereas 69.29% were of negative opinion about it and 6.42% did not mention anything. The findings indicated that if proper initiative and care are taken, public libraries could compete with the other media.

Padmamma *et al.* (2001)[53] has assessed children's views on public library through a survey of child users of Chickmangalore City Central library, Karnataka. The study revealed the perceptions of child users on the existing facilities, services, and resources as: almost all of the respondents feel good about collection of books, magazine and newspapers; but they said that the library does not provide the user services like new arrival services, inter-library loan, paper clipping service, reference service, over night issue, and book exhibition and computer facility. The study offers suggestions for the proper library services to the children and concludes with the statement that the user satisfaction should be the ultimate objective of the library.

Nikam and Rajashekara (2003)[54] have analysed the reading habits of public library users in two public libraries of Mysore city of Karnataka State. The result of the study revealed that (1) More than half of the public library users (51%) are between 16-25 years age group; (2) 79% of the users are male and only 21% are female; (3) 45% of users are degree holders, users with masters degree (16%), and others form minority; (4) Nearly half of the users (47%) are students; and (5) A majority of the users (71.5%) visit the library for reading.

Salma and Yelwa (2004)[55] have investigated the students' attitudes towards public library services and resources of the central library in Borno State of Nigeria and has provided the following information: (1) A majority of the students (64%) who patronise the library have not registered with the library; (2) 36% of the students visit the library for examination purposes, 20% visit the library to study using library books, 20% came to the library to borrow and return books and 12% used the library to read newspaper and magazines; (3) 40% of the students describe the resources and services as inadequate for their needs, 28% said they were adequate for their needs, while 12% gave a rating of highly inadequate; (4) 64% of the students responded "very good" on the conduciveness of the environment, 28% said it is "excellent", and equal responses of 4% each for "good" and "fairly good" were also registered.

Sunil Kumar (2005)[56] has undertaken a research project to assess the information needs of rural communities and this study aimed at the development of a model for a Rural Library and Community Resource Centre. For the survey, the researcher selected a sample of 375 persons from the village 'Bohar' of Rohtak district in Haryana. The model for a well functioning Rural Library and Community Resource Centres (RLCRCs) has the proposals of (1) well developed infrastructure for the smooth flow of information, (2) rural Book Trust should be established for encouraging the publication of books on local contents, (3) NGOs should be encouraged to take part in the integrated rural library programmes, (4) a strong government policy in this regard, (5) trained library personnel should be appointed for managing and running the activities of RLCRC, and (6) the curriculum of Library Science course should need to be revised to accommodate rural information services as a part of the study.

COMPUTERISATION OF PUBLIC LIBRARIES

Keenan *et. al.* (1981)[57] have given a report of the details of the research project on Bibliographic Information Retrieval On-line services (BIROS). It was carried out jointly by Manchester Polytechnic and Lancashire County Library. The objectives of this project were to look at the impact of the services on the library service generally, on the staff and on the users, to gather information about the motivations of users and their reactions to the services, and finally to evaluate the overall success of the services. To complement this project the British Library assisted the experimental development of on-line information services in four other public libraries of Birmingham, Liverpool, Lancashire, and Sheffield. The project resulted in the introduction of a set of guidelines for the introduction of on-line services. This study revealed the following facts: (1) An on-line service increases the demand for books and increases inter-library loans; (2) Much time has to be spent by the staff for training, updating knowledge, for practising search skills, and for actually carrying out searches; and (3) The type of end-users attracted to this service depended on the nature of services offered.

Venkata Ramana and Vinod Kumar (1997)[58] have emphasised the importance of a need-based planning for public library automation in their study report and indicated the following important facts to develop and execute effective plans to implement the library information storage and retrieval process in public libraries: (1) It requires the financial support from funding agencies, talent, education, creativity, determination, management and above all vision on the part of the library professional and other support staff and (2) The professionals should get themselves trained and take the lead in operating the systems.

Karisiddappa (1999)[59] has discussed the growth of technology from stone age to information age, possible areas of technology application in public libraries in library operations like online bibliographical services, creation of computerised bibliographic database, networking with the regional and national networks, and creation of non-bibliographic databases. It described the role of different satellite based nation wide computer communication network such as NICNET, GISTNIC, and DISNIC to meet the growing information needs of the public at large. The need for providing Internet facility in public libraries and also the trained staff who have necessary skills in this facility are emphasised.

Barber et al. (2000)[60] have reviewed in detail the case of new technologies to provide high value added services in the context of public libraries in Buenos Aires city and surrounding areas. The main results of the survey are: (1) The percentage of automated functions of libraries surveyed is-Acquisition

(31.50%), cataloguing (65.80%), serial control (21.90%), circulation (28.8%), Reference (34.20%), and OPAC (26%); (2) 71.2% of units surveyed do not belong to library network; (3) 47.9% of units have an Internet connection; (4) 15.1% of libraries have their own website, 27.4% of libraries use e-mail for reference service; and (5) 32.9% provide online library catalogue with in-home access, 11% provide online library catalogue with Internet access, 17.8% have other catalogues and databases on CD-ROM. The study concluded with the remarks that the main deficiencies observed in IT services in the public libraries are lack of adoption of standard for information exchange and processing, use of database administrators instead of integrated library systems, lack of information quality control, and less use of information and communication technologies for service provisions.

Eve and Brophy (2000)[61] in their study on ICT (Information and Communication Technology) based services offered by public libraries in U.K. indicated that (1) only 20% of respondents use the ICT facilities in the library; (2) 96% rated ICT as very or quite important; (3) 43% remarked that the main reason for non-use of ICT facilities is having access elsewhere, 26% indicated that they had no Internet in using this facility, 18% said they didn't know how to, 2% indicated that no help was available to use this facility and 11% have other reasons; and (4) 29% of the respondents indicated that their main use of the facilities is for leisure, 26% replied that it was for research, 20% used this facility for study and 10% for other reasons. The study illustrated that libraries are increasingly becoming important locations for accessing ICT to support a range of activities, from formal study to job seeking, to building and maintaining social network using the Internet.

Larkin-Lieffers (2000)[62] carried out a study on the older users' attitudes, experience, and issues concerning public library computer technology in Canada. Six adults with the age restriction of 65 years or more, and in-person users of the public library participated in the study. Interviews were chosen as the research method. The main findings of their study are: (1) Three of the participants were able to use computers;

(2) Three participants used computers on an average of once a week for e-mail, word processing, and financial spread sheets; (3) All participants thought computers are highly useful and were impressed with their capabilities; (4) Two of the six participants frequently used OPAC, two other participants tried the OPAC but found them difficult to use, and the remaining two had never tried the OPAC; and (5) The reasons for not using the OPAC were OPAC user interface was too different from the home computer, OPAC interface was difficult to use and results were disappointing particularly in subject searches, librarians gave instructions too quickly, confusing or absent written instructions in OPAC, and OPAC was in constant demand.

Turner and Kendall (2000)[63] have analysed the use of the Internet facilities at Chester Library between August 1998 and May 1999. The main findings can be summed up as: (1) The most numerous group of Internet users was full time employed users (38%) and the next largest group was unemployed people (22%) student users made up of 20% of total sample, the remaining groups constituted 20% of the total sample including 9% part-time workers and 5% retired users; (2) The overall average of total users split almost in half with 51% male and 49% female; (3) 80% of the entire sample constituted persons aged between 16 and 35 years; and (4) 39% of total users stated that web-based e-mail was their sole reason for using the Internet in Chester Library, they used it for searching information on a specific subject (36%), 27% of total users were using Internet for visiting specific websites; and (5) A majority of the users (75%) had not received any formal training in Internet use.

Dutch and Muddiman (2001)[64] have assessed the impact of Information and Communication Technology (ICT) on the development of public libraries in U.K., and examined national and local information policy, community networking and public library policy. The findings are summarised as: (1) The government recognised the central role of public libraries in the information age and stated that every public library should be connected to the National Grid for Learning by 2002; (2) An important recent report commissioned by U.K.

Government's Social Exclusion Unit recommended that by April 2002 deprived neighbourhoods should have at least one publicly accessible community based ICT facility and envisages a network of local ICT resource centres based in schools, libraries, community centres and other public locations; (3) Department of Trade and Industry (2000) estimated that a total of approximately 6500 public ICT access points could eventually be expanded to a network including 19,000 post offices and 4716 public libraries; (4) The important aim of the research project on Public Libraries and Social Exclusion (Muddiman *et al,* 2000) was to assess the potential of U.K. Public library ICT developments for tackling social exclusion; (5) The U.K. National Lottery supported New Opportunities Fund (NOF) has provided Pd.100 million of funding to complete the people's network through a service of local infrastructure projects in U.K. public libraries. (6) It was targeted that by the end of 2002, all of the U.K.'s 4300 public libraries will function as ICT bearing centres and provide public access to ICT, and (7) U.K. public library policy has been concerned primarily with the mechanics of developing a network which involves the provision of access to ICT through existing library service points.

Thomas (2001)[65] has studied the state of application of IT in the public library field in India, their future plans and the problems they face in this process. The findings of the study revealed that 8% of the libraries computerised are two State central libraries, two district libraries and a voluntary organisation library. They are T.S. Central State Library, Chandigarh; H. K. M. State Library, Bhuvaneswar; District Central Library, Coimbatore; City Central Library, South zone, Bangalore; and Ramakrishna Mission Vivekananda Library, Bhuvaneswar. Only 28% libraries were planning to automate. The major problem the library encountered was with regard to updating of databases and correctness of entries.

ROLE OF PUBLIC LIBRARIES

Smith (1984)[66] has reviewed the involvement of the public libraries in literacy education. The public libraries in U.S.A.

were selected for this study. The important findings of the study revealed that (1) public libraries in urban and sub-urban communities are involved more in literacy education than libraries in rural communities, (2) public libraries located in large communities and serving demographically heterogeneous areas provide more literacy education services than libraries is smaller and homogeneous communities, (3) larger libraries have more literacy education programmes than smaller libraries, (4) public libraries that have a wide range of non-print materials and equipment are more active in literacy education than libraries with limited non-print resources, (5) more libraries that involved in literacy education provide in-service training to their staff than libraries which do not provide these services and (6) the main barriers to the literacy education are the low profile of public libraries in the community, staffing patterns, and lack of staff expertise.

Khan (1991)[67] has described the role of public libraries in India in literacy and adult education in terms of information services, educational, and cultural functions. Information services to be provided are: (1) Creating awareness of literacy and adult education among rural people; (2) Information regarding literacy/adult education agencies in respect of their location, objectives, persons to be contacted, their activities/operations and such others; and (3) Dissemination of current information on vital issues related to population education, environmental education, health, hygiene, nutrition, and such others. Educational role: (1) Providing adequate instructional material to these programmes, (2) Changing/modifying attitudes towards learning, (3) Providing positive learning environment, (4) Providing library space to conduct literacy/adult education programmes. (5) Assisting in framing of suitable curricula, and (6) Assisting in all possible ways in promoting social education. The author also stressed the importance of public libraries to be a centre of socio-cultural activities.

Laxman Rao and Ratna Rao (1997)[68] have conducted a study on the role of public libraries in national and social movements in Andhra Pradesh during the pre-independence period. The social movements were against caste system, evils of drinking, widow marriages, women's education etc. The various national movements were independence movement, swadeshi movement, non-cooperation, salt satyagraha, national awakening and such others. The findings of the study indicated that the role played by the libraries in these movements helped to redefine the purpose and function of libraries.

Haniff Uddin (2000)[69] has emphasised the importance of establishing rural libraries in each and every village of Bangladesh. They are: (1) To sensitise the people to better health, water supply and sanitation, (2) To find out government policy, (3) To provide better crops, (4) To prevent and control environmental pollution, (5) To provide text books and teaching aids, (6) To provide sport facilities, and (7) To prevent and control social problems. The study explored the inter linkages between libraries and rural development and also highlighted some rural aspects of the country.

Deshpande (2000)[70] has studied the importance of public libraries in developing countries and has pointed out the salient characteristics of a public library and grass root services. The services which can be offered to the public are detailed in the study, which are educating the illiterates, providing information services for women, giving children's service, conducting adult education classes, providing information on social evils, giving information service to the farmers, creating science temper, and providing information services to the disadvantaged.

Stanffer (2005)[71] has traced the growth of public libraries in Utah, a State in West America and has described their role in the establishment of a recognised social order in the State by stressing the eradication of the social evil, "polygamy." Major events in the development of public libraries and their important role as social stabiliser are listed as follows: (1) The establishment of libraries in Utah was influenced by social and cultural factors unique to Utah, in particular, the practice of polygamy; (2) The several women's organisations striving to eradicate social ills including polygamy, established many public libraries; (3) The first public library in Utah has been founded in Nauvoom, Illinois in 1845; (4) Ten of the city's prominent Mormon and non-Mormon women founded the Ladies Public Library Aid Society in 1890; (5) In 1904, Zoe Faddis, a librarian requested funds from Carnegie, U.S. Industrialist; her strongest argument for the money was the eradication of polygamy; and (6) The first public library law in Utah came in to effect in 1898.

COLLABORATIONS WITH OTHER INSTITUTIONS

Bandy (2002)[72] made a survey in 2001 to find out the level of interaction between the school and public libraries in Australia. One page questionnaire with 5 questions were distributed to all 1496 public library branches and 115 schools in Australia. The results of this survey are given under two headings. The important public library responses are: (1) Nearly half of the public librarians (49%) responded that the level of interaction with local school librarians is "low", (2) The highest percentage of the public librarians (46%) stated that lack of time is the factor that determined the current level of interaction, (3) More than half of the school library staff (55%) did not visit the library, and (4) The highest percentage of them (44%) reported that knowledge of school library issues and developments was "low". The important school library responses are: (1) Nearly half of the teacher librarians (46%) indicated that the current level of interaction with the local public library is "very low", (2) A majority of the teacher librarians (72%) responded that interaction with the local public library during the last five years are "stable", (3) A majority of them (67%) reported that lack of time is the factor that determines the current level of interaction, (4) 55% reported that public library staff did not visit the school, (5) Half of them stated that knowledge of public library issues and developments is "low", and (6) 55% are not regular public library users.

Rodger (2005)[73] has examined collaborations among public institutions providing informal lifelong learning opportunities to children and adults in the United States, through a survey of chief executive officers and staff of the public libraries, museums, public television stations, and public radio stations. He has investigated the extent of collaborations between and among these institutions, the influence of the size of institutions on the incidence of collaborations, forces driving collaboration and the impact of collaborations on the institutions. The findings are listed as: (1) Public libraries were collaborating primarily with art museums and other kinds of museums (78.3%) and, secondarily with public broad casters (17.7%) and other public libraries (4.1%); (2) Public libraries that were engaged in collaboration had significantly higher operating revenues, had significantly larger staff, and were located in metropolitan areas with significantly higher population ranks; (3) The most important forces driving collaboration were as follows: to expand educational opportunities, to meet community needs, to expand-diversify an audience or user base, to enhance the institutions' stature, to enhance use of collections and programmes, to be a good civic player in the community; and (4) 78.8 % of the respondents rated the impacts of collaboration on their organizations as positive.

EVALUATION OF PUBLIC LIBRARY EFFECTIVENESS

D' Elia and Walsh (1985)[74] made an evaluative study of public library performance. Questionnaires were distributed in each of the four branches of the Ramsey County Public Library (U.S.A.) to the patrons. A number of measurements are done for evaluating library performances and they are: (1) Measurement of library use: circulation of materials, number of services used, duration of visits, and frequency of visiting the library; (2) Measurement of evaluation of services: quality of collections, availability of collections, satisfaction with physical facilities and library staff, and convenience of hours; (3) Measurement of overall evaluations of and satisfaction with library services; and (4) Measurement of individual characteristics: Importance of use, style of use and purpose of use. The analysis of the data has revealed that (1) there was no statistically significant relationship between the number of non fiction borrowed and the libraries used; (2) there was statistically significant relationship between the number of activities in which the patrons engaged and the use of library; (3) there were statistically significant relationships between patrons' evaluations of the quality of collections, the availability of collections, the staff, the over all evaluation of the library and the general satisfaction with the library; and one or more of the different libraries used by the patrons; and (4) there were statistically significant relationships between the patrons' evaluations of the physical facilities and the convenience of hours and one or more of the different libraries used by the patrons.

Van House (1986)[75] has conducted a study on public library effectiveness in terms of theory, measures and determinants. This study has taken two kinds of empirical approach. The first is "outcome studies" which seek to define the organisational effectiveness and to develop indicators of it. The second is "determinant studies" which attempt to identify the determination of organisational effectiveness. The data were collected from Baltimore Public Library (U.S.A). The investigation was on four output measures namely title and subject/author fill rates and reference and circulation per capita. Fill rate is the materials availability in the library. A model of relationships among user characteristics, library resources and effectiveness was also developed. The important findings of the study are: (1) The success of the transaction depends on both the library and the user; (2) The users' success in the library depends on his ability to use information generally and the library specifically, which depends in part on user characteristics such as education; (3) The success of the transaction is measured by the output measures; and (4) The search success may affect the users' perceptions of the library.

Ikoja-Odongo (2004)[76] has surveyed the attitudes of politicians, civil servants, and leaders of Uganda library associations towards public library services in Uganda. The following major problems were realised in the survey: (1) Uganda lacks a policy for public libraries, their development and maintenance, (2) Ugandan public libraries do not cover the whole country, (3) The libraries are starved of grants from central government, (4) Information materials are inadequate, mostly out of date and sometimes irrelevant, (5) Literacy levels and illiteracy are the major problems affecting the use of public libraries, and (6) Reading habits of the people are very low.

PUBLIC LIBRARIES ACTS

Raju (1990)[77] has attempted an evaluative study of the working of Andhra Pradesh Public Libraries Act, 1960 and its contribution towards the development of public services in the State. The evaluation of this Act and public library services in Andhra Pradesh revealed that the State Public Library System failed to provide an effective public library service. The library cess is not effectively collected and remitted by the local administrator and thus planning and phasing of services are in the face of uncertainty. Financial constraints remain the major bottleneck in universalising free public library service in the State. The government gives no due importance to the improvement of library system in the State. The study led to the conclusion that only an imaginative leadership in the State can save the situation from ending in a catastrophe.

Shiva and Rochna (2003)[78] have pointed out the need of legislation for efficient functioning of public libraries and the following major suggestions were made in this regard. (1) Legislation should have provision for better financial support. (2) Legislation can be recommended to authorise local board/authority to levy a special tax for the library service. (3) It should carry norms and procedures to provide grant-in-aid to public libraries. (4) Legislation would allow district library to use tax money as collateral for the improvement of public libraries. (5) Legislation can be recommended to appoint full time district library officers to manage the library at district level. (6) Legislation must include ideas to give clear account of different levels of authorities and their responsibilities. In conclusion, they observe that the Library Acts of the different States must be brought up to a common platform for comparison, to include better/specific laws in rest.

Nasirudheen (2004)[79] has evaluated Kerala Public Libraries Act, 1989, its objectives, constitution of the library authorities, library finance, in the light of UNESCO principles for public library legislation, Model Public Libraries Bill (1963) of the Ministry of Education, Government of India, the Model Public Libraries Act (1972) of Ranganathan and the ten State public libraries Acts in India. The author has observed that (1) the preamble of the Kerala Public Libraries Act does not include the statement of the objectives; (2) the Act aims at bringing about uniform and comprehensive public library law applicable to all the existing library authorities and organisations in the State; (3) the Act provides very typical provisions with respect to the constitution of library authorities at State, district, and taluk levels; library services; affiliation of libraries etc; (4) the Act provides for a democratically elected State Library Council with the representatives of bonafied users of the grant-in-aid libraries in the State; (5) the Act provides a token representation to library professionals in the State Library Council; and (6) the Act provides for the library cess for mobilising the State library fund maintained by the State Library Council.

CONCLUSION

The studies reviewed show that mainly they are focused on library movement in different countries, library services, and public library use and user study. Another fact to be noted that even though many studies on public library services to the disabled people have been conducted abroad, no such studies have been carried out in India. In Kerala, major studies have been conducted only in public library movement, Act, and Kerala Granthasala Sanghom. It can be seen that no comprehensive study has been conducted to reveal the present situation of the public libraries in Kerala.

References

1. Ramanujan Nair, P. (1974), *Library Movement in Kerala.* Trivandrum: Writer's Club.

2. Menon, V. K. N. (1974), The Trivandrum Public Library. In *Trivandrum Public Library Platinum Jubilee Souvenir*, 14 -17.

3. Hamsath, K. (1979), Public Libraries in Union Territory of Lakshadweep. In *Twenty Fifth all India Library Conference, 14-18 May 1979, at Trivandrum: Souvenir*, 141-142.
4. John, P. A. and V. K. G. Nair (1979), Public Library Movement in Kerala. In *Twenty Fifth all India Library Conference, 14-18 May 1979, at Trivandrum: Souvenir*, 161-167.
5. Ramachandra Rao, P. (1981), The Significance of the Library Movement in Andhra, 1900-1948. *Library Herald*, 20, No. 2- 4 (July-March): 151-158.
6. Shantaram, G. M. (1985), History of the Public Library Movement in Maharashtra; 1805-1921. *CLIS Observer* 2, No. 3-4 (July-October), 22-24.
7. Job, M. M. (1990), Public Libraries in Ethiopia. *Herald of Library Science* 29, No. 3-4, (July-October) 173-179.
8. Sewa Singh (1991), Public Library Development in Punjab. *Granthana*, 2, No. 2 (July): 147-154.
9. Wiele, Nic Van De (1991), Public Libraries. *Journal of Library Information Science*, 16, No. 1 (June): 48-59.
10. Pasilithil, A. (1992), The Kerala Granthasala Sanghom and its Socio-cultural Contributions. PhD Thesis, University of Kerala.
11. Anis Khurshid (1998), City Public Library System for Karachi Metropolis. *Library Herald*, 36, No. 3 (October-December): 135-151.
12. Kalia, D. R. (1998), A Review of State Public Library System in India. *CLIS Observer*, 15, No. 1-2, 46-51.
13. Jones, David J. (2005), Public Library Development in New South Wales. *The Australian Library Journal* 54, No. 2 (May), *http://alia.org.au/publishing/alj/54.2/full text/jones.html* (accessed May 21, 2006).
14. Odini, Cephas (1990), Planning for Public Library Development in Developing Countries with Special Reference to African Countries. *Libri.*, 40, No. 1 (March): 33-48.
15. Singh, R. S. P. (1991), Public Library Movement in Bihar. *Granthana*, 2, No. 2 (July): 193-203.
16. Bouri, Elizebeth N. (1994), Public Libraries Development Reconsidered: The Case of Egypt. *International Information and Library Review*, 26: 151-168.

17. Sahib Singh Verma (2002), A Study of Public Libraries and Literacy Movement in India with Special Reference to Delhi, Haryana, and Rajasthan: A Research Report. *Library Herald*, 39, No. 3 (September): 187-190.

18. Jones, David J. (2004), Critical Issues in Public Library Planning: The New South Wales Experience. *Australian Library Journal* 53, No. 4 (November), *http: //alia.org.au/publishing/alj/53.4/full text/ jones.html* (accessed May 21, 2006).

19. Hennen, Thomas J. (2005), Great American Public Libraries. *American Libraries* (October): 42-48. *www.ala.org/al-online Templatafm?section=october 2005*.

20. Doll, Carol A. (1984), A Study of Overlap and Duplication Among Children's Collections in Selected Public and Elementary School Libraries. *Library Quarterly*, 54, No. 3, 277–289.

21. Serebnick, Judith and Frank Quinn (1995), Measuring Diversity of Opinion in Public Library Collections. *Library Quarterly*, 65, No. 1: 1- 38.

22. Cole, Natalie (2000), The Influence of Attitudes on Public Library Stock Management Practice. *Libri*. 50, No. 1 (March): 37-47, *http:// lirijournal.org/2000-1 toc.html* (accessed May 21, 2006).

23. Goudy, Frank Wm (1982), General Revenue Sharing and Public Libraries: An Estimate of Fiscal Impact. *Library Quarterly*, 52, No. 1: 1-20.

24. Guruswamy Naidu, N. (1990), Public Library Finances. New Delhi, Ess Ess Publications.

25. Ramaiah, L. S. (1993), Public Libraries and Public Finances in India. *Herald of Library Science*, 32, No. 3-4 (July-Oct.), 171-179.

26. Merrifield, Mark (1995), The Funding of Rural Libraries. *Library Trends* 44, No. 1 (Summer), 49-62.

27. Sarada, K. (1986), *Rural Library Services in India*. New Delhi, Ess Ess Publications.

28. Richardson, Selma K. (1987), Children's Services of Public Libraries in the United States. *International Library Review*, 18: 15-24.

29. Saiful Islam, K. M. (1990), Public Library Systems and Services. *Herald of Library Science*, 29, No. 3-4: 163-171.

30. Ottensmann, John R., Raymond E Gnat, and Michael E. Gleeson. (1995), Similarities in Circulation Patterns Among Public Library

Branches Serving Diverse Populations. *Library Quarterly*, 65, No. 1: 89-118.

31. Wigg, Ristina (1995), Across Towns and Across Times: Library Service to Young People in Rural Libraries. *Library Trends*, 44, No. 1 (summer): 88 -111.

32. Aslam, M. (1998, Rural Libraries in India: As Community Information Centres. *Granthana*, 5, Nos.1 & 2 (July): 139-146.

33. Padmamma, S. *et al.* (2001), Public Library Service for Women. *Indian Journal of Information and Library Science*, 14, No. 3-4 (July-December), 177-181.

34. Vijayakumar, M. and Kumar N. (2001), Problems and Prospects of Rural Libraries. *SRELS Journal of Information Management*, 38, No. 2 (June): 165 -176.

35 Malarvele Ilangovan and Susan E. Higgins (2003), Library Provision to the Tamil Community in Singapore. *LIBRES (Library and Information Science Research Electronic Journal)* 13, No.1 (March), *http://libres.curtin.edu.au/libres 13n1* (accessed May 21, 2006).

36. Sule, Nathaniel N. *et al.* (2003), The Contributions of Rural Library Services to Literacy Development in Nigeria: A Review of the Past Century and Prospect of the New Millennium. *Library Progress (International)*, 23, No. 2: 133-141.

37. Brown, Anita (2004), Reference Services for Children: Information Needs and Wants in the Public Library. *Australian Library Journal* 53, No.3 (August), *http://alia.org.au/publishing/alj/53.3/full.text/brown.html* (accessed May 21, 2006).

38. Ranjith, K. S. (2004), *Rural libraries of Kerala*. TVM: CDS.

39. Griebel, Rosemary (1995), Partnering Services between Public Libraries and Library Services for the Blind: A Canadian Experience. Proceedings of Sixty Sixth IFLA Council and General Conference, 13-18 August, at Jerusalem, *Israel. http://www.ifla.org.*

40. Mcharazo, Alli A. S. (2000), Public Libraries and Distance Education in Tanzania: Issues and Dilemmas. *Libri.*, 50, No. 4 (December): 295-301, *http://libri journal.org/ 2000-4 toc.html* (accessed May 22, 2006).

41. Leong, Ivan Chew Boon and Susan.E Higgins (2002), Public Library Services for Wheelchair-Bound Young People in Singapore. *LIBRES (Library and Information Science Research*

Electronic Journal) 12, No. 1 (March), *http://libres. curtin.edu.au/ libres12n1* (accessed May 21, 2006).

42. Myhill, Christine E. (2002), ICT for Access to Information Services for Disabled People: An Overview of Projects and Services at Gateshead Library Services. *Journal of Management* 36, No. 3: 176-181, *www.emeraldinsight.com.*
43. Ng'ang'a, S. K. (2004), Delivering Services to the Visually Impaired through Public Libraries: The Kenyan Experience. *Information Development*, 20, No. 2, 130-133.
44. Vang, Vang (2005), Public Library Services to the Hmong-American Community: Much Room for Improvement. *IFLA Journal* 31, No. 4, 315-323.
45. D'Elia, George (1980), The Development and Testing of a Conceptual Model of Public Library User Behavior. *Library Quarterly*, 50, No. 4, 410-430.
46. Spiller, David (1980), The Provision of Fiction for Public Libraries. *Journal of Librarianship*, 12, No. 4 (October): 239-264.
47. Ramaraj Urs, R. (1984), Survey of the Reading Habits of the Clientele of Public Library System of Rural District of Bangalore. *ILA Bulletin*, 20, No. 1-2 (April- September): 14-20.
48. Khaiser Jahan Begum and Ramesh, C. P. (1991), Factors Inhibiting the Public Library Use. In *Education through Public Libraries: A Practical Approach*. Proceedings of the National Seminar on Public Library Movement, April 19-21 in Madras, edited by C. Palanivelu and K. S. Raghavan. 332-343. Madras: Directorate of Public Libraries.
49. Chandraiah, I. (1993), Circulation Libraries: A Study. *Granthana*. 4, No. 1 and 2 (January and July): 37-40.
50. Kar, P. K. (1996), Users Reading Habits and Satisfaction in Public Libraries: A Sociological Exploration in Some Select Towns of Orissa. *Indian Journal of Information, Library and Society*, 9, No. 3-4 (July–December), 240-245.
51. Satyanarayana, M. (1996), Use of Public Library: A Case of Deposit Holders of Visakhapatnam District Central Library. *Annals of Library Science and Documentations*, 43, No. 3, 118-115.
52. Kumbar, Mallinath, and B. S. Biradar (1997), Use of Mass Media and Public Library by the Rural Community: A Study. *Annals of Library Science and Documentation*, 44, No. 3, 86-92.

53. Padmamma, S. *et al.* (2001), Children's Views on Public Library. *Indian Journal of Information and Library Science*, 14, No. 3-4 (July - December).

54. Nikam, Khaiser and N. Rajashekara (2003), Reading Habits of Public Library Users: A Survey. *SRELS Journal of Information Management*, 40, No. 4 (December): 337-363.

55. Salma, Joel H. and Idris Mohammed Yelwa (2004), A Survey of Student's Attitudes Towards Public Library Services. A Case Study of Central Library in Borno State of Nigeria. *International Library Movement*, 26, No. 2, 61-70.

56. Sunil Kumar (2005), Rural Library and Community Resource Enters (RLCRCs) in India with Special Reference to States having Library Legislation: Problems and Prospects. *SRELS Journal of Information Management*, 42, No. 3, (September), 275-280.

57. Keenan, Stella, Nick Moore, and Anthony Oulton (1981), On-line Information Services in Public Libraries. *Journal of Librarianship*, 13, No. 1 (January): 9-24.

58. Venkata Ramana, V. and E. A. Vinod Kumar (1997), Need Based Planning for Public Library Automation. In *Public Library Systems: Services and Networking*. Vol. 1,edited by L. S. Ramaiah *et al.* 61-67. New Delhi, Ess Ess Publications.

59. Karisiddappa, C. R. (1999), Application of Modern Technology to Public Libraries. *Granthana*, 6, Nos. 1-2 (Jan.): 113-123.

60. Barber, Elsa *et al.* (2000), Information Society and Information Technology: The Situation at the Public Libraries in Buenos Aires City and Surrounding Areas, Argentina. *International Information and Library Review*, 38, No. 1, (March): 1-14.

61. Eve, Juliet and Peter Brophy (2000), Vital Issues: The Perception, and Use of ICT Services in UK Public Libraries. *LIBRES (Library and Information Science Research Electronic Journal)* 10, No. 2 (September), *http://libres.curtin.edu.au/ libres10n2 /vital.html* (accessed May 21, 2006).

62. Larkin-Lieffers, Patricia A. (2000), The Older Adult and Public Library Computer Technology: A Pilot Study in a Canadian Setting. *Libri*. 50, No. 4 (December): 225-234, *http: // librijournal.org/ pdf/2000-4 toc.html* (accessed May 21, 2006).

63. Turner, Katherine and Margaret Kendall (2000), Public Use of the Internet at Chester Library, U.K. *Information Research* 5, No. 3

(April), *http:// information r.net/ir//5.3/paper 75.html* (accessed May 22, 2006).

64. Dutch, Martin and Dave Muddiman (2001), The Public Library, Social Exclusion and the Information Society in United Kingdom. *Libri.* 51, 183-194. *http://librijournal.org / 2001-4 toc.html* (accessed May 21, 2006).
65. Thomas, V. K. (2001), Computerisation of Public Libraries in India." *CLIS Observer* 18, No. 3 (July-December), 92-98.
66. Smith, Ester Gottlieb (1984), The Literacy Education Gap: The Involvement of Public Libraries in Literacy Education. *Library and Information Science Research,* 6, 75-94.
67. Khan, H. A. (1991), Role of Rural Libraries in the Promotion of Literacy and Adult Education. *Granthana,* 2, No. 2 (July): 135-144.
68. Laxman Rao, N. and N. Rartna Rao. (1997), Role of Public Libraries in National and Social Movements in Pre-independent India: A Study with Reference to Andhra Pradesh. In *Public Library Systems: Services and Networking.* Vol. 1, edited by L. S. Ramaiah, *et al.* 258-260. New Delhi, Ess Ess Publications.
69. Hanif Uddin (2000), The Role of Rural Libraries in the Rural Development of Bangladesh. *IASLIC Bulletin,* 45, No. 3, 97-104.
70. Deshpande, K. S. (2000), Public Libraries: Community Fountain of Information, Education and Culture. *SRELS Journal of Information Management,* 37, No. 3 (September), 165-182.
71. Stanffer, Suzanne M. (2005), Polygamy and the Public Library: The Establishment of Public Libraries in Utah before 1910. *Library Quarterly* 75, No. 3 (July): 346-70, *http://www.journals.uchicago.edu/ LQ/journal/issues/V75n3/750305/750 305.html* (accessed 21 May, 2006).
72. Bandy, Alan (2002), Essential Connections: School and Public Libraries for Lifelong Learning. *Australian Library Journal,* 51, No. 1 (February), *http://alia.org. au/ publishing/alj/51.1/fulltext/essential connections.html* (accessed May 21, 2006).
73. Rodger, Eleanor Jo *et al.* (2005), Partnerships and Collaboration Among Public Libraries, Public Broadcast Media, and Museums: Current Context and Future Potential. *Library Quarterly,* 75, No. 1 (January): 42-66, *http.//www.journals.uchicago.edu/ LQ. journalcontents /v75n1.html* (accessed May 22, 2006).

D'Elia, George and Sandra Walsh (1985), Patron's Uses and Evaluations of Library Services: A Comparison Across Five Public Libraries. *Library and Information Science Research,* 7, 3-30.

75. Van House, Nancy A. (1986), Public Library Effectiveness: Theory, Measures, and Determinants. *Library Information Science Research,* 8, 261-283.

76. Ikoja-Odongo, J. R. (2004), Public Library Politics: The Ugandan Perspective. *Information Development,* 20, No. 3, 169–180.

77. Raju, A. A. N. (1990), Constraints on the Public Library Services in Andhra Pradesh. *CLIS Observer,* 7, No. 3-4, 69-72.

78. Shiva Kanaujia and Rochna Srivasthava (2003), Public Library Legislation in Changing Information Scenario. *Library Progress (International)* 23, No. 2, 107-110.

79. Nasirudheen, T. P. O. (2004), Impact of Kerala Granthasala Sanghom on the Formulation of the Kerala Public Libraries Act, 1989. Ph.D. Thesis, University of Calicut.

3

PUBLIC LIBRARIES IN MALABAR: GENESIS AND DEVELOPMENT

INTRODUCTION

This chapter aims to study the genesis and development of public libraries in Malabar. A brief note on the physiographic of Malabar which has an important role in the cultural and political development of the area has been given. Educational, literary, political, cultural, and other social backgrounds which help the birth and growth of libraries in Malabar have been traced in this chapter. The workers' unions, students' unions, religious organisations, social reformers, political workers have their own role in the birth and growth of public libraries in Malabar and they also have been traced in this chapter. Ultimately the library movement led to the phase of organised movement which was started in the first half of the twentieth century. The organised movement of public libraries in Kerala particularly in Malabar has been arranged in a chronological order so that the evolution can be properly understood in a historical perspective. Now the public libraries in Kerala is under the Kerala State Library Council which is the controlling authority formed as per the Kerala Public Libraries (Kerala Granthasala Sanghom) Act, 1989. The activities and functions of the State Library Council and the present situation of libraries in Malabar in general terms have also been discussed in this chapter.

MALABAR

Malabar, earlier a part of Bombay presidency was transferred to Madras presidency on May 20, 1800 (Sreedhara Menon 1996).[1] Up to the formation of Kerala State on November 1, 1956, it was a district of the erstwhile Madras State. On November 1, 1956 Travancore and Cochin, the erstwhile States; Malabar; and Kasaragod of South Canara districts of the erstwhile Mysore State were formed in to Kerala. On January 1, 1957 Malabar district was trifurcated into Cannanore, Kozhikode and Palghat districts. On June 16, 1969 Malappuram district, on November 1, 1980 Wayanad district, and on May 24, 1984 Kasaragod district were formed (Ramachandran Nair 1986).[2] At present Malabar has 6 districts with 22 taluks and 661 villages (Bhatt 1998).[3]

Map of Malabar

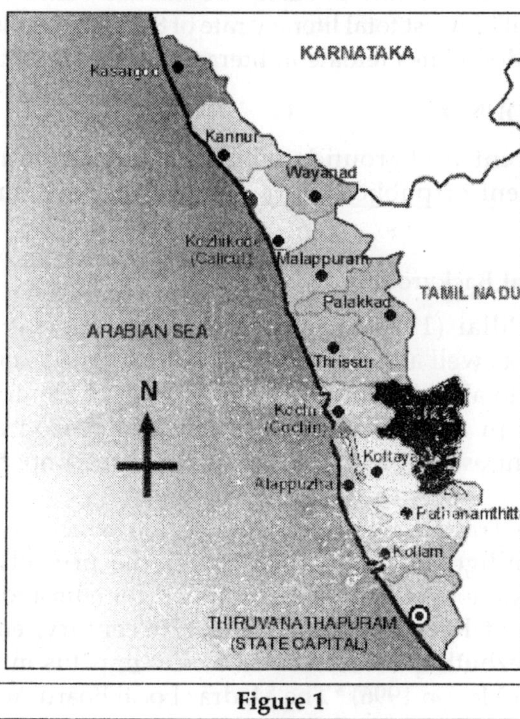

Figure 1

Kerala has the highest literary rate in India. The literacy rates of the districts of Malabar are given in Table 1.

Table 1
Literacy Rate of Malabar

District	*Total Population (%)*	*Male (%)*	*Female (%)*
Kasaragod	85.17	90.84	79.80
Kannur	92.80	96.38	89.57
Kozhikode	92.45	96.30	88.86
Malappuram	88.61	91.46	85.96
Wayanad	85.52	90.28	80.80
Palakkad	84.31	89.73	79.31
Kerala	90.92	94.20	87.7

Source: Census Report, 2001.

Table 1 shows that in Malabar, Kannur comes first with the highest total literacy rate of 92.8%, followed by Kozhikode where the literacy rate is 92.45%. Palakkad ranks the sixth position with lowest total literacy rate of 84.31%. It is also noted that male dominates female in literacy rate in all districts.

BACKGROUNDS

The different backgrounds which helped in the rise and development of public libraries in Malabar are illustrated below.

Educational Background

Kunhan Pillai (1970)[4] remarks that "in ancient Kerala, education as well as access to houses of recorded knowledge was open to all and there was a high level of literacy in this area." As in ancient period, in modern period also the government as well as public is aware of the importance of education.

Unlike Travancore and Cochin region which had strong roots in indigenous education under the princely rulers, Malabar did not get strong State support for education till the formation of Kerala State. During 17th century, education through "ezhuthupally" received a new impetus in Malabar (Sreedhara Menon 1996).[5] The Madras Local Board Act of 1834 and subsequent Elementary Education Acts were the early attempts for speedy establishment of elementary schools in Malabar (Malabar Gazetteer 1935).[6] Basel evangelical mission took the lead in spreading English education in Malabar. They established many schools in Malabar at different places like Thalassery, Vadakara, Kozhikode, and Palaghat. Colleges established early in Malabar are Zamorin's college, Calicut in 1877; Brennen College, Tellichery in 1891; Malabar Christian College, Calicut in 1907 (Innes 1951).[7] The Malabar Education Society was established in 1926 at Calicut. Its objectives were the promotion and advancement of education, award of scholarships to poor deserving students, maintenance of educational institutions, libraries, reading rooms, hospitals, boarding houses etc. (Sreedhara Menon 1962).[8] The Labour Department of Government of Madras had established many elementary schools for the depressed classes in Malabar in 1930-31 (Innes 1951).[9] The contribution of the Malabar District Board in education was most remarkable. It had started many schools in Malabar. Single-teacher schools were established in the remote villages of Malabar. Many social workers started Schools. Ganapath School in Kozhikode is an example for this. Many rulers of royal houses like Chirakkal, Nileswaram, Kadathanad, and Samudiri opened schools in Malabar area (Ganesh 1997).[10] The caste organisations such Sree Narayana Dharma Paripalanayogam (S.N.D.P.), Nair Service Society (N.S.S.), Sadhuparipalana Sabha, Yogakshema Sabha and various Christian organistions started educational institutions of their own (Cherian 1999).[11] Various Muslim organisations like Malabar Muslim Association and Kerala Muslim Association propagated education among Muslims and stressed the need for western education (Cherian 1999).[12] The Muslim Education Society (M.E.S.) established in 1964 runs a number of schools and colleges and has helped the Muslim community to forge ahead in the social and educational fields (George 2002).[13]

The growing number of educational institutions and the rise in the literacy helped in the growth of number of reading rooms. Thus educationally benefited youths became aware of the power of knowledge and they started to establish reading rooms and libraries in different parts of Malabar to uplift the educationally and socially backward communities. They collected books from homes and started many libraries in small rooms.

Literary Movement

The growth of the publishing industry started in Malabar during the first half of the 19th century. With the advancement of printing technology several literary publications came into existence. The first newspaper "Rajyasamacharam" by Basel mission at Thalassery (Kannur) started publication in June 1847 (Priyadarsanan 1981).[14] Another newspaper, "Keralopakari" started by a German missionary in 1874 (Hari Sharma 1964).[15] The literary activities of Basel mission included the compilation of a lexicon, publication of journals, textbooks, and grammar for the schools. (Sreedhara Menon 1996).[16] In 1884 the proprietor of the English newspaper "Malabar Spectator" started a Malayalam newspaper "Kerala Sanchari", which highlighted the various socio-political issues of Kerala. The newspaper "Malayala Manorama" came into existence in 1890. Swadeshabhimani K. Ramakrishna Pillai, the pioneer of fearless journalism was the editor of the papers "Darpanam", "Kerala Panchika", "Malayali" and "Swadeshabhimani" during 1899 and 1910. "Kerala Kaumudhi" was started in 1911, and "Mathrubhumi" started its publication in 1923. "Al-Ameen" newspaper was started by Muhammad Abdu Rahiman in 1924 from Calicut with the objective of bringing Muslims into the stream of national movement. In 1924 another newspaper "Kerala Kesari" was published from Vadakara (Kozhikode), its publisher was Moyarathu Shankaran (Vijayan 2000).[17] A periodical "Muslim" was published with the object of generating new insights in the social and intellectual life of Muslims. Vakkam Abdul Khadar Maulavi, a social reformer was its editor (Sreedhara Menon 1996).[18] In January 1935, "Prabhatham" the weekly newspaper was published by Kerala Congress Socialist Party (Namboothiripad 1976).[19] In 1942 the Communist Party of India began to publish a daily "Deshabhimani"(Namboothiripad. 1964).[20]

These dailies were subscribed to in village libraries and people were very curious to know the current events. The newspapers catered to the needs of the growing reading public. Newspapers served as an important means of mobilisation of public opinions. News about different social reforms like Vaikam and Guruvayoor temple entry satyagrahas and national movement received wide coverage in the newspapers. People often had to travel many kilometers for a newspaper. They wanted a centre for reading newspapers. This was one of the causes for the birth of reading rooms in the different parts of the State.

Dramas, novels, poems etc. depicting the life of ordinary human beings began to appear in those days. By this time, social and religious organisations entered the field of publication. Very soon, a "Progressive Literary Movement" was developed (Vijayan 2000).[21] Consequently reading rooms and libraries increased in number. The establishment of Sahithya Pravarthaka Sahakarana Sanghom (Co-operative Society for the Literary Works) in 1949 promoted the publishing industry, and it acted as a catalyst agent in the library movement (Lenin 1982).[22]

Political Awakening and Libraries

Along with the political awakening, a large number of reading rooms and libraries were opened in Malabar..They became the meeting places of people in the evening and they discussed various social, economic and political issues. Many agitations such as salt sathyaghraha and toddy shop picketing were conducted as part of nationalist movement under the auspices of the libraries.

The national movement in the real sense was started in Malabar only with the setting up of the Malabar Home Rule League in 1916. On 4th and 5th May, 1916 the Malabar District Congress meeting held at Palakkad under the chairmanship of Annie Bezant resolved to establish autonomous local administrative units, which would have full freedom in establishing schools and libraries in every village (Pillai 1986).[23] After the Malabar rebellion, under the initiative of Devdar

Malabar Reconstruction Trust (DMRT) which was established in 1922 under Gopalakrishna Ghokale's "The Servants of India Society" established many adult education centres, reading rooms, schools, and orphanages in Malabar (Udayabanu 1982).[24]

During public agitation against British imperialism and against the atrocities of landlords, P. Eashwaran, a congress worker came to Mayyil, a rural area in Kannur in 1932. He organised the young people of this place and conducted Hindi classes in a shed. Along with attending the Hindi classes, people actively participated in national movements. This shed was later converted as "Velam Pothujana Vayanasala" in 1934. This library was a centre for political activity and peasant movements against landlords and it played an important role in the political, cultural and educational development of this area. (Velam Public Library, Administrative Committee 1984).[25]

In Kalliassery, a rural place in Kannur, a reading room namely "Sree Harshan" was opened in April 1935, which was a work-centre for K.P.R. Gopalan, Keralayeen, and A.K.Gopalan, the activists of Kerala Congress Socialist Party (Rairappan 2001).[26] During this period many libraries were established in the surrounding villages such as Bakkalam, Parassinikadavu, Anchampeedika, Keecheri, and Kolachery. These libraries were centres of national movement and peasant movement (Poduval 1982).[27]

Under the leadership of K.P.R Gopalan, a meeting of 44 libraries in Chirakkal thaluk was convened at Bakkalam, Kannur in 1934 (Thozhilali Library and Reading Room, Chovva 1982).[28] When E.M.S. Namboothiripad was the general secretary of the Kerala Pradesh Congress Committee in 1938, he issued a circular to its all village committees to establish reading rooms and conduct night classes under their responsibility as part of the constructive social service programmes of the Congress. He stressed the role of public libraries and adult education programmes in uplifting the people (Namboothiripad 1964).[29] In the *Golden Jubilee Souvenir of Kodiyeri Public Library* (1986),[30] it was stated that during 1938, night classes were held in this library, to teach five languages

Hindi, Tamil, English, Malayalam, and Sanskrit and 38 students attended the classes and 5 teachers engaged the classes.

The Communist Party was formed in the Vivekananda Library at Pinarayi village in Kannur district on September 3, 1939. This library was established in 1935 in memory of the arrival of the then president of Indian National Congress, in Kannur. From this library, a procession went to the palace of Kottayam Raja to protest against the unnecessary levy. The secretary of this library was arrested then in connection with the "Quit India Movement" and this library did not function thereafter (Mukundan Master 2001).[31]

The veteran Communist leader in Kerala, Azhikodan Raghavan was the secretary of the public library Deshabhivardhini Vayanasala, Kakkad, a rural area in Kannur during 1940-41. A majority of the population of this area was labourers. This library was the centre of many social activities during that period (Kumaran 2001).[32] In the year 1943 when cholera spread in Malabar, many relief centres were started and some of them converted as libraries. When A. K. Gopalan, a veteran Communist leader was released from jail, one such relief centre was converted into reading room under his initiative. This is Mavilayi Public Library, Thalasserry, Kannur. Its main objectives were to help the downtrodden people, elevate them and make them conscious of irreligious works and superstitions. This library was renamed Moidu Memorial Library. Moidu, a young Muslim from a conservative family won acclaim for his social work. (Murali 1993).[33]

The working class enthused with the leaders' words, actively participated in the establishment of reading rooms. In the initiative of Kundanjeri Kunhiraman Master and N. E. Balaram libraries were established in Eranholi, Thalassery and, under the leadership of K. T. Madhavan Master libraries were established in Mattanur. Libraries were established under the initiative of M. K. Kelu in Vadakara and Sugreevan Kunhiraman Master in Quilandy. P. C. Raghavan Nair, P.V. Kunhunni Nair, and E .P. Gopalan took initiative for establishing libraries in south Malabar (Poduval 1982).[34] They were the centres for holding study classes, night classes, political discussions, and many cultural activities. They also made people conscious of irreligious works and superstitions.

Role of Workers' Unions

The leaders of peasant movements, A. K. Gopalan, K. A. Keraleeyan, K. P. R. Gopalan, P. Krishna Pillai, T. S. Tirumumbu and such other leaders, were also the pioneers in the establishment of reading rooms such as Deshapriya Vayanasala, Mottammal, Kannur; Balabodhini Library, Kanchangad; and Deshiya Yuvajana Sangham Vayanasala, Kannur. When All India Students Federation sent a procession to Chirakkal, Kannur, they noted that informal peasant unions had set up reading rooms in the forest regions of north-east (EK 1939).[35] The Malabar Karshaka Sangham (peasant union) officially formed in May 1938 led many peasant processions to the houses of the local janmis (landlords). The libraries of the area gave enthusiastic receptions to these processions in the premises of libraries.

The Cigar Workers' Union formed in Cannanore in 1934 resolved to set up reading rooms.Accordingly Thalassery Cigar Workers' Union started a reading room namely Sree Narayana Beedi Thozhilali Vayanasala (Cigar Workers' Reading Room) in March 20, 1934 to increase their knowledge. In 1940 they started to publish a hand written magazine "Thozhilali" (Labourer). During 1940-46, Hindi English, Malayalam and Tamil languages were taught in the night classes as part of the reading room. This reading room was kept open from 10 a.m. to 9 p.m. every day (Prabhatham 27 March, 1939).[36] Other libraries set up by cigar workers at their work place are Pothujana Vayanasala, Edachovva, Kannur; Udaya vayanasala, later renamed as AKG Memorial Library, Marutha road, Palakkad (1950); Deshiya Reading Room& Library, Thalassery, Kannur (1953). Weaving labourers also started reading rooms such as Jankeeya Vayanasala, Karaltheru, Thalassery (1953) (Kerala. State Planning Board 1997).[37] During the period 1920-1930 when movements like peasant movements and political movements were not alive in

Malabar, the teachers union took active part in establishing reading rooms in Malabar (Kutty Master 2004).[38]

Role of Students' Organisations

Students' Union in Kannur established a library namely Sree Narayana Library and Reading Room at Punnol, Kannur in 1928. (Kerala. State Planning Board 1997).[39] Muslim students' organisation of Kozhikode started a public library at Idiyangara in 1951 with the fund obtained from cultural programmes conducted by the Yuvasahithi Samajam (Youngmen's Literary Association). It is CIESCO, Kozhikode (Citizen's Intellectual, Educational, Social, and Cultural Organisation) formed at Idiyangara, Kozhikode, which started a library and was affiliated to Kerala Granthasala Sanghom in 1957. In 1974 it started mobile libraries for women (Mammad Koya 1994).[40]

Role of Religious Organisations

The lower caste movements of early decades of 20th century had emphasised the link between power and knowledge (Dilip Menon 1994).[41] The Sudhujana Paripalana Sabha (Poor People Welfare Society) established by Ayyankali in 1907; The Keraliya Kammala Samajam (Kerala Artisans Association), started in 1911; Araya Mahajana Sabha (Fishermen's Congress) 1920; Namboodiri Yoga Kshema Sabha (Namboodiri Welfare Association); Nayar Samajams (Nayar Society) did a lot for the upliftment of their community (Ganesh 1997).[42]

Religious associations also showed interest in establishing libraries. Christian missionaries and Muslim associations also started libraries in Malabar. Muslim Brotherhood Library established at Kuttichira, in 1928 is the first library established in the Muslim majority area of Kozhikode. This organisation inculcated reading habits among the Muslims of this area (Mammad Koya 1994).[43] YMMA (Young Men's Muslim Association) formed in 1928 as part of nationalist movement established Muhammad Abdu Rahiman Smaraka Library, at Mattul (Kannur) in 1928 (Kerala. State Planning Board 1997).[44] The scheduled castes and scheduled tribes libraries were established in areas with predominantly backward communities for their intellectual and social upliftment. C.M.P. Nair library, Hosdurg, Kasaragod; Jai Hind Reading Room and Library, Kadamkode, Hosdurg are examples of such libraries (District Library Council, Kasaragod 2001).[45] As part of Harijan Balika Sadanam (Harijan Girls Home) a library named K. C. Narayanan Memorial Library was opened in 1943 (Mathrubhumi 16 September, 1943).[46]

Social Reform Movements and Birth of Public Libraries

Many libraries were established as part of social reform movements. Sree Narayana Guru, the social reformer asked his followers to establish libraries as part of monasteries and to ensure that a library includes books on all religions, as this would ensure communal harmony (Sree Narayana Guru 1990).[47] His followers and the workers of "Sree Narayana Dharma Paripalana Yogam" formed on May 15, 1903 (Mitra 1993)[48] were enthused with his speeches and established many libraries in Malabar in his memory such as Sree Narayana Vilasam Library, Alavil, Kannur; Sree Narayana Memorial Library, Mokeri, Kozhikode; Sree Narayana Memorial Library, Mangattiri, Malappuram; and Sree Nararyana Library, Olavakkode, Palakkad. Another social reformer Sree Vagbhatananda Guru established 'Athma Vidya Sangham', a spiritual organisation. This Sangham established many libraries in the name of this spiritual master. He had shown much interest in the functioning of the libraries (Udayabanu 1982).[49] 'Vagbadanada Vilasam', Kuthuparamba, Kannur (May 1929); Pattiam Gurudevavilasam Library, Thalassery, Kannur (August 29, 1936); Sree Vagbadananda Library, Azheekode, Kannur (1939); Sree Vagbadananda Gurudeva Memorial Library, Kuthuparamba, Kannur (1956); Sreė Vagbadananda Library, Eranhipalam, Kozhikode (1939) are libraries established by Athma Vidya Sangham.

In Chalapuram, a rural place in Kozhikode, reading rooms were opened as part of the movement against untouchability, casteism, outdated customs and traditions, and for the upliftment of poor and backward communities. Kasturba

Memorial Library, Cherpulassery, Palakkad; Karalmanna Public Library (Palakkad), Sanmarga Darshini Library& Reading Room, Kozhikode (1929), Sengupta Library, Kozhikode (1933), Thozhilai Vayanasala (Labourers' Reading room), Chovva, Kannur(1932) are some examples of the centres of nationalist movement, and also against the social evils.

Cultural Background

During the 1950s, due to the initiative of eminent literary figures like Thikkodian, K.T. Mohammed, and S. K. Pottekkatt, a Central Cultural Committee was formed. Under the auspices of this Committee, local libraries were formed. Many arts and sports clubs started libraries such as A. K. G. Arts & Sports Club & Library, Kattipoyil, Kasaragod; Labour Sports Club Library and Reading room, Keechery, Kannur; and Youngmen's Arts Club & Library, Muchukunnu, Kozhikode. Namboothiripad (1964)[50] puts the cultural development of Kerala of this period in these words: "The Congress Socialist Party which developed within the Indian National Congress and which later on converted itself into the Communist Party in Kerala did many services to the cultural renaissance of Kerala." Young congress workers and the communists organised several cultural programmes like dramas highlighting the social, political, and economic problems under the auspices of libraries and attracted more people to national movements. The libraries acquired the reading materials published by the various political, religious, and social organisations. The increased use of libraries and reading rooms raised them to the level of cultural centres of the locality.

The educational awareness, national movement, the emergence of political parties, the rapid growth of political consciousness, the formation of religious organisations, the social reform movements during the twenties and thirties of the twentieth century accelerated the genesis and growth of public libraries and hastened the birth of a library movement in Kerala.

There were several instances to mark the enthusiasm and the heart-felt attachment of the people for the development of the libraries. P.C. Lakshmi, a retired teacher form Thanur Devdar High School took membership in the Thanur Sanchara Library, Malappuram. After her retirement she went to her native place, Kannur and until her death she sent subscriptions to the library. Before her death she expressed her desire to contribute to the building fund of the Thanur Sanchara Library and her last wish was fulfilled by her brother P. C. Raghavan (Granthalokam April 1979).[51]

Kodungalore Kunhukuttan Nambiar, a local ruler contributed a good collection of rare manuscripts (palm leaves) to Champathil Chathukutty Mannadiyar Memorial Library. Kerala Varma Valiya Koyi Thampuran, Raja Raja Varma also made contribution to this library. Unfortunately after 1977, it ceased functioning (Muthumaster 1997).[52] Ruler of Nileswaram province, Kasaragod donated a land of 10 cents for building a library for the people of Achamthuruthi, a small island resided mostly by the tenants of the ruler. On this land Sree Narayana Guru Library was established on December 4, 1944 (Krishnan 2001).[53]

Many activities such as chittis, auctions etc. were undertaken by the people for the purpose of raising funds for construction of library buildings. Cultural programmes were also organised for raising money. They received generous contributions from many people in the form of money and construction materials to build libraries.

Though several libraries and reading rooms sprang up during early period under the influence of social reform movements and national movements, many were short lived because the library workers who were also political workers were arrested during this period. Many libraries were destroyed in Malabar immediately after the independence because of political rivalry, e.g. Public Library, Irinavu, Kannur; Deshapriya Vayanasala, Mottammal, Kannur; Public Library, Chalavara (Palakkad).

EARLY DEVELOPMENTS IN TRAVANCORE AND COCHIN

The history of public libraries in Travancore started with the establishment of the Trivandrum Public Library in 1829, one among the oldest libraries of this type in existence in India. It was founded by Col. Edward Codogan, a British Resident in Travancore. This library at its inception was for the use of the Europeans of Trivandrum and for those invited to the Durbar of the Maharaja (Menon 1974).[54] Under the reign of Sree Moolam Thirunal it was opened to the public in 1898. In 1958 it was declared as the State Central Library of Kerala (Kerala 2002).[55]

The first attempt to collect books in Malayalam and organise public libraries was made during the reign of Vishakam Thirunal Maharaja (1880-1885) and thus Sugunaposhini Vayanasala at Vanchiyoor was established in 1880 (Ramanujan Nair 1974).[56] Under the reign of Sree Moolam Thirunal, rules were framed to give grant-in-aid to libraries By 1917-18 there were about 47 libraries and reading rooms in Travancore receiving aid from the Education Department of the State. (Ramanujan Nair 1974).[57] Three all Travancore library conferences were held under the auspices of Jnanapradayini Library at Neyyattinkara in 1925, Sree Chithira Thirunal Library at Trivandrum in 1933 and Diwan Nanu Pillai Memorial Library at Neyyoor in 1935. These conferences helped to convince the general public of the urgent need for a strong library movement in the State. The Education Reform Committee of Travancore made certain recommendations regarding government's role in the development of libraries. In the light of these recommendations, the Director of the Department of Education prepared a scheme in 1932 to establish a central distributing library and a number of rural libraries. In 1935 the government opened 64 libraries as part of government primary schools and each of these libraries was given annual grants (Ramanujan Nair 1974).[58]

The following are the libraries established early in Travancore: Suganaposhini Vayanasala, Vanchiyoor (1880); Kottayam Public Library (1882); Leo XI Public Library &Reading Room, Kaippuzha, Kottayam (1900); Chithira Thirunal Smaraka Library, Trivandrum (1913); Raja Raja Varma Library, Oachira (1913); Lalithavilasini Library and

Reading Room, Padmanabhapuram (1916); Marthandavilasam Library, Eraniel (1917); Sree Moolam Silver Jubilee Library, Thodupuzha (1919); Avoor Deshabhandu Library, Avoor (1925); Jnanapradayini Library at Neyyanttinkara (1925); Sree Avittam Thirual Library, Kuriyathi (1934) etc.

All Travancore Granthasala Sanghom

The "All Travancore Granthasala Sanghom" was formed in 1945 under the initiative of P. N. Panicker, the leading figure in public library movement in Kerala at P.K. Memorial Library, Ambalapuzha. Forty seven libraries took membership in the Sanghom in 1945. P.N. Panicker was elected the secretary and K.M. Kesavan the president (Panicker 1974).[59] The Sanghom was registered as per the Travancore Company Act on May 27, 1947 (Lenin 1982).[60] During the working period of the Sanghom, many libraries were established in Travancore.

In Cochin

In Cochin, rural libraries were started as part of the adult education programme of the Government since 1926. These libraries were under the direct control of Village Development Committes (Ramanujan Nair 1974).[61] An important event in the history of library movement in Cochin is the establishment of the literary organisation called "Samastha Kerala Pusthakalaya Samithi" (All Kerala Library Association) under the leadership of Chenkulath Cheriya Kunhirama Menon at Trichur in March 1931. The main objectives of this organisation were (1) to conduct campaign work stressing the necessity of establishing libraries in about 6000 rural areas, (2) to convince the government, locals bodies, and the rich sections of the society the importance of establishing more libraries, (3) to establish a book depot in order to collect books from the different publishers and to distribute them to the libraries, and (4) to publish a periodical named "Granthavihara" with the subscription rate of Re. 1 per issue (Balakrishnan 1989).[62] The public libraries in municipalities were under the control of the Director of Education and the government rural libraries were under the control of the Director of Panchayats (Krishna Kurup

1946).[63] There were three types of libraries in Cochin by 1946 and they were public libraries, rural libraries, and village libraries. They all received grants from the government (Isaac 1971).[64] The "Cochin Granthalaya Sanghom" was formed at Trissur on October 5, 1946 with R. Krishnankutty Nair, the Secretary and M.K. Raja, the Chairman (Krishna Kurup 1946).[65] Libraries established early in Cochin are the following: Ernakulam Public Library (1869), Trichur Public Library (1873), Chittur Municipal Library (1910), Kodungalloor Public Library (1912), Yogakshema Library and Reading Room, Trichur (1915), Grameena Vayanasala, Cheruthuruthi (1929), Sri. Kerala Varma Public Library, Vadakkanchery (1934), Sri. Appan Thampuran Smaraka Vayanasala, Ayyanthole (1936) etc.

Travancore-Cochin Granthasala Sanghom

With the integration of the States of Travancore and Cochin, the 'All Travancore Granthasala Sanghom' and Cochin Granthalaya Sanghom merged together and formed the "Travancore-Cochin Granthasala Sanghom" in 1949 (Ramanujan Nair 1974).[66] In the library conference at Ernakulam Public Library under the chairmanship of Tottakkad Krishna Menon on March 11, 1949, it was decided to merge the libraries in both erstwhile States of Travancore and Cochin together. Accordingly a committee with twenty nine members; Tottakkad Krishna Menon, the president; and W. O. George and K. R. Sashtri, the covenors was constituted. In the meeting of this committee on April 3, 1949, a sub-committee including P.N. Panickar and P.V. Krishnan Nair was constituted for drafting rules and guidelines. Then the libraries in Cochin were merged together with the libraries in Travancore and formed the "Travancore-Cochin Granthasala Sanghom". The Library Department of Cochin was abolished. (Murali 1997).[67]

LIBRARY MOVEMENT IN MALABAR

The Madras government contributed much for the development of public libraries in Malabar which is a part of

Madras Presidency. The Madras government allocated Rs. 20, 000 for the public libraries in Malabar in the budget of 1920-21 (Ravi 1992).[68] The private interests also contributed in the establishment of libraries in Malabar such as Victoria Memorial Library, Tellicherry; Payyannur Public Library, Kannur; and Alathur Public Library, Palakkad. The District Board Authorities invited Ambattu Sivarama Menon, a member of Administrative Committee for Libraries of Madras government to Malabar and he delivered lectures in Cannanore, Tellicherry, Calicut, Tirur, and Palghat in June 1931 and stressed the need for the establishment of public libraries. (Krishna Kurup 1946).[69] Thus the visit of Sivarama Menon is considered as the beginning of library movement in Malabar.

Early Established Libraries

Some of the libraries established early in Malabar are the following:

Calicut Public Library (1890) which was later handed over to Calicut municipality and it functioned under its control till 1952; Victoria Library, now renamed Maulana Kalam Azad Memorial Library, Tellicherry (1901); Sree Narayana Vilasam Vayanasala, Alavil, Kannur (1926); Cannanore Public Library, Kannur (1929); Samadarshini Library, Kozhikode (1929); Sanmargadarshini Library and Reading Room, Kozhikode (1929); Mahatma Library, Palghat (1931); Thozhilali Library and Reading Room, Chovva, Kannur (1932); Sengupta Library, Kozhikode (1933); Paral Public Library, Paral, Tellicherry, earlier known as "Kerala Chandrika" (1934); Aikyakerala Library, Kozhikode (1934); Tagore Library and Reading Room, New Mahe (1934), Kodiyeri Public Library, Tellicherry (1936), Gurudeva Vilasam Library and Reading Room, Pathayakunnu, Tellicherry (1936); Deshaposhini Vayansala, Kozhikode (1937); SJM Library and Reading Room, Kandakkai, Kannur (1938); Sree Vagbhadananda Gurudeva Smaraka Vayansala, Eranhipalam, Kozhikode (1939); Sanjayan Smaraka Library and Reading Room, Payyannur (1944); Chathamangalam Public Library, Chathamangalam (1944) etc.

Malabar Vayanasala Sanghom

The meeting of library workers held at Gramabandu Vayanasala, Tirur on April 17, 1937 resolved to upgrade the defunct libraries of Malabar and to hold a library conference in the following month. For this purpose a working committee with K. Damodaran the secretary was elected (Mathrubhumi 20 April, 1937).[70] Accordingly the first Malabar library conference was held in June 1937 at town hall, Calicut. K. Kelappan, the president of Malabar District Board was the chairman of this conference. About 300 delegates from various places such as Badagara, Quilandy, Thottada, Kannur, Malapparambu, Kottapparambu, Nellayi, Kozhikode, Tirur, Beypore, Nadakkavu, Chirakkal, Puthiyara, Cherukulathoor, Kalliassery, Athirakam, Pinarayi, Nilamboor, Kodiyeri etc have attended the meeting. The meeting recommended to form a separate library committee for each taluk and for Malabar district; to start a library in each elementary school; to conduct night classses, Hindi classes, and to establish rural industrial centres, Harijana Seva Sangham, Seva Samiti, and such other activities as part of libraries; to establish circulating libraries; and to form "Vayanasala Sanghom" to coordinate the works of all libraries in Malabar. Accordingly the "Malabar Vayanasala Sanghom" was formed at Calicut town hall on June 11, 1937 with E. Raman Menon, president; Maduravanam C. Krishna Kurup, vice president; K. Damodaran, secretary; P.T. Narayanan Nair, joint secretary; and A. Balagopalan, treasurer (Mathrubhumi 13 June, 1937).[71]

Kerala Granthalaya Sanghom

The Kerala Granthalaya Sanghom was formed to extend the works of the "Malabar Vayanasala Sanghom" all over Kerala. E. Raman Menon was the chairman of the Sanghom. Nalappattu Narayana Menon, Balamani Amma, K. Godavarma, Panampilli Govinda Menon, Joseph Mundassery, S. Guptan Nair, and C. Unniraja, were members of the executive committee (Kerala Granthasala Sanghom 1971).[72] As per XXI (Charitable Society) Act of 1860, the "Malabar Vayanasala Sanghom" was registered as "Kerala Granthalaya

Sanghom" on December 6, 1943 (Mathrubhumi 10 December, 1943).[73]

This organisation did a lot for the establishment and development of libraries in Malabar. It organised the first north Malabar library conference on November 30, 1946 at Calicut town hall under the chairmanship of veteran political leader K. Kelappan. This meeting resolved to take the following decision: (1) To give a memorandum to the government describing the existing condition of the public libraries in Malabar, (2) To request the government to draft and pass a public library bill in the legislation, (3) To appoint a committee to enrich the children's literature section in the libraries, (4) To establish a research library in Calicut, (5) To increase the women membership in the libraries, and (6) To consult with the library associations in Travancore and Cochin for implementing one administrative structure in all libraries in Kerala (Mathrubhumi 4 December, 1946).[74] The Sanghom organised several meetings of library workers and conducted training programmes for them. It invited S. R. Ranganathan, the chairman of the "Indian library Association" and he visited the libraries in Malabar in January and February 1945. It is an important event in the history of the library movement. He made speeches on various aspects of libraries in many places such as Sree Shailam, Badagara, Thalasserry, Paral, Kannur, Chirakkal, Payyannur, and Kalliassery. He had discussions with library workers, education officers, and members of Local Administrative Departments and made suggestions for the development of libraries in Malabar (Krishna Kurup 1946).[75] It conducted the first book exhibition in Kerala at Calicut in May 1945 as part of the Madras State education conference (Krishna Kurup 1960).[76] The Sanghom became defunct in 1953 as some of its workers were arrested, since they were the political workers (Lenin 1982).[77]

Local Library Authority (LLA)

The first library law in the country, Madras Library Act was passed in 1948. It came into effect on April 1, 1950. Under the provision of the Act, Local Library Authorities have been constituted one for the city of Madras and one each for the fifteen revenue districts including Malabar. Every Local Library Authority elects one of its members its director, he is the chief executive of the Authority. The District Educational Officer functions as the secretary of the Authority. In case the Authority ceases to exist, the secretary will carry out its work as usual till its reconstitution. The term of office of a member of Local Library Authority is three years. The Authority appoints an executive committee of seven members and delegates powers to this committee. Sub committees are also formed to enquire into or advise on matters connected with LLA.

Local Library Authorities have the powers to provide necessary infrastructure to the libraries, and conduct lectures and hold classes for library staff and workers. The movable and immovable properties of all public libraries in the area are vested in the Local Library Authority of that area. Periodical inspections of branch libraries and rural libraries are done by the Director of the Authority twice a year. The Authority recommends grants to libraries run by the panchayats, grama sanghm, and private agencies. Private agencies have to consult the Authority with regard to their bye-laws and the list of books they want to purchase.

Each LLA levies and collects library cess in the form of a surcharge on the property or house tax through local bodies. The State government contributes an amount equal to the amount collected by levying library cess. The other sources of income of the Authority include contributions, gifts and income from endowments made for the benefit of public libraries; special grants from governments; fees, fines; and other amounts collected from the libraries.

Each LLA maintains and runs one district central library and various branch libraries. The branch library is opened in each village with a population of not less than five thousand. Full time librarians are appointed in these libraries. The staff in the libraries under the LLA are qualified, and salaried and have the status of government employees. Part-time librarians are working in the book delivery stations. (Madras. Education and Public Health Department 1949).[78]

Malabar Local Library Authority

In order to manage, administer, and run library services in the Malabar region a Local Library Authority was constituted under the provision of Madras Public Libraries Act (1948) in 1950 (Madras. Education and Public Health Department 1949).[79] Calicut was the head quarter of Malabar LLA. The first meeting of the LLA under the chairmanship of Special Officer for Libraries R. Janardhana Kurup was conducted at Government Training School, Calicut on August 6, 1950. K. P. Kesava Menon was elected the first chairman, and K. Kunju Kaimal was the first secretary. An executive committee was elected with C. Achutha Menon, Madhuravanam C. Krishna Kurup, and P. P. Ummer Koya the members. Two more members from panchayat boards were taken into the committee (Local Library Authority, Malabar 1950).[80]

As per the Act, the district board, the municipal councils, and the panchayat boards collected library cess from April 1 onwards. With the formation of Malabar LLA, the government sanctioned a sum of Rs. 8,000 as advance for putting into effect library services as expeditiously as possible. There is a provision of Rs.1 lakh out of which Rs. 46,000/- for libraries under district board and municipal councils and Rs. 54, 000/- for libraries under panchayats and grama sanghoms were allocated in the budget estimate for 1950-51 towards grants to the public libraries (Local Library Authority, Malabar 1950).[81]

The old Calicut Muncipal Library was taken over by the LLA on July 15, 1952 and it was the District Central Library of the LLA (Local Library Authority, Malabar 1952).[82] Many municipal libraries, panchayat libraries, and firka central libraries in Malabar were handed over to the LLA. The Municipal Library, Cannanore; Municipal Library, Tellicherry; Payyannur Reading Room & Library, Payyannur; Muncipal Library, Palaghat; Muncipal Library, Calicut; Perinthalmanna Panchayat Library, Perinthalmanna; Firka Central Library, Kumbala; and Firka Central Library, Tellicherry were such transferred libraries (Local Library Authority, Malabar 1952-56).[83]

The LLA gave some aid to the local private libraries like Victoria Public Library, Tellichery; Payyannur Public Library; and Alathur Public Library. for "meeting the charges on dailies and periodicals approved by the Malabar LLA" The LLA were also giving grant to grama sangham libraries such as Vidyaposhini Reading Room, Karumankkad; Madhavan Nair Memorial Library, Cholapuram; Kunnamangalam Grama Sangham Library; Kottakkal Grama Sangham Library; and Pattuvam Grama Sangham Library. (Local Library Authority, Kozhikode 1959).[84]

After the reorganisation of States and after the formation of the present constituent State of Kerala, the State government split Malabar region into three revenue districts viz. Calicut, Cannanore, and Palghat and consequently three Local Library Authorities were constituted on April 1, 1959, one for each district as per government notification no. Ed (d) 3-2447/57/ EHD dated 18.6.57. A district central library, branch libraries, rural libraries, and book delivery stations were functioning under each Library Authority.

Local Library Authority, Cannanore

The first meeting of the LLA, Cannanore was held in 1959 and Govardhan Das was elected the chairman. The head quarter of this LLA was at Tellicherry. The District Central Library was functioning at Kannur. Many libraries in Cannanore such as Victoria Memorial Muncipal Library, Tellicherry; the Firka Central Library, Tellicherry; the Firka Central Library, Kumbala, and Hajee Memorial Library under the Cannanore municipality were transferred to the Cannanore LLA (Local Library Authority, Cannanore 1959-64).[85]

Local Library Authority, Kozhikode

The first meeting of the LLA, Kozhikode was held on May 24, 1959 at the office of District Educational Officer, Kozhikode. A. Balagopalan was elected the chairman (Local Library Authority, Kozhikode 1959).[86] The Calicut Municipal Library which was handed over to the LLA, Kozhikode on July 15, 1959 functioned as District Central Library (Local Library

Authority, Kozhikode 1959).[87] In addition to this, 4 branch libraries at Badagara, Panthalayini, Manjeri, and Tirur; 4 rural libraries at Kottakal, Manjeri, Perambra, Vattoli; and 5 book delivery stations at Kunnamangalam, Koduvalli, Elathur, Beypore and Ramanattukara were under its control at the time of its formation (Sreedhara Menon 1962).[88] Several libraries such as community centres under Wyanad colonisation scheme at Ambalavayal, Chulliode, Cheeral, and Nellarchal were transferred to the LLA (Local Library Authority, Kozhikode 1973).[89] The government handed over 33.5 cents of land of Calicut to the LLA, Kozhikode in 1965 (Local Library Authority, Kozhikode 1965).[90] The public libraries under the district board, corporations, municipalities, panchayats, private management, and grama sanghams and firka central libraries were aided by the LLA.

After the formation of the new Malappuram district, the activities of the LLA, Kozhikode were extended to the Malappuram district also. The District Central Library, Malappuram was opened on October 2, 1977 and the distributing librarian, Palghat was posted as district central librarian of Malappuram on work arrangement. The branch library at Ponnani and Malappuram came under the control of the LLA, Kozhikode. (Local Library Authority, Kozhikode 1977).[91]

Local Library Authority, Palghat

The first meeting of the LLA, Palghat was held in the office of District Educational Officer, Palghat on May 30, 1959. K. Narayanan Nair was elected the chairman. The district central library, eight branch libraries, and nine rural libraries were functioning under the LLA, Palghat in 1959. Many libraries under the panchayats and the municipalities in the Palghat district were transferred to the LLA, Palghat (Local Library Authority, Kozhikode 1959).[92]

The government in the notification no. 24769/A3/84 H. Edn. dated 1-11-85 has ordered to reconstitute six LLAs, one each for the revenue districts of Kozhikode, Malappuram, Wayanad, Palakkad, Cannanore, and Kasaragod (Kerala

Gazette 1985).[93] As per G. O. no. M3-97063/83 dated 27-1-86, LLA committee of Kozhikode, Cannanore, and Palakkad was dissolved. But the chairman of the LLA, Kozhikode filed a writ petition against this order in the High Court of Kerala, and a stay order was obtained. As per government notification no. Ed (d) 3-2447/57/EHD dated 18.6.87; LLA of Kozhikode, Palakkad, and Cannanore were continued.

But the proposed six LLAs did not come into existence. Since 1987, no committee was constituted for the LLAs of Cannanore, Kozhikode, and Palghat and all powers of the LLA were vested upon the secretary.

The LLAs, since its formation has tried its best to form public libraries in the urban and the rural areas under its jurisdiction. The main problem they faced was the shortage of funds, as the cess collected by the local bodies was not handed over to them. This situation adversely affected the development and day to day functioning of the libraries under the LLAs.

KERALA GRANTHASALA SANGHOM

In the meeting of north Malabar library conference under the chairmanship of K.P. Kesava Menon in February 1957, initiative was taken to form "Kerala Granthasala Sanghom." In the administrative committee meeting of the "Travancore-Cochin Granthasala Sanghom" on September 15, 1958, it was decided to rename "Travancore-Cochin Granthasala Sanghom" as "Kerala Granthasala Sanghom". Accordingly an elected administrative committee comprised of members from all taluks in Kerala was constituted. In the meeting of the administrative committee convened on 28 September 1958, a working committee with Panampalli Govinda Menon the president, K. Damodharan and N.P.Manmadan the vice presidents, and P.N. Panicker the secretary was formed (Murali 1997).[94] The main objective of the Sanghom was to function as the central organisation for all libraries in the State and to work for their improvement.

The activities of the Sanghom were then extended to Malabar. Though the Madras Libraries Act was in force in the

Malabar area, a number of libraries in this area were organised and administered by the Sanghom. The Thanur Sanchara Library, Malappuram which was affiliated to "Kerala Granthasala Sanghom" on February16, 1957 is the first library to be affiliated from the Malabar area (Lenin 1982).[95] Public meetings, symposia, seminars, and workshops were periodically held under the direction of the Sanghom. The Sanghom received "Krupskaya" award from UNESCO in 1975 for its literacy works (Bhaskara Panicker 1982).[96] The most outstanding achievement of the Sanghom was the establishment of the grass roots democracy in the State.

The government dismissed the Sanghom on the issue of mis-management by an ordinance on March 16, 1977 and the powers of the Sanghom were transferred to the newly constituted "Control Board" (Lenin 1982).[97] It was a nominated body. The Control Board was reconstituted several times and it was abolished in 1991 with the enactment of Kerala Public Libraries (Kerala Granthasala Sanghom) Act.

KERALA PUBLIC LIBRARIES (KERALA GRANTHASALA SANGHOM) ACT, 1989

The enactment of the Kerala Public Libraries (Kerala Granthasala Sanghom) bill is an important event in the history of development of public libraries in Kerala. After several attempts, Education minister K. Chandrasekharan (in charge of libraries) presented the libraries bill in the assembly. The assembly gave unanimous approval to the bill on February 23, 1989. The Act got presidential assent on May 16, 1989. Thus the Kerala Public Libraries (Kerala Granthasala Sanghom) Act, 1989 came into force in Kerala as per government notification no. 1951/ Leg.C1/89/Law dated 18-5-1989. The rules and regulations of this Act were published in 1991 for the working of the libraries affiliated in the State Library Council (Kerala Gazette 1991).[98] As per this Act, three tier systems of library councils are controlling the library functions in the State. They are State Library Council, District Library Council, and Taluk Library Union. Every library has a library committee to manage its functions.

KERALA STATE LIBRARY COUNCIL

The first elected State Library Council came into existence on April 27, 1994. (Das 1997).[99] The important duties and powers of the State Library Council are:

1. To advise the government on all matters regarding library administration,
2. To co-ordinate the works of the district library council and the taluk library unions,
3. To supervise and direct all matters relating to library services in the State,
4. To carry on propaganda on the importance of library development in the State by providing lectures, conference etc., and
5. To conduct other activities such as imparting training to librarians, promoting distance education, adult education, and eradication of illiteracy (Kerala Public Libraries Act 1989).[100]

It organises various programmes and services such as conducting certificate course in Library Science, children's section, women's section, jail libraries, sanatorium libraries, juvenile home libraries, reading contest, book banks, orphanage libraries, academic study centres, rural book-circulating programmes, rural information centres, career guidance centres, and model village libraries.

PRESENT SITUATION

As per the State Library Council's record, there are 6490 public libraries affiliated to the State Library Council in 2003-04 and they are classified into six grades from A to F based on standards formulated by the Council for the purpose of giving grants. Standard for grading of libraries and rates of annual grant are furnished in Table 2.

The government grants to the State Library Council for the 5 years from 1999-2000 to 2003-04 are shown in Table 3.

The data given in Table 3 reveal that there is no steady increase of government grants to the libraries during the period from 1999-2000 to 2005-06 and maximum was in 2005-06 and

Table 2
Standard for Grading of Public Libraries and Rates of Annual Grant in 2003-04

Grade	*Books*	*Issue (Annually)*	*Paper (Dailies)*	*Periodicals*	*Building*	*Rate of annual grants (Rs.)*	*Librarians' allowance (Annual) (Rs.)*
A	8,000 and above	12,000	5 (Malayalam) 2 (English)	20	Own	10,000	6,000
B	5,000 to 8,000	8,000	5 (Malayalam) 2(English)	15	Own	8,000	6,000
C	4,000 to 5,000	6,000	5 (Malayalam) 2 (English)	12	Own	6,000	6,000
D	3,000 to 4,000	5,000	5(Malayalam) 2 (English)	10	Own	4,000	6,000
E	2,000 to 3,000	4,000	5(Malayalam) 1(English)	10	Own or rented	3,000	3600
F	1,000 to 2000	2000	5 (Malayalam)	7	Own or rented	2,000	3,600

Source: State Library Council Annual Report, 2003-04.

Table 3
Government Grant to the State Library Council from 1999-2000 to 2005-06

(*Rs. in lakh*)

Source	*1999-2000*	*2000-2001*	*2001-2002*	*2002-2003*	*2003-2004*	*2004-2005*	*2005-2006*
Grant from the Govt.	620.28	509.00	530.00	658.00	642.20	943.20	724.32
Cess	263.03	198.46	193.86	234.31	425.49	311.80	691.94
Total	883.31	707.46	723.86	892.31	1067.69	1255.0	1416.26

Source: Kerala State Library Council, Annual Reports, 1999-2005.

minimum was in 2000-01. This fluctuating trend will adversely affect the proper development of the public libraries. It can be also seen that there is a variation in the cess collected.

The public libraries in Malabar fall under five categories. They are (1) Libraries run independently, (2) Libraries run by local bodies, (3) Libraries formerly under the Local Library Authority, (4) Libraries run as part of Sports and Arts Club, and (5) Libraries run by other governing bodies. The first four categories of libraries are affiliated to the State Library Council and are provided grant-in-aid by the Council. But for the libraries run by the local bodies, the grant is provided only for books. The libraries under other governing bodies get the revenue form different sources such as donation, membership fee and private agencies. The public libraries, grade-wise and district-wise are given in Table 4.

Table 4
Public Libraries in Malabar in 2003-04 (Grade-wise and District-wise)

Grade	*Kasaragod*	*Kannur*	*Kozhikode*	*Malappuram*	*Wayanad*	*Palakkad*	*Total*
A	8	50	43	24	9	45	179
B	10	90	87	58	9	56	310
C	16	107	74	58	18	57	330
D	33	132	64	49	60	51	389
E	46	168	68	70	25	48	425
F	64	64	100	52	19	41	340
Total	177	611	436	311	140	298	1973

Source: District Library Council's Records, 2003-04.

As figured in Table 4, there are 1973 well functioning public libraries in Malabar in 2003-04. But as per the records, 2152 libraries are affiliated to the State Library Council in Malabar. Kannur has the largest number of public libraries in Malabar and also in Kerala and Wayanad has the lowest number. The economic and educational backwardness of Wayanad has a positive correlation in this slowness; besides this, the library movement started later in this district, whereas in Kannur it started during the national movement itself. The growth of public libraries during the period from 1999-2000 to 2005-06 is furnished in Table 5.

The data in Table 5 show the libraries which are affiliated to the Kerala State Library Council and their growth from 1999-2000 to 2003-04. It reveals that each year new libraries varying between 2 and 25 were established in all the districts.

Table 5
Growth of Public Libraries in Malabar from 1999-2000 to 2005-06

District	*1999-2000*	*2000-2001*	*2001-2002*	*2002-2003*	*2003-2004*	*2004-2005*	*2005-2006*
Kasaragod	158	165	172	174	183	185	193
Kannur	596	621	639	655	672	680	693
Kozhikode	405	427	438	445	453	460	470
Wayanad	113	121	124	132	140	142	145
Malappuram	284	297	305	310	317	318	326
Palakkad	339	361	371	378	387	391	395
Total	1895	1992	2049	2094	2152	2176	2222
Kerala	5943	6136	6250	6364	6490	6495	6594

Source: Kerala State Library Council: Annual reports 1999-2000 to 2005-06.

CONCLUSION

Changes in the socio-political context in the first half of the 20th century, especially during the nationalist movement helped the genesis of public library movement in Malabar. It was a people's movement. This movement flourished with the establishment of several reading rooms in different parts of Malabar which created national consciousness among them.

With the enactment of Madras Libraries Act in 1948, the library administration in Malabar was a part of government missions and LLAs were formed for this purpose. A number of libraries were formed on their initiative. But the public library development in all its aspects did not take place in its full dimension due to the improper administration and lack of fund. When Kerala Granthasala Sanghom became the apex body of the public libraries in 1956, there was a rapid growth of public libraries in Malabar in its number. Even though it had several objectives they couldn't be successfully implemented in all the libraries due to lack of effective planning and lack of funds. During the period of Control Board administration in 1977, there was stagnation in the growth of the library movement because the bureaucrats became the official bearers of the Board.

The Kerala State Library Council formed as per the Kerala Public Libraries (Kerala Granthasala Sanghom) Act, 1989 assumed the charge of public libraries in Kerala adopted several development programmes to convert the libraries into a social institution to fulfil their educational, cultural, informational, and recreational role. But its reflection was seen only partially in the libraries due to lack of fund, lack of scientific organisation, and lack of effective services. So it can be concluded that the multidimensional development of public libraries in Malabar is in a slow pace.

References

1. Sreedhara Menon, A. (1996), *A Survey of Kerala History*. Rev. ed. Chennai: Ananda Book Depot, 355.
2. Ramachandran Nair, Adoor K. K., ed. (1986), *Kerala District Gazetteers*. Trivandrum: State Editor, Kerala Gazetteers, 25-36.
3. Bhatt, S. C. (1998), *The Encyclopaedic District Gazetteers of India*, Vol. 2, New Delhi, Gyan Publishing House.
4. Kunhan Pillai, Elamkulam (1970), *Studies in Kerala History*. Trivandrum: The Author, 267.
5. Sreedhara Menon, A. (1996), *A Cultural Heritage of Kerala*, 2nd ed. Madras: V. Subramanian, 193.
6. Madras (1935), *Malabar Gazetteer* (Malayalam). Vol. 3, 147.
7. Innes, C. A. (1951), *Madras District Gazetteers*, Vol. 1. Madras: Government of Madras, 296-297.
8. Sreedhara Menon, A., ed. (1962), *Kerala District Gazetteers: Kozhikode*. Trivandrum: State Editor, Kerala Gazetteers, 742.
9. Innes, C. A. *op. cit.*, 7, 299.
10. Ganesh, K. N. (1997), *Keralathile Innalekal* (Malayalam), Rev.ed. Trivandrum: Government of Kerala, Department of Cultural Publications, 288-289.
11. Cherian, P. J. (1999), *Perspectives on Kerala History: The Second Millennium, Kerala State Gazetteer*. Trivandrum: Government of Kerala, Kerala Gazetteers, 464.
12. *Ibid.*, 465.
13. George, K. M. (2002), The Malayalis: The People their History and Culture. Vol. 4 of *Malayali Social and Cultural Life*. New Delhi, Cosmo Publications, 121.
14. Priyadarshanan, G. (1981), Malayalathile Adyathe Moonnu Pathrangal. In *Kerala Granthasala Sanghom Kannur Jilla Smaranika*

(Malayalam), 27-33. Kannur: Granthasala Sanghom Advisory Committee, Kannur.

15. Hari Sharma, A. D. (1964), Keralathile Pathrapravarthanam: Praramba Kaalam. In *Kerala Granthasala Directory* (Malayalam). Trivandram: Granthasala Sanghom, 27.

16. Sreedhara Menon, A. (1996), *A Survey of Kerala History*. Rev. ed. Chennai, Ananda Book Depot., 421.

17. Vijayan, M. N., ed. (2000), *Nammude Saahithyam, Nammude Samooham, 1901-2000* (Malayalam). Vol. 2. Thrissur: Kerala Sahithya Academy, 687-695.

18. Sreedhara Menon, A., *op. cit.*, 16, 407.

19. Namboothiripad, E. M. S. (1976), *How I Became a Communist*. Trans. P. K. Nair. Trivandram: Chintha Publications, 174.

20. ——(1964), *Keralam Malayalikalude Mathrubhumi* (Malayalam). 2nd ed. Trivandram: Kerala Libraries Cooperative Society, 328.

21. Vijayan, M. N., ed. *op. cit.*, 17, 706.

22. Lenin, K. M. (1982), S. P. S. S. Mayulla Bandham. In *Keralathile Granthasala Prasthanam* (Malayalam). Ed. P. N. Panicker, 132-134. Trivandram: Steps.

23. Pillai, A. K. (1986), *Kongressum Keralavum* (Malayalam). Kottayam, D. C. Books, 258.

24. Udayabhanu, P. (1982), Prasthanathinte Adiverukal. In *Keralathile Granthasala Prasthanam* (Malayalam). Ed. P. N. Panicker, 31-32. Trivandram: Steps.

25. Velam Public Library, Kannur. Administrative Committee (1984), Velam Pothujana Vayanasala. In *Velam Pothujana Vayanasala Suvarna Jubilee Souvenir* (Malayalam), 13-14.

26. Rairappan, K. P. R. (2001), Interview by Investigator. Kalliassery, Kannur, 21 February.

27. Poduval, A. K. (1982), Vayanasala Prasthanam. In *Keralathile Granthasala Prasthanam* (Malayalam). Ed. P. N. Panicker, 29-30. Trivandram: Steps.

28. Thozhilali Library and Reading Room, Chovva (1982), Fiftieth Annual Meeting Report.

29. Namboothiripad, E. M. S. *op.cit*, 20, 321.

30. Kodiyeri Public Library. Souvenir Committee. 1986. Pinnitta ara noottaand: Oru samkshipta avalokanam. In *Kodiyeri Public Library golden jubilee souvenir* (Malayalam), 129-136.

31. Mukundan Master, K. 2001. Interview by investigator. Thalassery, Kannur, 10 May.

32. Kumaran, T. C. 2001. Interview by investigator. Kakkad, Kannur, 15 August.

33. Murali Kadachira. 1993. Mavilayi mannile prakashagopuram (Malayalam). *Dheshabimani*, 21 April, 2, Kannur edition.

34. Poduval, A.K. 1982. Vayanasala prasthanam. In *Keralathile granthasala prasthanam* (Malayalam). Ed. P. N. Panicker, 28-30.Trivandram: Steps.

35. EK. 1939. Nirakshraraya krishikkar (Malayalam). *Prabhatham*, January 11, 17.

36. *Prabhatham*, March 27, 1939

37. Kerala. State Planning Board. 1997. *Onpatham paddhathi panchayath vikasana rekha, 1996: Kodiyeri panchayath* (Malayalam). Vol.145. Trivandrum: State Planning Board.

38. Kutty Master, V. P. 2004. Interview by investigator. Vadakara, Thalassery, 22 May.

39. Kerala. State Planning Board, op. cit., 37.

40. Mammad Koya Parappil, P.P. 1994. *Kozhikode muslimngalude charithram* (Malayalam). Kozhikode: Focus, 182-183.

41. Dilip M. Menon. 1994. *Caste, nationalism, and communism in south India: Malabar, 1900-1948*. New Delhi: Foundation Books.

42. Ganesh, K.N. op. cit., 10, 289.

43. Mammad Koya Parappil, P. P. op.cit, 40, 179.

44. Kerala. State Planning Board. 1997. *Onpatham paddhathi panchayath vikasana rekha, 1996: Mattul panchayath* (Malayalam). Vol.140. Trivandram: State Planning Board.

45. District Library Council, Kasaragod. 2001. Hosdurg talukile public librarikalude charithram (Malayalam), unpublished papers.

46. Mathrubhumi, September16, 1943, Kozhikode edition.

47. Sree Narayana Guru. 1990. In *Sree Narayana Guru swantham vachanangalilude*. Ed. C. R. Keshavan Vaidyar, 124. Kottayam: DC

Books. Orginally published in *Vivekodayam*, Makaram-Meenam (Malayalam months), 1912.

48. Mithra, C.R. 1993. *Sree Narayana Guruvum samuhya viplavavum* (Malayalam). Trans. C. P. Sivaraj. Kottayam: NBS, 65.
49. Udayabhanu, P. *op. cit.*, 24, 31.
50. Namboothiripad, E. M. S. *op., cit.*, 20 , 336.
51. *Granthalokam*.1979, April.
52. Muthumaster, V. (1997), Granthasalaprasthanam Palakkad Jillayil (Malayalam). In *Kerala State Library Council Seminar Report*, 15-18.
53. Krishnan, K.V., Secretary, Sree Narayana Guru Library, Achamthuruthi, 2001. Interview by Investigator. Kasaragod, April 3.
54. Menon, V. K. N. (1974), The Trivandrum Public Library. In *Trivandrum Public Library Platinum Jubilee Souvenir*. Ed. Rosscote Krishna Pillai, 14-17. Trivandrum: Government. of Kerala. State Librarian.
55. Kerala (2002), State Central Library. *http://www.kerala.gov.in/pub_library/index.htm.*
56. Ramanujan Nair, P. (1974), *Library Movement in Kerala*. Trivandrum: Writers Club, 2.
57. *Ibid.*, 7.
58. Ramanujan Nair, P. (1974), Strong Library Movement in Kerala. In *Trivandrum Public Library Platinum Jubilee Souvenir*, 111-115.
59. Panicker, P. N. (1974), Library Movement in Kerala. *Herald of Library Science*, 13, No. 3-4: 253- 258.
60. Lenin, K. M. (1982), Randam Sammelanam. In *Keralathile Granthasala Prasthanam* (Malayalam). Ed. P. N. Panicker, 71-78. Trivandram: Steps.
61. Ramanujan Nair, P. *op.cit*, 56, 11.
62. Balakrishnan, A. (1989), *Kesariyude Mukhaprasangangal* (Malayalam). Kottayam: D.C. Books, 194.
63. Krishna Kurup, Madhuravanam C. (1946), *Keralathile Granthalaya Prasthanam*. Kozhikode: Kerala Granthalaya Sanghom, 6.
64. Isaac, K.A.1971. Library movement in Kerala. In Silver jubilee souvenir of Kerala Granthasala Sanghom, 103-111. Trivandrum, Kerala Granthasala Sanghom.

65. Krishna Kurup, Madhuravanam C. *op., cit.*, 63, 8.

66. Ramanujan Nair, P. *op., cit.*, 58.

67. Murali, Pirappankode. (1997), Keralathile Granthasala Prasthanam (Malayalam). *Granthalokam* 49, No. 9 (September): 45-74.

68. Ravi, N., ed. (1992), Library Movement in Madras. In *The Hindu Speaks on Libraries*. Madras: Kasthuri and Sons, 3.

69. Krishna Kurup, Madhuravanam C. *op., cit.*, 63, 2.

70. *Mathrubhumi* (1937), Malabar Vayanasla Conference (Malayalam). April 20, Kozhikode edition, 8.

71. *Mathrubhumi* (1937), Malabar Vayanasala Conference: Vayanasalakal Parishkarikkuvan Chila Nirdeshangal (Malayalam). June 13, Kozhikode edition, 3-6.

72. Kerala Granthasala Sanghom (1971), Granthasala Sanghom: Oru laghu Charithram (Malayalam). In *Kerala Granthasala Sanghom silver jubilee souvenir*, 23-25.

73. *Mathrubhumi* (1943), December 10, Kozhikode edition.

74. *Mathrubhumi* (1946), Uthara Kerala Granthalaya Sammelanam (Malayalam). December 4, Kozhikode edition, 2.

75. Krishna Kurup, Madhuravanam C. *op., cit.*, 63, 6.

76. ——(1960), Granthalaya Prasthanam: Innaleyum Naaleyum. *Granthalokam* 12, No. 2 (February): 71-75.

77. Lenin, K. M. (1982), Malabarilekku. In *Keralathile Granthasala Prasthanam* (Malayalam). Ed. P. N. Panicker. Trivandram: Steps, 139-144.

78. Madras. Education and Public Health Department. 1949. *The Madras Public Libraries Act, 1948 (Madras Act XXIV of 1948), and the Rules Made there under.*

79. *Ibid.*, 3.

80. Local Library Authority, Malabar. 1950. Minutes, August 6.

81. —— (1950), Minutes book.

82. —— (1952), Minutes, July 15.

83. —— Minutes book, 1952-1956.

84. Local Library Authority, Kozhikode. 1959. Minutes book.

85. Local Library Authority, Cannanore. Minutes book, 1959-1964.

86. Local Library Authority, Kozhikode. 1959. Minutes, May 24.

87. —— (1959), Minutes, July 15.

88. Sreedhara Menon, A. ed., *op., cit.*, 8, 685.

89. Local Library Authority, Kozhikode (1973), Minutes book.

90. —— (1965), Minutes book.

91. —— (1977), Minutes book.

92. —— (1959), Minutes book.

93. Kerala. Gazette. 1985. XXX (November 1).

94. Murali, Pirappankode. *op. cit.*, 67: 45-74.

95. Lenin, K. M. (1982), Sanghathinte Ghadana. In *Keralathile granthasala prasthanam* (Malayalam). Ed. P. N. Panicker, 171-178. Trivandram: Steps.

96. Bhaskara Panicker, P. T. (1982), Granthasala Sanghavum Saksharatha Padhathiyum. In *Keralathile Granthasala Prasthanam* (Malayalam). Ed. P. N. Panicker, 235-240. Trivandram: Steps.

97. Lenin, K. M. (1982), 1945 Muthal Control Board Vare. In *Keralathile Granthasala Prasthanam* (Malayalam). Ed. P. N. Panicker, 297-300. Trivandram: Steps.

98. *Kerala Gazette*. 1991. February 15, 1.

99. Das, I. V. (1997), Kerala State Library Council, Kerala Granthasala Sanghom (Malayalam). In Seminar Report of Kerala State Library Council at Palakkad, 9-12.

100. Kerala Public Libraries Act. 1989, c. 2, Sec. 8, No. 1.

4

ORGANISATION, ADMINISTRATION, RESOURCES, AND USERS OF PUBLIC LIBRARIES IN MALABAR

INTRODUCTION

The preceding chapter described the various socio-political backgrounds which helped the birth of public libraries in Malabar and the organised library movement in Kerala, particularly in Malabar. The present chapter analyses the existing status of public libraries in Malabar in terms of their general characteristics, organisation; different kinds of resources such as collection, finance, staff, physical facilities, and technology; users; membership; and administration. An evaluative study on these aspects is also made based on the *IFLA/UNESCO Guidelines for Public Library Development, 2001*, to measure the effectiveness and efficiency of the libraries.

GENERAL CHARACTERISTICS OF THE LIBRARIES

The general characteristics of the selected libraries under study are described by their district, grade, year of establishment, status, location, and registration.

District

The sampled libraries under study belong to six districts of Kasaragod, Kannur, Kozhikode, Wayanad, Malappuram, and Palakkad; and their distribution, district-wise is furnished in Table 1.

Table 1
Public Libraries in Malabar (District-wise)

District	*No. of Libraries*	*Percentage*
Kasaragod	21	11.2
Kannur	57	30.5
Kozhikode	40	21.4
Wayanad	18	9.6
Malappuram	28	15.0
Palakkad	23	12.3
Total Libraries	187	100

The data in Table 1 indicate that among the 187 libraries selected for the study, Kannur district has the highest number of libraries (30.5%), followed by Kozhikode (21.4%), Malappuram (15.0%), Palakkad (12.3%), and Kasaragod (11.2%). Wayanad has the lowest number of libraries (9.6%). From this it is clear that Kannur is in the fore-front of establishing a large number of libraries and Wayanad registers slowness in this progress.

Grade

The libraries belong to six grades from A to F. The libraries are graded based on the total number of books and periodicals including newspapers in the libraries, the total number of books lent out in a year, and ownership of the library building. There are also some libraries under the control of other governing bodies in the study area which are not graded. The libraries, grade-wise are furnished in Table 2.

Table 2
Public Libraries in Malabar (Grade-wise)

Grade	*No. of Libraries*	*Percentage*
A	28	15.0
B	27	14.4
C	33	17.6
D	31	16.6
E	35	18.7
F	28	15.0
Other	5	2.7
Total	187	100.0

The data in Table 2 reveal that among the libraries under study, more number of libraries is in E grade (18.7%), followed by C (17.6%), D (16.6%), A(15%), F (15.0%), B (14.4%), and the libraries under other governing bodies are less in number (2.7%).

Location

The libraries under study are located in urban and rural areas. The Census definition of "rural" is a place of under 5,000 population; and "urban", a place with a minimum population of 5,000. The libraries, location-wise are given in Table 3.

Table 3
Public Libraries in Malabar (Location-wise)

Location	*No. of Libraries*	*Percentage*
Rural	150	80.2
Urban	37	19.8
Total	187	100

Table 3 shows that the number of libraries is more in the rural area (80.2%) than in the urban area (19.8%).

Year of Establishment

The year of establishment of the libraries under study vary from 1901 to 2002. The libraries by the year of establishment are furnished in Table 4.

Table 4
Public Libraries in Malabar (By the Year of Establishment)

Year of Establishment	*No. of Libraries*	*Percentage*
Before 1947	19	10.2
1948-67	69	36.9
1968-87	52	27.8
After 1988	47	25.1
Total Libraries	187	100.0

The data as shown in Table 4 indicate that only 10.2% of the libraries under study were established before 1947, and most of them have been established as part of the national movement. More than one third of the libraries (36.9%) were established during the period 1948-67; 27.8% of the libraries were established during 1968-87; and, 25.1% of the libraries were established after 1988 till the period of study. The Granthasala Sanghom, which was established in 1945 had an active role in the development of public libraries in Kerala. More number of libraries were established during 1948-67 with the constant efforts of the Kerala Granthasala Sanghom.

Status

A majority of the libraries are working independently under the State Library Council and some libraries, even though under the State Library Council, are working as part of other institutions such as arts and sports clubs, local administrative units such as municipalities and panchayaths, and women's clubs. Libraries which are attached to a parent institution are provided with buildings to house the library, financial assistance for purchase of books, furniture and such others by the concerned parent institution. The libraries status-wise are given in Table 5.

Table 5
Public Libraries in Malabar (Status-wise)

Status	*No. of Libraries*	*Percentage*
Independent	165	88.2
Part of Parent Institution	22	11.8
Total	187	100.0

The data in the table (Table 5) indicate that 88.2% of the libraries under study are working independently and only 11.8% are working as part of parent institutions.

Registration

Registration as per Societies Registration Act is necessary for the libraries to get financial assistance from the funding agencies such as RRRLF. So, many of the libraries have registered as per this Act. The libraries by their status of registration are furnished in Table 6.

Table 6
Public Libraries in Malabar (By the Status of Registration)

Status of Registration	*No. of Libraries*	*Percentage*
Registered	123	65.8
Not registered	64	34.2
Total	187	100

As detailed in Table 6, most of the libraries under study (65.8%) have been registered as per Societies Registration Act, and 34.2% of the libraries have not been registered. Most of the libraries which are not registered are the newly established libraries.

DIFFERENT SECTIONS IN THE LIBRARY

The different sections commonly found in the public libraries on the basis of materials are general books section, reference section and periodical section The data regarding the different sections of the libraries, grade-wise are furnished in Table 7.

Table 7
Different Sections in the Public Libraries

		General Books Section		*Reference Section*		*Periodical Section*	
Grade	*Total Libraries*	*No.*	*%*	*No.*	*%*	*No.*	*%*
A	28	28	100	28	100	28	100.0
B	27	27	100	18	81.5	26	96.3
C	33	33	100	19	72.7	30	90.9
D	31	31	100	18	58.1	27	87.1
E	35	35	100	19	54.3	32	91.4
F	28	28	100	12	42.9	25	89.3
Other	5	5	100	5	100	5	100.0
Total	187	187	100	128	68.40	173	92.5

From Table 7, it is found that all libraries have a separate general books section. All libraries in A grade, B (81.5%), C (72.7%), D (58.1%), E (54.3%), F (42.9%), and all libraries under other governing bodies having a reference section. Here a reference section means only that the reference books are arranged in separate almirahs which are placed in the general book section. A separate room for this section is not provided in these libraries. In other libraries, the reference books are kept along with general books. All libraries of A grade (100%), B (96.3%), C (90.9%), D (87.1%), E (91.4%), F (89.3%), and all libraries under other governing bodies having a periodical section. In other libraries, periodicals are kept in the general book section. There is no separate newspaper section in the public libraries under study and they are kept along with magazines and journals.

LIBRARY RESOURCES

The IFLA/UNESCO (2001)[1] says about the importance of resources for the success of the library: "To fulfil its roles satisfactorily the public library must have adequate resources, not just when it is established but also on a continuing basis, to enable it to sustain and develop services that meet the needs of the local community." The resources in a library can be categorised into five and they are: (1) information resources, (2) finance, (3) human resources, (4) physical facilities, and (5) technology. All these in sufficient quantity are inevitable for the proper development of libraries.

Information Resources

The information resources include both book materials and non-book materials. Book materials include monographs; pamphlets; journals, both current and bound volumes; newspapers; reports; and such others. The non-book materials include maps, charts, graphs, photographs, paintings, manuscripts, CDs, DVDs, floppies, cassettes, and such others.

Books

Books are the major information resource in a library. They should cover all subjects in a balanced proportion and also include adequate reference books, text books, and children's books.

Selection of Books

Value and quality of service will depend on the collection. So when the books are selected, due care must be employed to select standard books in various subjects and in all languages used by the community and other languages. A good collection depends upon a good selection policy, and it should be based on the user needs.

Selection Committee

There may be a book selection committee in many libraries comprising specialists in different subjects and languages. The data regarding the number of libraries in each grade having a book selection committee are furnished in Table 8.

Table 8

Public Libraries Having Book Selection Committee (Grade-wise)

Grade	*Total Libraries*	*No.*	*Percentage*
A	28	20	71.4
B	27	14	51.9
C	33	11	33.3
D	31	14	45.2
E	35	14	40.0
F	28	10	35.7
Other	5	2	40.0
Total	187	5	45.5

The analysis of the Table 8 shows that a majority of the libraries in A grade (71.4%) and more than half of the libraries in B grade (51.9%) have a book selection committee. More than half of the libraries in other grades and the libraries under other governing bodies have no such committee. On the whole, only 45.5% of the libraries have a book selection committee. The books selection committee is mainly comprised of executive members of the library committee. An analysis of the constitution of the library committee shows that subject experts are co-opted as members in the books selection committee in 58.69% libraries, and in a majority of the libraries (82.92%), the librarians are co-opted as members. In 54.5% of the libraries, which have no separate books selection committee, the library committee itself selects the books. In a very few libraries (17.65%), the members of the library make suggestions for purchase of books.

Book Selection Policy

No library under study adopts a book selection policy incorporating norms for distribution of funds between adult and juvenile books, fiction and non-fiction, periodicals and newspapers; discarding of old books; types of materials to be included; for which categories of books for which multiple copies have to be purchased and such other matters.

Selection Tools

A majority of the libraries (84.4%) use publishers' catalogues as an important book selection tool, 80.7% consider suggestions of the readers, 64.7% select books directly from the book shops, 27.8% select books from book exhibitions, and a few libraries (18.2%) seen book reviews for selection of books.

Book Stock

The different categories of books available in the libraries are analysed on the basis of grade, district, and location and the findings are furnished in Figures 1, 2 and 3 respectively.

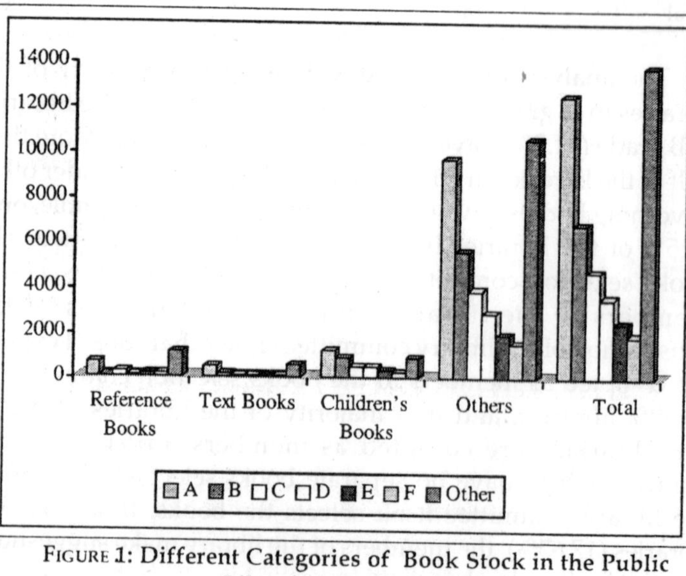

FIGURE 1: Different Categories of Book Stock in the Public Libraries, Grade-wise

It can be seen from Figure 1 that among the grant-in-aid libraries, a mean collection of more than 500 reference books are stocked by only A grade libraries (Mean 667.00 with SD 826.91), ranging between 31 reference books and 3200 reference books and the libraries under other governing bodies (Mean 1106.67 with SD 601.81), ranging between 412 reference books and 1470 reference books. A mean of more than 500 text books for the student community were acquired only in A grade libraries (Mean 508.35 with SD 1100.77), having to a maximum of 4543 text books and in the libraries under other governing bodies (Mean 557.00 with SD 626.50), ranging between a minimum of 114 text books and a maximum of 1000 text books. A and B grade libraries, and the libraries under other governing bodies have a mean of more than 500 children's books. The respective figures are: A grade libraries (Mean 1195.88 with SD 839.90), ranging between a minimum of 100 children's books and a maximum of 2800 children's books; B grade libraries (Mean 834.08 with SD 673.94) ranging between 27 children's books and 2235 children's books; and the libraries under other governing bodies (Mean 897 with SD 395.81), varying from a minimum of 618 children's books to a maximum of 1350 children's books. The libraries under other governing bodies have the highest mean of 13677 total books, ranging from a minimum of 5817 books to a maximum of 20125 books, followed by A grade libraries (Mean 12439.04 with SD 4513.73), ranging from a minimum of 3595 total books to a maximum of 22345 total books. F grade libraries have the lowest number of book collection (Mean 1864.73 with SD 1239.16), ranging from a minimum of 600 books to a maximum of 2560 books.

District-wise analysis as furnished in Figure 2 shows that the libraries in Kozhikode is in the fore-front with the highest average number of reference collection (Mean 443.36 with SD 798.42) ranging from a minimum of 5 books to a maximum of 3200 books. The libraries in Wayanad have the highest average number of text book collection (Mean 464.81 with SD 1115.79) ranging up to a maximum of 4543 books. The libraries in Kasaragod have the highest average number of children's

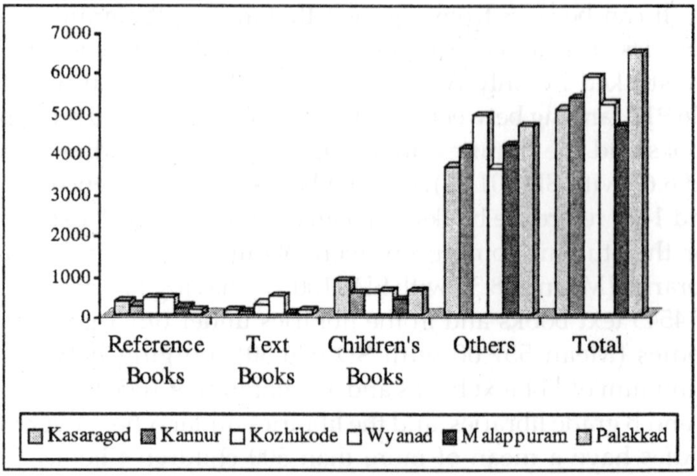

FIGURE 2: Different Categories of Book Stock in the Public Libraries, District-wise

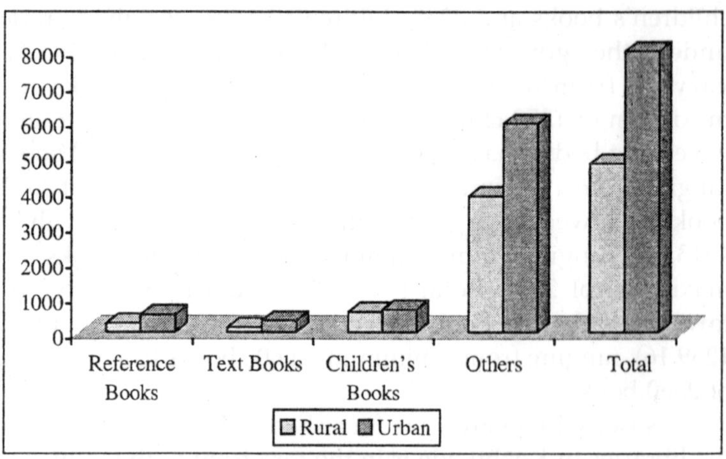

FIGURE 3: Different Categories of Book Stock in the Public Libraries, Location-wise

collection (Mean 863.89 with SD 790.22) ranging from a minimum of 168 books to a maximum of 2800 books. The libraries in Palakkad have the highest average number of total books (Mean 6437.91with SD 4800.97) ranging between a minimum of 1339 books and a maximum of 17543 books, followed by Kozhikode (Mean 5844.37 with SD 4488.93) ranging between 475 books and 20125 book, and the lowest in Malappuram (Mean 4654.11 with SD 3763.59) ranging from a minimum of 600 books to a maximum of 18253 books.

Figure 3 show that the mean number of different categories of books stocked in the libraries is more in the urban areas than in the rural areas. The respective figures in the urban areas are: reference books (Mean 490.37 with SD 717.56), text books (Mean 323.19 with SD 958.00), children's books (Mean 634.44 with SD 616.82), others (Mean 5922.83 with SD 4745.36) and total books (Mean 7985.03 with SD 5731.71). Whereas the book stock in different categories in the rural areas is (Mean 252.60 with SD 423.73), text books (Mean132.99 with SD 278.36), children's books (Mean 574.73 with SD 570.27), others (Mean 3853.34 with SD 3057.89) and total books (Mean 4772.27 with SD 3616.95).

The IFLA/UNESCO Guidelines (2001)[2] proposed that "the minimum stock level for the smallest service point should not be less than 2500 books." But the analysis of the data shows that F Grade libraries which are the smallest service unit have only an average of 1865 books. This finding does not agree with the IFLA/UNESCO Guidelines. It also indicates that there is a general pattern of descending order of number of books in different categories from A to F grades. The size of the collection in the libraries is determined largely by the annual library grant provided by the state library authority.

Per-Capita Book Stock

Per-capita book stock is a resource indicator which can be used to evaluate the library's performance. The district wise per-capita book stock are furnished in Table 9.

The IFLA/UNESCO Guidelines (2001)[3] proposed that "an established book collection should be between 1.5 and 2.5 books per capita." It is evident from Table 9 that no district under study agrees with this standard. Kannur comes first with a per capita book stock of one book, whereas Malappuram comes last with 0.36 per capita book stock.

Table 9
Per Capita Book Stock of the Public Libraries at the End of 2003-04

District	*Total Population (Census 2001)*	*Total Book Stock*	*Per-Capita*	*Rank*
Kasaragod	1203342	568026	0.47	4
Kannur	2412365	2401671	1.00	1
Kozhikode	2878498	1275658	0.44	5
Wayanad	786627	491960	0.63	2
Malappuram	3629640	1316168	0.36	6
Palakkad	2617072	1364471	0.52	3

Note: *Total book stock is compiled from the statistical data collected by the State Library Council.*

Average Cost of Books

The average cost of books can also be used as a library performance indicator. The average cost of books in the libraries, district-wise is shown in Table 10.

Table 10
Average Cost of Books in the Public Libraries in 2003-04 (District-wise)

District	*Total Books*	*Total Cost (in Rs.)*	*Average Cost (in Rs.)*	*Rank*
Kasaragod	5,68,026	1,29,57,199	22.81	3
Kannur	24,01,671	5,18,05,519	21.57	4
Kozhikode	12,75,658	3,95,00,209	30.96	1
Wayanad	4,91,960	1,23,56,641	25.12	2
Malappuram	13,16,168	2,73,21,319	20.76	5
Palakkad	13,64,471	2,62,86,860	19.27	6

Note: Total books and cost are compiled from the statistical data collected by the State Library Council.

From the data as shown in Table 10, it is found that the average cost of books in all districts is much less. These figures indicate that most of the books purchased in the libraries are not of standard quality or relevance to the users.

Fiction and Non-Fiction Collection

The distribution of fiction and non-fiction collection in the book stock, grade-wise, district-wise, and location-wise is presented in Tables 11, 12 and 13.

Table 11
Fiction and Non-Fiction Collection in the Public Libraries (Grade-wise)

	Fiction		*Non-Fiction*	
Grade	*Mean*	*SD*	*Mean*	*SD*
A	7743.05	2951.89	4480.00	3517.47
B	4817.67	1113.39	1853.29	1789.97
C	3656.25	1489.67	1064.19	909.16
D	2623.93	976.14	859.27	688.06
E	1842.41	631.10	664.81	538.44
F	474.61	711.11	452.43	677.91
Other	3654.00	62.23	6742.50	8160.98
Total Books	3571.39	2505.99	1556.72	2263.22

The data in the table (Table 11) reveal that, an average of more than 5000 fiction books is stocked only in A grade libraries (Mean 7743.05 with SD 2951.89). The lowest collection of fiction is in F grade libraries (Mean 474.61 with SD 711.11). The highest average number of non-fiction was acquired by the libraries under other governing bodies (Mean 6742.50 with SD 8106.98), followed by A grade libraries (Mean 4480.00 with SD 3517.47), B grade (Mean 1853.29 with SD 1789.97), and C grade (Mean 1064.19 with SD 909.16). In all other grades, the non-fiction collection is less than on an average of 1000 books. It can be noted that in the libraries under other governing bodies, the size of the non-fiction collection is larger than that of fiction; in the grant-in-aid libraries, the situation is vice versa.

Table 12
Fiction and Non-Fiction Collection in the Public Libraries (District-wise)

	Fiction		*Non-Fiction*	
District	*Mean*	*SD*	*Mean*	*SD*
Kasaragod	3413.28	2255.57	1437.61	1393.63
Kannur	3358.46	2247.60	1835.20	3053.56
Kozhikode	3827.27	2592.36	1197.90	1542.59
Wayanad	3285.00	2695.35	1898.60	2529.47
Malappuram	3343.52	2331.51	1449.35	1941.90
Palakkad	4502.44	3420.57	1290.27	1247.27
Total	3571.39	2505.99	1556.72	2263.22

Among the districts, Palakkad tops first with the mean collection of 4502 fiction books. The number of fiction collection in the libraries in other districts figures on an average of a little more than 3000. The libraries in Wayanad have the highest average of non-fiction collection (Mean 1898.60 with SD 2529.47), followed by Kannur (Mean 1835.20 with SD 3053.56), whereas the libraries in Kozhikode have the lowest number of non-fiction collection (Mean 1197.90 with SD 1542.59).

Table 13
Fiction and Non-Fiction Collection in the Public Libraries (Location-wise)

	Fiction		*Non-Fiction*	
Grade	*Mean*	*SD*	*Mean*	*SD*
Rural	3407.71	2523.44	1341.52	1682.80
Urban	4389.76	2291.48	2668.54	4006.70
Total	3571.39	2505.99	1556.72	2263.22

Location-wise analysis as shown in Table 13 shows that the average number of fiction books acquired by the public libraries is more in the urban areas (Mean 4389.76 with SD 2291.48) than in the rural areas (Mean 3407.71 with SD 2523.44). It also reveals that the total collection of non-fiction books stocked by the libraries is more in the urban areas (Mean 2668.54 with SD 4006.70) than in the rural areas (Mean 1341.52 with SD 1682.80).

The findings reveal that the recreational needs of the local community are considered by the public libraries by providing a large number of fiction books. The investigator has personally observed that nearly 60% of the fiction collection, in the libraries which are affiliated to the State Library Council is of cheap quality, mostly detective novels; and non-fiction collection does not cover all subjects. It is also noted that the quality of the fiction and non-fiction collection in the libraries under other government bodies is far better.

Language-wise Book Collection

The collection in the public libraries should include reading materials in the primary and minority language of the community and in other languages. The stock of books in different languages, grade-wise, district-wise, and location-wise are presented in Figures 4, 5 and 6 respectively.

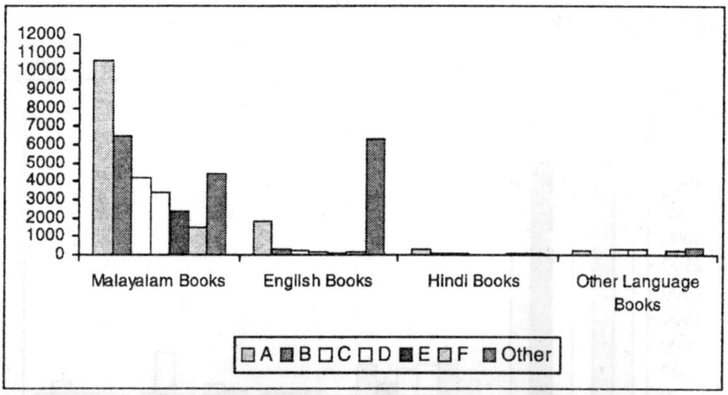

FIGURE 4: Collection of Books in the Public Libraries in Different Languages, Grade-wise

From Figure 4, it is found that the highest average number of Malayalam books is stocked by A grade libraries (Mean 10563.84 with SD 2795.89), ranging from a minimum of 5,088 Malayalam books to a maximum of 15,624 books; followed by B grade libraries (Mean 6440.17 with SD 1245.83), ranging from a minimum of 4,493 Malayalam books to a maximum of 9,740 Malayalam books. The libraries in other grades have an average of less than 5,000 Malayalam books. The lowest number of Malayalam books (Mean 1508.00 with SD 452.24) is stocked in F grade libraries. Among the grant-in-aid libraries, an average of more than 1,000 English books is collected in A grade libraries (Mean 1818.80 with SD 2125.49), ranging from a minimum of 48 to a maximum of 8,808 English books and an average of below 500 English books is stocked by the libraries of all other grades. An average of more than 5,000 English Books is stocked only in the libraries under other governing bodies (Mean 6329.50 with SD 6777.62), ranging from a minimum of 1,537 to a maximum of 11,122. The highest average number of Hindi books is acquired in A grade libraries (Mean

300.32 with SD 370.92), ranging from 15 to 1506 Hindi books, whereas only an average of below 100 Hindi books is stocked in the libraries of other grades. The highest mean of other language books is stocked in D grade libraries (Mean 330.20 with SD 723.85), followed by C grade libraries (Mean 323.86 with SD 658.23).

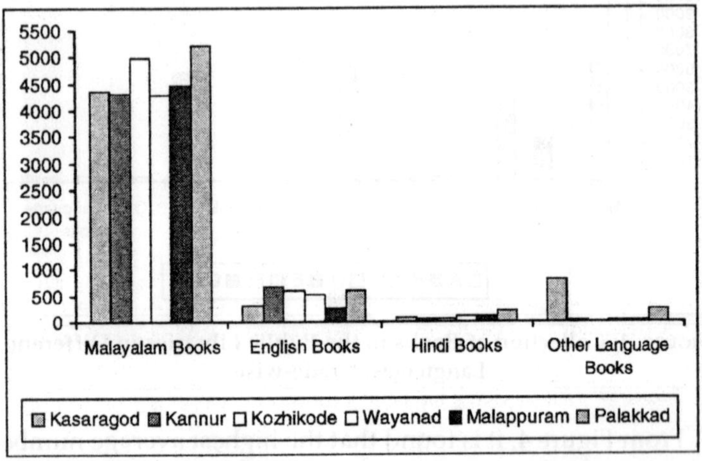

FIGURE 5 : **Collection of Books in the Public Libraries in Different Languages, District-wise**

District-wise analysis shows that the highest average number of Malayalam books (Mean 5217.33 with SD 3858.62) is available in the public libraries in Palakkad, followed by Kozhikode (4995.97 with SD 2812.99), and the lowest in the public libraries in Wayanad (4281.35 with SD 3619.27). The highest average number of English books (Mean 663.14 with SD 1893.81) is stocked by the public libraries in Kannur, followed by Kozhikode (Mean 603.18 with SD 1553.06), and the lowest number of English books is available in the public libraries in Malappuram (Mean 270.54 with SD 377.23). The highest average number of Hindi books (Mean 213.60 with SD 406.78) is available in the public libraries in Palakkad, and the lowest in the libraries in Kozhikode (Mean 59.72 with SD 71.88). Among districts, the public libraries in Kasaragod and

Palakkad have more "other language" books. Kasaragod is near Karnataka State where the native language is Kannada and Palakkad is near Coimbatore, a district in Tamil Nadu where the native language is Tamil. So the libraries in Kasaragod collect more Kannada books and the libraries in Palakkad collect more Tamil books to serve the Kannada people and Tamil people in the respective local community. In Kasaragod, the libraries have an average of 813 of "other language" books and in Palakkad the libraries have an average of 223 other language books. In other grades, the average number of "other language' books is only below 40.

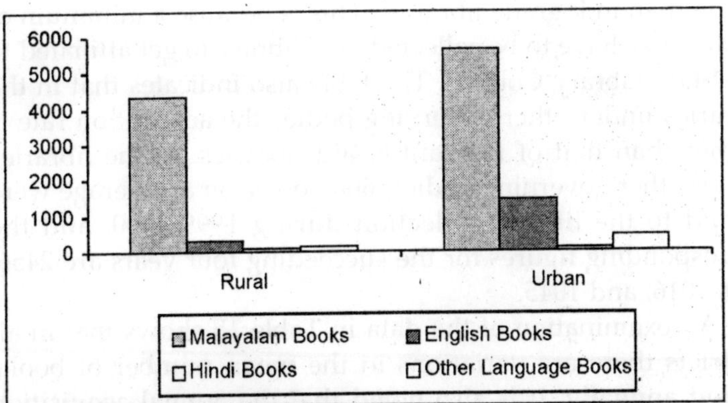

FIGURE 6: Collection of Books in the Public Libraries in Different Languages, Location-wise

Location-wise analysis shows that a greater average of Malayalam books is available in the libraries in the urban areas (Mean 5662.29 with SD 3055.86); also English books (1427.30 with SD 2786.60) and "other language" books (429.33 with SD 737.92), whereas a greater average of Hindi books is available in libraries in the rural areas (96.11 with SD 207.91).

The analysis of the data reveal that 87.52% of the collection in the public libraries under study is Malayalam books, while English, Hindi and other languages occupy a very small percentage.

Acquisition of Books

The acquisition of books in the libraries during 1999-2000 to 2003-04 grade-wise, district-wise, and location-wise is shown in Tables 14, 15, and 16 respectively. The acquisition rate is a performance indicator to measure the efficiency of the library service.

An examination of the data in Table 14 shows that in the libraries of all grades and in the libraries under other governing bodies, there are variations in the mean number of books added annually. In A grade libraries, the annual acquisition rounded to a mean of 400 books from 1999-2000 to 2003-04, while in all other grades, it is below an average of 300 books during these periods. It can be noted that addition of books is more in F grade than in E grade libraries. This is because a minimum of 1000 books have to be collected by a library to get affiliated to the State Library Council. The table also indicates that in the libraries under other governing bodies the acquisition rate is higher than that of in grant-in-aid libraries. In the libraries under other governing bodies, 600 books, on an average were added to the library collection during 1999-2000, and the corresponding figures for the succeeding four years are 2456, 700, 1016, and 1045.

An examination of the data in Table 15 shows that in all districts there are variations in the mean number of books added annually. It is also noted that the annual acquisition rate is low in the public libraries in Malappuram compared to those in other districts, where there is an annual acquisition of only an average of below 200 books per year.

Table 16 reveals that the annual acquisition of books is more in the urban area than in the rural area during 5 years from 1999-2000 to 2003-04.

The analysis of the data revealed that totally an average of 337 total books were purchased in the public libraries during 1999-2000 and the corresponding figures for the succeeding four years are 260, 229, 260, and 259 respectively, which reveal that there is no steady increase in the acquisition rate of books from 1999-2000 to 2003-04. In a majority of the grant-in-aid libraries, the grant allotted by the State Library Council is the

Tabble 14

Annual Acquisition of Books in the Public Libraries from 1999-2000 to 2003-04 (Grade-wise)

	1999-2000		*2000-01*		*2001-02*		*2002-03*		*2003-04*	
Grade	*Mean*	*SD*	*Mean*	*SD*	*Mean*	*SD*	*Mean*	*SD*	*Mean*	*SD*
A	377.92	250.48	388.91	273.04	377.92	250.48	412.87	254.51	427.00	284.50
B	232.35	213.50	248.80	207.64	188.35	85.55	266.75	211.89	219.50	95.31
C	131.29	85.45	206.87	157.66	156.04	93.63	208.54	158.17	207.09	258.95
D	215.54	309.04	213.00	214.81	208.04	198.92	271.63	269.26	252.38	300.90
E	216.78	242.90	188.75	155.56	193.75	159.77	184.39	157.88	195.75	226.91
F	264.50	326.31	243.00	258.31	244.70	319.26	195.19	236.77	216.71	249.51
Other	600.00	134.21	2456.00	287.42	700.00	210.35	1016.00		1045.00	264.82
Total	336.61	1134.21	260.33	284.42	228.75	210.35	260.06	235.91	259.02	264.82

Table 15
Annual Acquisition of Books in the Public Libraries from 1999-2000 to 2003-04 (District-wise)

	1999–2000		*2000-01*		*2001-02*		*2002-03*		*2003-04*	
District	*Mean*	*SD*	*Mean*	*SD*	*Mean*	*SD*	*Mean*	*SD*	*Mean*	*SD*
Kasaragod	241.44	251.30	371.19	586.00	234.88	169.73	332.29	307.18	283.19	250.15
Kannur	260.30	265.70	218.80	187.71	198.11	190.78	238.59	243.30	233.35	224.77
Kozhikode	298.15	312.02	348.29	242.22	281.33	244.85	305.61	263.54	327.18	365.53
Wayanad	246.92	295.00	269.83	362.82	364.00	326.99	341.39	171.23	390.15	320.24
Malappuram	157.65	127.57	164.62	122.29	176.52	145.20	198.43	158.50	175.85	95.15
Palakkad	214.31	302.31	207.79	185.08	170.57	145.3	152.43	124.50	147.29	124.15
Total	336.61	1134.21	260.33	284.42	228.75	210.35	260.06	235.91	259.02	264.82

Table 16

Annual Acquisition of Books in the Public Libraries from 1999-2000 to 2003-04 (Location-wise)

	1999 s–2000		*2000 - 01*		*2001 - 02*		*2002 - 03*		*2003 - 04*	
Location	*Mean*	*SD*	*Mean*	*SD*	*Mean*	*SD*	*Mean*	*SD*	*Mean*	*SD*
Rural	254.74	275.16	237.82	205.32	224.97	201.18	243.05	212.45	247.58	247.41
Urban	705.04	2608.01	363.00	512.96	245.50	250.76	337.23	315.48	313.04	335.94
Total	336.61	1134.21	260.33	284.42	228.75	210.35	260.06	235.91	259.02	264.82

only source for book purchase. During these periods there is no increase in the allocation of funds for book purchase. So there is a little variation in the average number of books purchased during these periods, but the highest is in 1999-2000 (Mean 336.61 with SD 1134.21) and the lowest in 2001-02 (Mean 228.75 with SD 210.35). The State Library Council provides only inadequate amount for the purchase of books, and hence the low acquisition rate in the grant-in-aid public libraries.

Periodicals

As books, periodicals are also an important information resource in public libraries. The category-wise particulars of the average number of periodicals subscribed to in the libraries, grade-wise, district-wise and location-wise are furnished in Tables 17, 18, and 19 respectively.

Table 17
Category-wise Subscription to the Periodicals in the Public Libraries (Grade-wise)

	Children's Periodicals		*General Periodicals*		*Subject Periodicals*		*Total*	
Grade	*Mean*	*SD*	*Mean*	*SD*	*Mean*	*SD*	*Mean*	*SD*
A	4.00	1.93	21.64	13.20	7.54	6.57	32.63	14.43
B	3.55	2.65	11.30	9.76	6.60	5.09	22.27	13.83
C	3.13	1.18	9.34	5.82	4.21	3.56	15.76	8.87
D	4.3	5.29	9.43	6.05	4.38	3.72	11.21	11.31
E	2.63	1.57	7.64	6.16	3.24	1.37	12.47	8.68
F	2.41	1.37	5.79	3.39	2.59	1.46	9.90	4.41
Other	5.50	2.12	33.00	23.99	4.00	1.63	37.80	23.88
Total	3.41	2.73	11.57	10.50	4.8	4.37	18.83	13.75

From Table 17, it can be seen that a mean of below 5 children's magazines are subscribed to in all grant-in-aid libraries. The average number of children's magazines subscribed to be the highest in A grade (Mean 4 with SD 1.93) and the lowest in F grade (Mean 2.41 with SD 1.37). But in the libraries under other governing bodies, a little higher than a mean of 5 children's magazines (Mean 5.5 with SD 2.12) are subscribed to.

The data also show that the average number of general magazines subscribed to is the highest in the libraries under other governing bodies (Mean 33.00 with SD 23.99) ranging from 11 periodicals to 58 periodicals, followed by A grade libraries (Mean 21.64 with SD 13.20) ranging from 3 periodicals to 49 periodicals. An average of 11 periodicals is subscribed to in B grade (Mean 11.30 with SD 9.76) ranges from 2 periodicals to 34 periodicals. Other grades have a mean of below 10 general magazines.

In A and B grade libraries, an average of more than 5 subject periodicals are subscribed to, the respective figures are: A (Mean 7.54 with SD 6.57) ranges from 5 to 29 periodicals, B (Mean 6.60 with SD 5.09) ranges from 5 to 19 periodicals. The libraries under other governing bodies subscribe to an average of a small number of subject periodicals (Mean 4 with SD 1.63) which varies from 1 to 6.

The libraries under other governing bodies come to the first position with the highest average number of periodicals subscription (Mean 37.80 with SD 23.88) ranges from 13 to 66 periodicals, followed by A grade libraries (Mean 32.63 with SD 14.43), ranges from 10 to 67 total periodicals. F grade libraries have the lowest number of periodicals (Mean 9.90 to SD 4.41) varies from 3 to 19 periodicals.

Table 18
Category-wise Subscription to the Periodicals in the Public Libraries (District-wise)

	Children's Periodicals		*General Periodicals*		*Subject Periodicals*		*Total Periodicals*	
District	*Mean*	*SD*	*Mean*	*SD*	*Mean*	*SD*	*Mean*	*SD*
Kasaragod	3.53	2.77	9.00	7.04	4.59	3.73	15.61	11.14
Kannur	2.89	1.59	11.80	11.01	4.83	4.82	18.06	13.85
Kozhikode	4.34	4.23	11.65	10.00	4.83	3.80	21.14	13.99
Wayanad	2.45	1.57	13.62	11.03	5.77	5.36	20.06	15.48
Malappuram	2.60	1.29	11.95	12.26	6.11	5.53	20.10	15.82
Palakkad	4.25	2.62	11.32	11.15	2.94	1.86	17.32	12.15
Total	3.41	2.73	11.57	10.50	4.8	4.37	18.83	13.75

District-wise analysis shows that Kozhikode occupies the first position in the subscription to children's periodicals (Mean

4.34 with SD 4.23) and Malappuram comes last in the list (Mean 2.60 with SD 1.29). The average number of general magazines subscribed to by the libraries is the highest in Wayanad (Mean 13.62 with SD 11.03) and the lowest in Kasaragod (Mean 9.00 with SD 7.04). The average number of subject periodicals subscribed to in the public libraries is the highest in Malappuram (Mean 6.11 with SD 5.53) and the lowest in Palakkad (Mean 2.94 with SD 1.86). The libraries in all districts have an average of above 15 periodicals. Kozhikode comes first, with a mean of 21 periodicals. Kasaragod comes last with a mean of only 16 periodicals.

Table 19
Category-wise Subscription to the Periodicals in the Public Libraries (Location-wise)

	Children's Periodicals		*General Periodicals*		*Subject Periodicals*		*Total Periodicals*	
Location	*Mean*	*SD*	*Mean*	*SD*	*Mean*	*SD*	*Mean*	*SD*
Rural	3.42	2.93	10.85	9.52	4.61	4.21	17.70	12.54
Urban	3.38	1.53	14.32	13.46	5.59	4.94	22.94	17.07
Total	3.41	2.73	11.57	10.50	4.8	4.37	18.83	13.75

It is clear from the Table 19 that in the urban and rural libraries there is only an insignificant variation between the mean number of the children's magazines subscribed to in rural libraries (Mean 3.42 with SD 2.93) and urban libraries (Mean 3.38 with SD 1.53). The mean number of general magazines subscribed to by the libraries is higher in the urban area (Mean 14.32 with SD 13.46) than in the rural area (Mean 10.85 with SD 9.52). The number of subject periodicals subscribed to in the libraries is more in the urban area (Mean 5.59 with SD 4.94) than in the rural area (Mean 4.61 with SD 4.21). The number of total periodicals subscribed to in the libraries is more in the urban area (Mean 22.94 with SD 17.07) than in the rural area (Mean 17.70 with SD 12.54).

The investigator personally observed that most of the libraries subscribe to Malayalam weeklies, which include both standard magazines such as "Mathrubhumi", "Deshabhimani", "Kalakaumudi", and "Malayalam" and others like

"Grihalakshmi", "Vanitha", and "Keralasabdam". It also includes agricultural magazines, career guidance magazines, and film magazines. "Granthalokam" the publication of the Kerala State Library Council is subscribed to in all the grant-in-aid libraries. In some of the libraries, English magazines such as "India Today", "Frontline", and "Readers Digest" are also subscribed to.

Bound Volumes

The findings of the survey indicate that only 25% of the libraries keep the bound volumes of some of the important periodicals.

Lending of Periodicals

The survey indicates that more than half of the libraries (54.30%) lend periodicals to the members, out of which 22% lend for a period of less than a week, 40% for one week, and 38% for above one week

Newspapers

The data available in the survey reveal that very few libraries in A grade (10.7%) subscribe to 3 English newspapers. Most of the libraries in A grade (60.7%), B grade (50%), C grade (50%), D (45%); and very few libraries in E grade (5.9%), and F (2.45%) subscribe to two English newspapers. A majority of the libraries in E grade (94.1%) and F grade (88.6%) subscribe to only one English newspaper. Two libraries under other governing bodies under study (40%) subscribe to only one English newspaper, other two (50%) subscribe to 5 English newspapers each.

A great majority of the libraries in A grade (85.7%), and more than half of the libraries in B grade (57.6%), C grade (56.3%), D grade (51.7%) and the libraries under other governing bodies (55.7%) subscribe to 5-10 Malayalam newspapers, whereas most of the libraries in E grade (64.7%) and F grade (60%) subscribe to only less than 5 Malayalam newspapers.

A very few number of libraries under study subscribe to other language newspapers. In Kasaragod, two libraries subscribe to 3 Kannada newspapers each; in Kozhikode, one library subscribes to one Hindi newspaper; and in Palakkad, two libraries subscribe to one Tamil news paper each.

Non-Book Materials

The survey shows that the majority of the libraries (88.2%) have no non-book material collection. A few libraries (11.8%) have the non-book materials and those are only a poor collection of some CDs and Floppies.

Special Collections

Special collections are the collections of special materials such as pamphlets and rare books; and those that meet the special needs of the community such as the culture of the people and local history; and materials meant to special groups such as disadvantaged groups and ethnic minorities.

No library under study has collections of pamphlets, manuscripts, rare books and such other materials. A few libraries (30.68%) possess a special collection of writings of eminent personalities like Gandhiji, Jawaharlal Nehru, and EMS Namboothiripad.

Organisation of Books

The collection in the library should be classified, catalogued and arranged in a scientific manner, so that maximum utilization is obtained from the stock of the library.

Classification System

The particulars of the classification schemes used in different libraries to classify the books are furnished in Table 20

An examination of the data in Table 4.20 indicates that only 4.3% of total libraries use Dewey Decimal Classification (DDC) to classify the books, which includes 10.7% of A grade libraries and 7.4% of B grade libraries. No libraries in C, D, E, and F grade use any recognized classification schemes to classify the books. It is also noted that 3 out of 5 libraries under other governing bodies (60%) under study classify the books using DDC scheme. Only an insignificant percentage of the total

Table 20
Classification Schemes Used in the Public Libraries (Grade-wise)

		Not Classified		*Local Method*		*Colon Classi-fication*		*Dewey Decimal Classi-fication*		*Modified DDC*	
Grade	*Total Libraries*	*No.*	*%*	*No.*	*%*	*No.*	*%*	*No.*	*%*	*No.*	*%*
A	28	25	89.3	0	.0	0	.0	3	10.7	0	.0
B	27	25	92.6	0	.0	0	.0	2	7.4	0	.0
C	33	31	93.9	0	.0	0	.0	0	.0	2	6.1
D	31	29	93.5	1	3.2	0	.0	0	.0	1	3.2
E	35	35	100	0	.0	0	.0	0	.0	0	.0
F	27	27	100	0	.0	0	.0	0	.0	0	.0
Other	5	1	20	1	20	0	.0	3	60	0	.0
Total	186	173	93.0	2	1.1	0	.0	8	4.3	3	1.6

libraries use a modified scheme of DDC with limited notations, suitable for rural libraries. The number of libraries use a local classification method is meagre. In this method, for each broad subject of the books, the first letter of the subject is given, then for each book, separate serial number is given. For example, Biography-B_1, B_2, B_3, B_4 and like this; Novel-N_1 N2 N3 and like this; Drama-D_1 D2 D3 D4 and so on. A majority of the libraries (93%) do not classify the books using a classification scheme.

Cataloguing System

Catalogue is an essential and indispensable tool for the members to have knowledge of the books available in the library. It helps the readers to locate the required books. The particulars of the cataloguing system adopted in different libraries are furnished in Table 21.

The data in the table (Table 21) show that a significant majority of the grant-in-aid libraries, A (92%), B (88%), C (87.9%), D (83.9%), E (87.9%), and F (92.3%) catalogue their books using a local cataloguing method. In this method the cataloguing details of the books such as serial number, author, and title are entered under the main subject headings such as novels, dramas, history, and science in a separate ledger or in loose sheets of paper. Only a small percentage of the total

Table 21
Cataloguing System Adopted in the Public Libraries (Grade-wise)

		Not Catalogued		*CCC*		*AACR*		*Other Methods*	
Grade	*Total Libraries*	*No.*	*%*	*No.*	*%*	*No.*	*%*	*No.*	*%*
A	25	0	.0	2	8.0	0	.0	23	92.0
B	25	1	4	1	4	1	4	22	88.0
C	33	3	9.1	1	3	0	.0	29	87.9
D	31	4	12.9	1	3.2	0	.0	26	83.9
E	33	3	9.1	1	3	0	.0	29	87.9
F	26	1	3.8	1	3.8	0	.0	24	92.3
Other	5	0	.0	1	20	2	40	25	40.0
Total	178	12	6.74	8	4.5	3	1.7	155	87.06

libraries (4.5%) use Classified Catalogue Code (CCC) to catalogue the books and a meager percentage of total libraries (1.7%) use Anglo American Catalogue Code (AACR). It is interesting to note that 40% of the libraries under other governing bodies use AACR, 20% use CCC and another 40% use other methods to catalogue the books.

A majority of the libraries (81.6%) use the ledger for catalogue, 6.2% use card catalogue and 10.3% use other forms such as loose sheets of paper. Two libraries under other governing bodies at Kozhikode and Kannur and two A grade libraries at Mananthavady (Wayanad) and Feroke (Kozhikode) under study are converting their traditional library catalogues into machine readable catalogues. They use locally developed software, their cost ranges from Rs. 12, 000 to 26,000/-.

Arrangement of Books

The scientific arrangement of books on shelves has an important role to ensure the maximum utilisation of books. The details of arrangement of books in the libraries are given in Figure 7.

From Figure 7, it is found that in nearly half of the libraries (48.11%), the books are arranged merely on the basis of accession number. Another 44.32% arrange books under broad subject headings such as novels, dramas, poetry, essays,

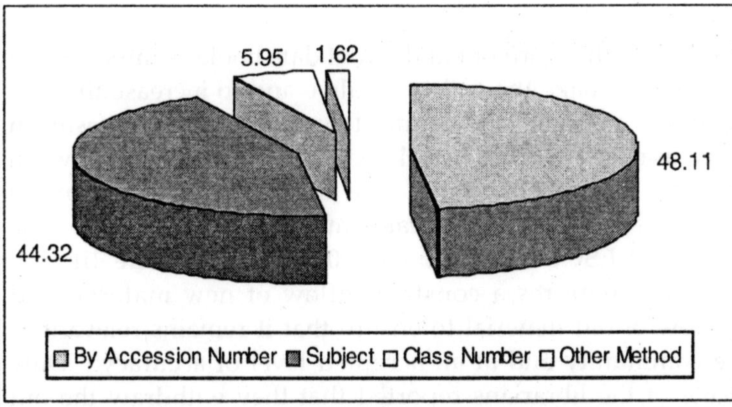

FIGURE 7: Method of Arrangement of Books in the Public Libraries

history, and science. Within subjects, books are arranged in different ways. In some of the libraries, books are arranged by separate numbers given to them. In others books are arranged alphabetically by author or title. In a very few libraries (1.62%), books are arranged alphabetically by authors' name or by title. In only 5.95% of the libraries books are arranged scientifically according to their class numbers. The data available in the survey reveal that in 3 out of 5 libraries under other governing bodies (60%) under study books are arranged by class numbers.

Preservation

Reading materials in all formats should be in good condition; this will create a good impression among the users and also will increase the durability of the documents. The investigator, during her visits, observed that the physical condition of most of the books in the libraries under the State Library Council is far from satisfactory, but it is far better in the libraries under other governing bodies. The data available in the survey show that as many as 72.19% libraries clean books regularly, 17.6% of libraries use pesticides, 76.47% bind the worn out books and 10% of the libraries cover the books using paper.

Discards

Discarding the worn out and out of date books is important in a library to make the collection alive and to increase the use. A smaller collection of standard current books will result in more usage than a large stock with a high proportion of worn out and outdated books. The quality of collections is maintained by acquisition rates matching discard rates. The IFLA/UNESCO Guidelines (2001)[4] state: "The library collection requires a constant inflow of new material and outflow of old material to ensure that it remains relevant to the community and at an accepted level of accuracy." Only 59.6% of the librarians reported that they withdraw the out dated and worn out books from the collection, and keep them separately.

Stock Verification

A vast majority of the libraries (95.19%) conduct stock verification regularly, out of which, 70.05% libraries conduct stock verification annually, 10.73% libraries conduct within 2 years, and 19.21% of the libraries conduct stock verification once in 3 years.

Access to Book Collection

There are two types of access to book stock, they are open access and closed access. The survey revealed that 45.71% of the libraries follow open access system and 54.28% follow closed access system.

Finance

Finance is the main source for all developmental work. The IFLA/UNESCO Guidelines (2001)[5] state: "Adequate levels of funding are crucial to the success of a public library in fulfilling its role." It includes both revenue and expenditure.

Revenue

The State government contribution and cess, equal to five per cent of building tax levied by the municipalities and corporations and land tax levied by the panchayaths is the primary source of revenue of public libraries under study. It is distributed to the public libraries through the State Library Council. The secondary sources of income include revenue from user fees such as membership fees, subscriptions and fine collected; donation from organisations such as Raja Rammohun Roy Library Foundation (RRRLF), municipalities, panchayaths and from Other individuals; and miscellaneous income from other activities such as sale of old newspapers. In the Government grants, the grants for books and periodicals and librarians' allowance form the major component. Funds are also made available for building, furniture, computerisation, and for special programmes and services. The item-wise revenue of the libraries for 5 years from 1999-2000 to 2003-04 is furnished in Table 22.

The analysis of revenue in Table 22 gives the clear picture and trend of the revenue of the public libraries through the period from 1999-2000 to 2003-04. It can be observed that there is a fluctuation in the provision of grant by the State Library Council to the public libraries for 5 years from 1999-2000 to 2003-04. The highest being in the year 2002-03 (Mean 63078.27 with SD 154334.68) and lowest in 1999-2000 (Mean 39414.01 with SD 77037.83).

User fee, which includes membership fee, subscription, and fine was the highest in the year 2003-04, membership fee (Mean 3276.19 with SD 28851.40), subscription (Mean 2789.62 with SD 6894.11) and fine (Mean 1970.80 with SD 3525.37).

Donation from public is not a regular source of revenue, so there is a variation in their figures in these 5 years. The donation from different organisations such as RRRLF, panchayaths, municipalities, and M. P. fund is the highest in 2002-03 (Mean 58654.38 with SD 209393.75) to a maximum of Rs.13, 46,480 from M. P. Fund and the lowest in 2000-01 (Mean 11219.86 with SD 36567.95). Miscellaneous revenue is the highest in 2003-04 (Mean 29821.14 with SD 200829.58) and the lowest in 2000-01 (Mean 10932.16 with SD 30732.02). It is evident from the above analysis that the income from different sources is insufficient to meet the different needs

Table 22
Revenue of the Public Libraries from 1999-2000 to 2003-04 (in Rs.)

	1999-2000		*2000-01*		*2001-02*		*2002-03*		*2003-04*	
Source of Revenue	*Mean*	*SD*	*Mean*	*SD*	*Mean*	*SD*	*Mean*	*SD*	*Mean*	*SD*
Grant	14703.53	36471.79	13403.15	25410.00	12548.80	16161.51	15295.61	20074.78	13282.21	14412..54
Member of Fee	820.78	2781.42	841.84	2942.44	871.36	3186.01	734.96	1660.72	3276.19	28851.40
Subscription	2068.80	6229.22	21057.61	7584.53	2227.77	7650.79	2009.29	3819.54	2789.62	6894.11
Fine	7715.33	1596.88	612.03	1722.87	929.35	2790.98	1607.76	3147.07	1970.80	3525.37
Donation from public	12360.79	23609.79	17936.82	37510.46	12430.24	16823.36	14038.60	22453.7	12207.99	18213.38
Donation from Different Organizations	13545.79	28927.90	11219.86	36567.95	13976.90	29385.16	58654.38	209393.75	29928.08	60910.67
Miscellaneous	12392.26	46640.91	10932.16	30732.02	14794.16	43401.79	15403.09	44067.39	29821.14	200829.58
Total	39414.01	77037.83	40710.39	81728.79	42236.53	67862.84	63078.27	154334.68	49461.94	79478.24

of the libraries. The government allocation for public library development from 1999-2000 to 2003-04 is given in Table 23.

Table 23
Government Grant for the Public Libraries from 1999-2000 to 2003-04

(Rs. in lakhs)

Year	*Government Grant*	*Expenditureon Education*	*Percentage*
1999-2000	620.28	2,48,094	0.25
2000-01	509.00	2,58,521	0.20
2001-02	530.00	2,44,423	0.22
2002-03	658.00	2,55,001	0.26
2003-04	642.20	3,10,177	0.21

Source: 1. For government grant, annual reports of Kerala State Library Council from 1999-2000 to 2003-04.
2. For expenditure on education, Economic Reviews of Government of Kerala from 1999-2000 to 2003-04.

As shown in Table 23, government allocated only a very small percentage of its expenditure on education for public library development from 1999-2000 to 2003-04 which varies from 0.20% in 2000-01 to 0.26% in 2002-03.

Per-Capita Income

The Per-capita income of libraries is a resource indicator, details of which are furnished in Table 24.

Table 24
Per-Capita Income of the Public Libraries in 2003-04
(District-wise)

District	*Total Population (census 2001)*	*Total Income (in Rs.)*	*Per-Capita (in Rs.)*	*Rank*
Kasaragod	1203342	4509935	3.75	4
Kannur	2412365	21951258	9.10	1
Kozhikode	2878498	16472512	5.72	3
Wayanad	786627	5449528	6.93	2
Malappuram	3629640	9349188	2.58	6
Palakkad	2617072	9149360	3.50	5

Source: Total income was compiled from the statistical data collected by the State Library Council.

The data in the table (Table 24) show that the per-capita income of libraries is the highest in Kannur (Rs. 9.10), followed by Wayanad (Rs. 6.93) and the lowest in Malappuram (Rs. 2.58). The per-capita income of the public libraries is found very less in the districts under study. It can be concluded that the paucity of fund is the main obstacle to the proper development of public libraries under study.

RRRLF Grant

An examination of the data received in the survey shows that 55.6% of the libraries have received RRRLF grant for purchase of books and furniture, and construction and extension of library building. The details of the grant received from this organisation, grade-wise, district-wise and location-wise are shown in Tables 25, 26, and 27 respectively.

Table 25

RRRLF Grant Received by the Public Libraries (Grade-wise)

Grade	*No. of Libraries*	*Mean (in Rs.)*	*SD*	*Minimum (in Rs.)*	*Maximum (in Rs.)*
A	27	77115.74	111107.74	.00	3,00,000.00
B	27	10,000.00	51961.52	.00	2,70,000.00
C	33	.00	.00	.00	.00
D	31	.00	.00	.00	.00
E	35	2550.00	15086.00	.00	89,250.00
F	28	1,785.71	9449.11	.00	50,000.00
Other	4	.00	.00	.00	.00
Total	185	13,466.89	53,737.85	.00	3,00,000.00

The data as furnished in Table 25 show that a maximum amount of Rs. 3 lakhs was received by the libraries from the RRRLF. The libraries under other governing bodies did not try to get grant from this organisation. The libraries of C and D grade also have not taken any initiative to get the RRRLF grant. A grade libraries received the highest amount (Mean 77115.74 with SD 111107.74).

Among districts, Kannur is in the fore-front in the receipt of grants from the RRRLF (Mean 17665.18 with SD 65434.25) and Malappuram comes last (Mean 6571.43 with SD 30243.98).

Table 26
RRRLF Grant Received by the Public Libraries (District-wise)

District	*No. of Libraries*	*Mean (in Rs.)*	*SD*	*Minimum (in Rs.)*	*Maximum (in Rs.)*
Kasaragod	21	14244.05	65274.43	.00	2,99,125.00
Kannur	56	17665.18	65434.25	.00	3,00,000.00
Kozhikode	40	11250.00	43467.49	.00	2,25,000.00
Wayanad	18	11111.11	47140.45	.00	2,00,000.00
Malappuram	28	6571.43	30243.98	.00	1,59,000.00
Palakkad	22	16772.73	58395.97	.00	2,70,000.00
Total	185	13466.89	53737.85	.00	3,00,000.00

Table 27
RRRLF Grant Received by the Public Libraries (Location-wise)

Location	*No. of Libraries*	*Mean (in Rs.)*	*SD*	*Minimum (in Rs.)*	*Maximum (in Rs.)*
Rural	150	12809.17	50326.93	.00	3,00,000.00
Urban	35	16285.17	67217.19	.00	3,00,000.00
Total Total	185	13466.89	53737.85	.00	3,00,000.00

Location-wise analysis shows that the amount received by the libraries from the RRRLF is higher in the urban (Mean 16285.17 with SD 67217.19) and lower in the rural area (Mean 12809.17 with SD 50326.93). The data also revealed that no library received grants from the RRRLF for computerisation during the survey period.

Expenditure

In the libraries, the expenditure is incurred for purchasing reading materials, payment of librarians' allowances, construction and maintenance of buildings, providing furniture and equipment, and to meet the contingent expenses for the day-to-day functioning of libraries and such other matters. The average item-wise expenditure of the libraries from 1999-2000 to 2003-04 are summarised in Table 28.

Table 28 indicates that there is a slight increase in the mean expenditure for books during the period from 1999-2000 to 2003-04 except in the year 2000-01. The expenditure for periodicals has also increased with a little variation from 1999-

Table 28
Expenditure of the Public Libraries from 1999-2000 to 2003-04

(in Rs.)

	1999-2000		*2000-01*		*2001-02*		*2002-03*		*2003-04*	
Items	*Mean*	*SD*	*Mean*	*SD*	*Mean*	*SD*	*Mean*	*SD*	*Mean*	*SD*
Books	6785.27	11813.19	6414.62	10863.31	7287.88	7556.37	8180.49	12525.98	9133.69	10567.33
Periodicals	4584.02	3841.39	4888.76	3823.93	5559.40	4133.61	5703.46	4307.94	5813.6	4533.61
Staff	9099.64	15652.12	8839.46	15597.3	8941.46	15442.89	9206.04	16998.12	9514.94	16854.01
Building	28817.3	54752.81	17808.04	41715.57	30322.19	62649.53	36754.15	94066.76	58194.53	137915.4
Furniture	5269.09	9991.12	6962.91	19958.54	7461.62	9252.23	9374.97	16074.47	7766	11280.02
Miscellaneous	14757.79	42244.11	503718.1	5187848.9	16510.61	39598.86	17699.38	34597.8	16839.52	34635.15
Total	25856.4	41942.97	25605.83	55787.23	30899.45	59271.49	36654.9	86489.78	32059.6	45422.44

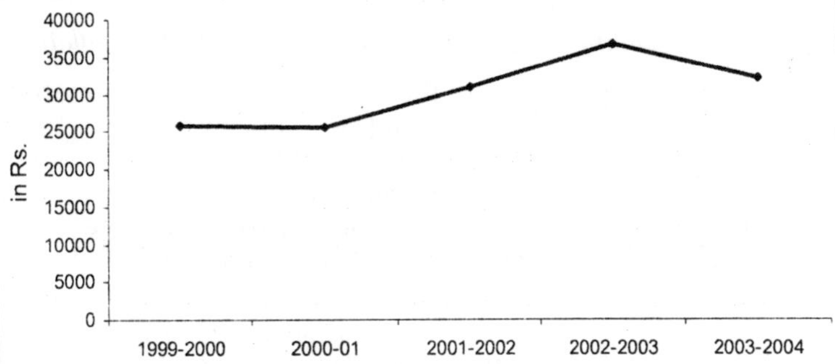

FIGURE 8: Total Expenditure of the Public Libraries from 1999-2000 to 2003-04

2000 to 2003-04. Since the librarians' allowance granted by the State library authority remains the same during 1999-2000 to 2003-04, there is a little variation in the staff expenditure during these periods. The expenditure for building and furniture is not recurring. The expenditure for building is the highest in 2003-04 (Mean 58194.53 with SD 137915.39) and the lowest in 2000-01 (Mean 17808.04 with SD 41715.57). The expenditure for furniture is the highest in 2001-02.

(Mean 9374.97 with SD 16074.47) and the lowest in 1999-2000 (Mean 5269.09 with SD 9991.12) The miscellaneous expenditure is the highest in 2000-01 (Mean 503718.10 with SD 5187848.92) and the lowest in 1999-2000 (Mean 14757.79 with SD 42244.11).

It can be deduced that the expenditure by the libraries is mostly determined by the revenue of the libraries. There is a fluctuation in the total expenditure of the libraries from 1999-2000 to 2003-04. From the analyses of the data it is revealed that only a very small amount is made available for the expenditure of the libraries for different purposes.

Per-Capita Expenditure

The per-capita expenditure for reading materials on literate population and on members, and per-capita expenditure on staff are used as the performance indicators to measure the library's effectiveness and efficiency.

Per-Capita Expenditure for Reading Materials on Literate Population

The per-capita expenditure of the libraries for reading materials on literate population is presented in Table 29.

Table 29
Per Capita Expenditure for Reading Materials on Literate Population in the Public Libraries in 2003-04 (District-wise)

District	*Total Literate Population (Census 2001)*	*Total Expenditure on Reading Materials (in Rs.)*	*Per Capita (in Rs.)*	*Rank*
Kasaragod	1024886	12,93,604	1.26	5
Kannur	2238675	60,75,817	2.71	1
Kozhikode	2661171	55,47,987	2.08	2
Wayanad	672723	11,24,700	1.67	3
Malappuram	3216224	39,10,349	1.22	6
Palakkad	2206453	33,73,926	1.53	4

Source: Total expenditure on reading materials was compiled from the statistical data collected by the State Library Council.

Table 29 indicates that Kannur records the highest per-capita expenditure of Rs. 2.71 for reading materials on literate population, followed by Kozhikode where it is Rs. 2.08. Malappuram records the lowest per-capita expenditure of only Rs.1.22 for reading materials. In all districts, the per-capita expenditure on reading materials is very meagre so that the provision of adequate standard reading materials to meet the various reading interests of the community cannot be fulfilled.

Per-Capita Expenditure for Reading Materials on Members

The per-capita expenditure for reading materials on members in 2003-04 is illustrated in Table 30.

Even though Malappuram lagged behind in the per-capita expenditure for reading materials on literate population, percentage of members with total literate population, and in the usage, it has the highest per-capita expenditure of Rs.57.09 on members in 2003-04. It may be due to the less number of members in the public libraries in Malappuram. Kannur, which occupies the first position in all above mentioned cases, ranks

Table 30
Per-Capita Expenditure for Reading Materials on Members in the Public Libraries in 2003-04 (District-wise)

District	*Total Members*	*Total Expenditure on Reading Materials (in Rs.)*	*Per Capita (in Rs.)*	*Rank*
Kasaragod	37,229	12,93,604	34.75	4
Kannur	1,86,518	60,75,817	32.57	6
Kozhikode	1,26,462	55,47,987	43.87	3
Wayanad	32,424	11,24,700	34.69	5
Malappuram	68,499	39,10,349	57.09	1
Palakkad	61,184	33,73,926	55.14	2

Source: Total expenditure on reading materials and total members was compiled from the statistical data collected by the State Library Council.

last in the per-capita expenditure for reading materials on members which is only Rs. 32.57. This shows that as the members increase in number, expenditure on the reading materials does not increase in direct proportion, and per-capita expenditure for reading materials on members is also too meagre to meet the various informational needs of the community.

Per-Capita Expenditure on Staff

The per-capita expenditure on staff is furnished in Table 31.

Table 31
Per-Capita Expenditure on Staff in the Public Libraries in 2003-04 (District-wise)

District	*Total Population (Census 2001)*	*Expenditure on Staff (in Rs.)*	*Per-Capita (in Rs.)*	*Rank*
Kasaragod	1203342	855349	0.71	5
Kannur	2412365	2974299	1.23	1
Kozhikode	2878498	2958601	1.03	2
Wayanad	786627	680461	0.87	4
Malappuram	3629640	1623804	0.45	6
Palakkad	2617072	2409457	0.92	3

Source: Expenditure on staff was compiled from the statistical data collected by the Sate Library Council.

The per-capita expenditure on staff, as shown in Table 31 indicates that Kannur comes to the first position with the per-capita expenditure of Rs. 1.23 on staff; followed by Kozhikode, where it is Rs. 1.03. Malappuram lags behind with the per-capita expenditure of only Rs.0.45 on staff. This illustration gives a discouraging picture which shows that the amount spent for the staff allowance is very meagre.

The analyses of the trend and patterns of financing of public libraries show that (1) though the government grant is a major source of revenue, the allocation is unsatisfactory, (2) the expenditure on reading materials and staff is not sufficient, (3) the per-capita revenue and expenditure is inadequate.

Human Resources

Human resources in the public libraries are professionals, semi-professionals and non-professionals. Professional staff are those who have a minimum qualification of graduate degree in Library Science, and semi-professionals are those who have only certificate course in Library Science and the non-professionals are those who are not professionally qualified; who include attenders, clerical staff and such others. Professionally trained and competent staff in adequate numbers are vital to select and organise resources and assist the users. The IFLA/UNESCO Guidelines (2001)[6] state: "Staff are a vitally important resource in the operation of a library. In order to provide the best possible service to the community, it is necessary to maintain well trained and highly motivated staff to make effective use of the resources of the library and to meet the demands of the community."

Categories of Staff

The staff working in the public libraries under study can be categorised into two, based on the duration of working hours. They are part-time and full-time librarians. The details, grade-wise, district-wise, and location-wise are given in Figures 9, 10 and 11 respectively.

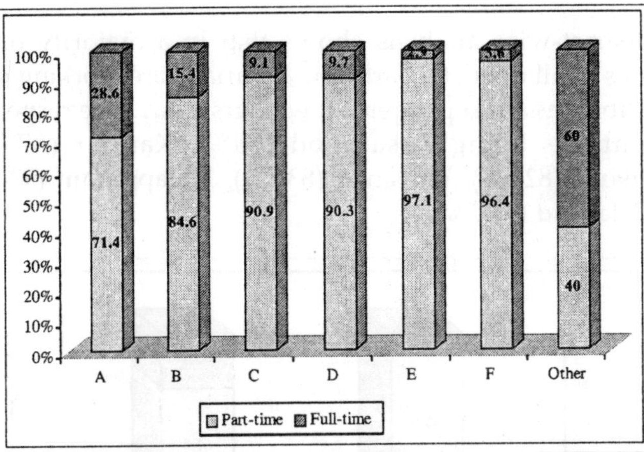

FIGURE 9: Categories of Staff in the Public Libraries, Grade-wise

The data in Figure 9 reflect that in a majority of the grant-in-aid libraries, librarians are part-time workers. The respective percentages are: A (71.4%), B (84.6%), C (90.9%), D (90.3%), E (97.1%), and F (96.4%). These libraries work below six hours a day, so that part-time librarians are engaged in these libraries. But in 60% of the libraries under other governing bodies, full-time librarians are employed, since these libraries offer services to the public for more than eight hours a day.

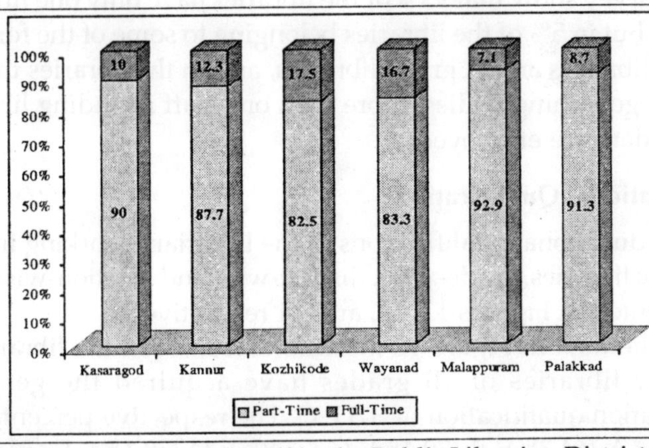

FIGURE 10 : Categories of Staff in the Public Libraries, District-wise

District-wise analysis shows that in a majority of the libraries in all districts, part-time librarians are working since these libraries are kept open a few hours a day. The respective percentages being Kasaragod (90%), Kannur (87.7%), Kozhikode (82.5%), Wayanad (83.3%), Malappuram (92.9%), and Palakkad (91.3%).

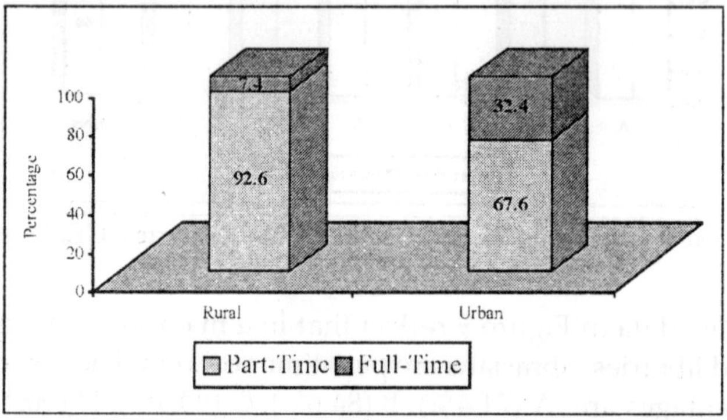

FIGURE 11: Categories of Staff in the Public Libraries, Location-wise

Location-wise analysis shows that part- time librarians working in the public libraries are more in the rural areas (92.6%) than in the urban areas (67.6%). The data collected in the survey show that 95% of the libraries have only one library staff. But in 5% of the libraries belonging to some of the former LLA libraries and A grade libraries, and in the libraries under other governing bodies, more than one staff including library attenders are employed.

Educational Qualifications

The educational qualifications of the librarians working in the public libraries, grade-wise, district-wise and location-wise are presented in Figures 12, 13, and 14 respectively.

The data in Figure 12 indicate that most of the librarians in the libraries of all grades have acquired the general education qualification of S.S.L.C. The respective percentages being: A (64.3%), B (70.4%), C (75.8%), D (58.1%), E (57.1%), and F (67.9%), while majority of librarians in the libraries under

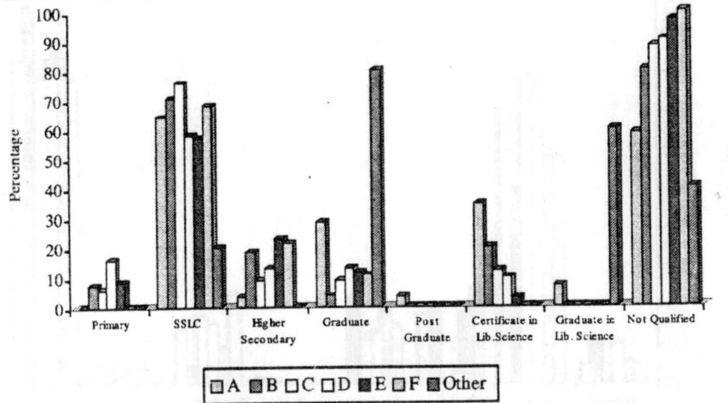

FIGURE 12 : **Educational Qualifications of the Librarians in the Public Libraries, Grade-wise**

other governing bodies (80%) are graduates. It also indicates that in 58.62% of A grade libraries, in a significant majority of libraries from B to F grades, B (80%), C (87.88%), D (90.32%), E (97.14%), F (100%), and only in 40% of the libraries under other governing bodies, the librarians have not undertaken any course of study in Library Science. On the whole, only a small percentage of the librarians (12.3%) has passed the certificate course in Library Science. The respective percentage in different grades of libraries being: A (34.48%), B (20%), C (12.12%), D (9.68%), E (2.86%), and no one in F grade libraries. Only a very few libraries in A grade (6.90%), and in a majority of the libraries under other governing bodies (60%), professional librarians are employed. These librarians have acquired a degree in Library Science, whereas in B to F grade libraries, there are no professional librarians.

District-wise analysis indicates that most of the librarians working in the public libraries in all districts, Kasaragod (57.1%), Kannur (57.9%), Kozhikode (75%), Wayanad (77.8%), Malappuram (50%), and Palakkad (73.9%) have acquired the general educational qualification of S.S.L.C. It also indicates that a majority of them have not acquired any educational qualification in Library Science. The respective percentages being: Kasaragod (77.27%), Kannur (87.72%), Kozhikode

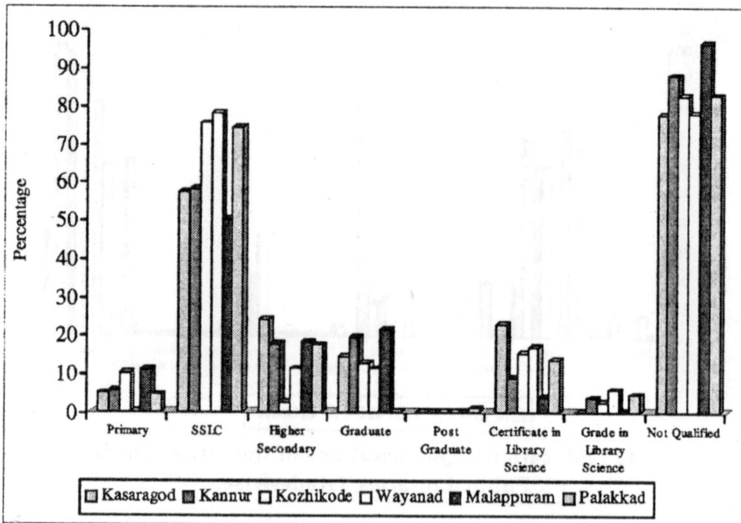

Figure 13: Educational Qualifications of the Librarians in the Public Libraries, District-wise

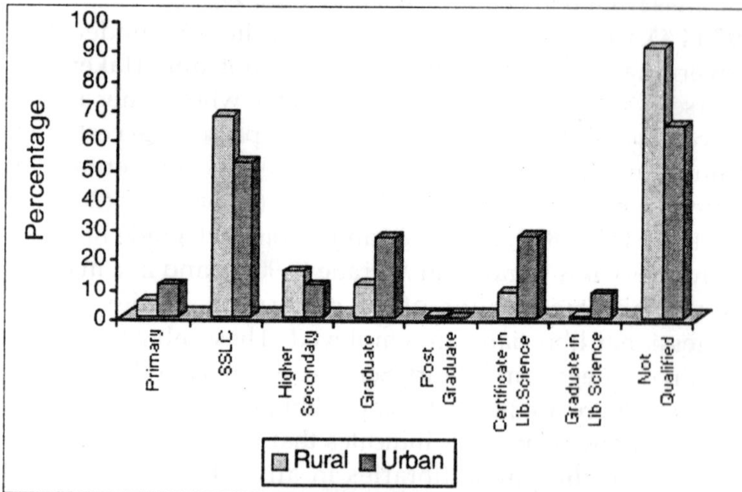

FIGURE 14 : Educational Qualifications of the Librarians in the Public Libraries, Location-wise

(82.5%), Wayanad (77.78%), Malappuram (96.3%), and Palakkad (82.61%).

From Figure 14, it can be seen that the higher percentage of librarians in both locations of rural (67.3%) and urban (51.4%) areas have the general educational qualification of SSLC, and a great majority of librarians in the rural area (90.67%) and 64.86% of librarians in the urban area have not undergone any course in Library Science.

The analysis shows that in a majority of the public libraries under study (64.2%) the librarians have acquired the general educational qualification of SSLC, 6.4% of them have only primary education, 14.4% have higher secondary education, and another 14.4% are degree holders. It also reveals that in a majority of the libraries (85.03%), the librarians have not undergone any course in Library Science, whereas a small percentage of the librarians (12.3%) have passed the certificate course in Library Science and the percentage of the library members who acquired a degree in Library Science is meagre. But in a majority of the libraries under other governing bodies (80%), the librarians are graduates. The IFLA/UNESCO Guidelines (2001)[7] state: "Small libraries open for limited hours do not require the continuous presence of a qualified librarian. They should however be under the supervision of a member of the qualified staff." But the data show that a greater majority of the libraries are not under the supervision of a qualified member of the staff.

The number of public librarians who have acquired computer knowledge, grade-wise, district-wise, and location-wise is furnished in Tables 32, 33 and 34 respectively.

Table 32
Computer Knowledge of Staff in the Public Libraries (Grade-wise)

Grade	*Total Staff*	*Acquired Computer Knowledge*	*Percentage*
A	28	9	32.1
B	27	8	29.6
C	33	5	15.2
D	31	5	16.1
E	35	5	14.3
F	28	2	7.1
Other	5	4	80.0
Total	187	38	20.3

From Table 32, it is clear that among the different grades of public libraries, the librarians of 32.1% of A grade libraries have acquired the basic knowledge of computer operation. The corresponding percentages of B to F grade libraries are 29.6%, 15.2%, 16.1%, 14.3%, and 7.1% respectively. In 80% of the libraries under other governing bodies, the librarians have a basic knowledge of computer operations.

Table 33
Computer Knowledge of Staff in the Public Libraries (District-wise)

District	*Total Staff*	*Acquired Computer Knowledge*	*Percentage*
Kasaragod	21	8	38.1
Kannur	57	11	19.3
Kozhikode	40	9	22.5
Wayanad	18	3	16.7
Malappuram	28	6	21.4
Palakkad	23	1	4.3
Total	187	38	20.3

District-wise analysis shows that only a very few librarians of the public libraries in all districts have basic computer knowledge. Kasaragod stands first with 38.1%, followed by Kozhikode (22.5%). Palakkad comes last with only 4.3%.

Table 34
Computer Knowledge of Staff in the Public Libraries (Location-wise)

Location	*Total Staff*	*Acquired Computer Knowledge*	*Percentage*
Rural	150	22	14.7
Urban	37	16	43.2
Total	187	38	20.3

The number of librarians who have acquired the basic computer knowledge is more in the urban (43.2%) than in the rural area (14.7%). On the whole, the number of librarians who have basic computer operating skill constitutes only a small percentage (20.3%).

Training

The IFLA/UNESCO Guidelines (2001)[8] stressed the importance of training to the staff as "training is a vital element of the activities of a public library. There must be a planned and continuous programme of training for staff at all levels, which should include both full-time and part-time staff. The rapid developments in information technology make the need for regular training even more essential." It also recommends that "0.5% to 1% of the total budget should be earmarked for training purpose." The findings of the survey indicate that the number of librarians who have participated in the training programmes is few (17.6%). No separate fund is allocated for training the librarians by the public libraries under study. These findings do not agree with the IFLA/UNESCO Guidelines, 2001.

Contacts

The IFLA/UNESCO Guidelines (2001)[9] stressed the importance of contacts as follows: "In addition to in-service training staff should be given opportunities to attend conferences and work shops, relevant to their ability to carry out their work." Analysis of the data revealed that more than half of the librarians (56.7%) have participated in the conferences or workshops conducted by the library authorities at district or taluk level or by the different libraries. The findings agree with the Guidelines to a limited extent.

Librarians' Allowance

The librarians' allowance as pre-fixed by the State Library Council is provided annually (Table 3.2). In the year under consideration an amount of Rs. 6,000 is given to the librarians of A to D grade libraries, whereas Rs. 3,600 is given to the librarians of E and F grade libraries. In addition to this, some of the libraries give separate allowances for the staff. The findings of the survey show that in a small percentage of libraries (4.84%), an amount ranges between Rs. 200 to Rs. 1300 per month is given as separate librarians' allowance. The former LLA libraries, panchayath/municipality libraries, and libraries formerly under Scheduled Caste Developing Corporation give salaries to the library staff in the State government scale. Only 13.37% of the librarians who are working in these libraries receive the salaries ranging between Rs.3, 150 to 7, 200 per month. The salary fixed by the library management is given to the staff in the libraries under other governing bodies.

Technological Resources

Adopting new methods of delivery of information using different technologies is an essential part of the public library. The IFLA/UNESCO Guidelines (2001)[10] state: "Public libraries must, whenever possible, make use of the new technologies to improve their services."

Computer Facility

The computer facilities now available in the public libraries, grade-wise, district-wise, and location-wise are given in Tables 35, 36, and 37 respectively.

Table 35
Availability of Computer Facilities in the Public Libraries (Grade-wise)

Grade	*TotalLibraries*	*No.*	*Percentage*
A	28	14	50.0
B	27	6	22.22
C	33	0	.0
D	31	0	.0
E	35	1	2.86
F	28	0	.0
Other	5	3	60.0
Total	187	24	12.83

The data in Table 35 reveal that only 50% of the libraries in A grade, B (22.22%), E (2.86%), and 60% of the libraries under other governing bodies use computers. Computers are not available in the libraries of C, D, and F grades.

Table 36
Availability of Computer Facilities in the Public Libraries (District-wise)

District	*Total Libraries*	*No.*	*Percentage*
Kasaragod	21	3	14.29
Kannur	57	8	14.04
Kozhikode	40	4	10.00
Wayanad	18	3	16.67
Malappuram	28	2	7.14
Palakkad	23	4	17.39
Total	187	24	12.83

District-wise analysis shows that only a small percentage of the public libraries in all districts under study have computer sets. The respective percentages are: Kasaragod (14.29%), Kannur (14.04%), Kozhikode (10%), Wayanad (16.67%), Malappuram (7.14%), and Palakkad (17.39%).

Table 37
Availability of Computer Facilities in the Public Libraries (Location-wise)

Location	*TotalLibraries*	*No.*	*Percentage*
Rural	136	14	10.29
Urban	27	10	37.04
Total	187	24	12.83

Location-wise analysis shows that the number of libraries which make use of computers is more in the urban area (37.04%) than in the rural area (10.29%). The analysis of the data also shows that computers are used in 4 out of 24 libraries to make catalogue entry using locally developed library software namely Linet 1.00 version, WINLIS, Machilogic and LIBMIS, and the cost varies from Rs.12,000 to 26,000. Others use computers for DTP, CD browsing, and to give computer training to children.

Internet Facility

The UNESCO/IFLA Guidelines (2001)[11] stressed the importance of provision of Internet in the public libraries as: "The vast amount of information that can be accessed via the

Internet is of variable quality and accuracy and a key role of the librarian is to guide users to accurate information sources, which will meet their requirements."

The State library authority provides one computer with internet facility to the taluk reference libraries in each district under study. CDs also are made available along with this facility for the use of the members. Nine libraries among the surveyed libraries have internet facility. The data collected in the survey show that on an average, a total of 15 to 20 members use this facility every day. An amount varies from Rs.5 to Rs.30 per hour is colleted as Internet charges. The IFLA/UNESCO Guidelines (2001)[12] state: "Since the provision of Internet facility is also an information service, it should be completely free, and a nominal charge can be levied for E-mail service." The collection of Internet charge is against the IFLA/UNESCO Guidelines, 2001. The financial constraints may urge the library committee to charge for this service, but it is advisable to make it nominal.

It is learnt that recently the library authorities have taken steps to computerise some of the public libraries in each district. Special grants were sanctioned by the State Library Council for this purpose. From the analysis it can be concluded that all libraries are far behind in the application of computer and telecommunication technologies. This may be due to lack of adequate funds and trained staff, and lack of interest on the part of the staff.

Physical Resources

Space and Building

The library buildings should be located in a central place close to shops, cultural centres etc. Space must be provided for each function and activity of library such as reading, book-storage, service points, operational and administration work.

The analysis of the data revealed that 73.8% of the libraries are housed in their own building. Table 38 furnished below shows the size of the building, grade-wise in terms of their plinth area.

Table 38
Size of the Public Library Buildings (Grade-wise)

(in sq. ft.)

	Plinth Area of the Library Building	
Grade	*Mean*	*SD*
A	1727.25	1520.38
B	1325.84	1372.73
C	719.61	921.84
D	457.86	290.37
E	452.15	402.40
F	450.51	416.50
Other	3166.67	2466.44
Total	939.03	1178.91

From Table 38, it is seen that the average size of the library building is the largest in the libraries under other governing bodies (Mean 3166.67 sq.ft. with SD 2466.44), followed by A grade libraries (Mean 1727.25 sq.ft. with SD 1520.38), and smallest in F grade (Mean 450.51 sq.ft. with SD 416.50). The size of the library buildings varies and it ranges from 16.14 sq. ft. to 6,000 sq. ft.

Table 39
Size of the Public Library Buildings (District-wise)

(in sq. ft.)

	Size of the Library Building	
District	*Mean*	*SD*
Kasaragod	845.55	767.35
Kannur	1036.06	1252.58
Kozhikode	956.89	1326.60
Wayanad	889.91	597.37
Malappuram	909.38	1489.38
Palakkad	644.53	644.90
Total	939.03	1178.91

The data in Table 39 indicate that the public libraries in Kannur own, on an average, the largest sized library buildings (Mean 1036.06 sq.ft. with SD 1252.58) compared to the libraries in other districts. The libraries in Palakkad own, on an average, the smallest sized (Mean 644.53 sq.ft. with SD 644.90) library buildings.

Table 40
Size of the Public Library Buildings, Location-wise

(in sq. ft.)

	Size of the Library Building	
Location	*Mean*	*SD*
Rural	818.53	986.40
Urban	1392.35	1676.86
Total	939.03	1178.91

Location-wise analysis shows that the average size of the library building is larger in the urban (Mean 1392.35 sq.ft. with SD 1676.86) than in the rural area (Mean 818.53 sq.ft with SD 986.40). The investigator has observed that 90% of the grant-in-aid libraries have 2 or 3 small rooms and are too insufficient to accommodate the book collection, to provide reading facility and for other functions. But the condition of libraries under other governing bodies is far better than that of grant-in-aid libraries. The findings of the survey do not agree with the IFLA/UNESCO Guidelines (2001)[13] which state that "the library should have adequate space to implement the full range of services." The great challenge in the public library building project is certainly the limited financial resources. It is also found that in most of the libraries, the cleanliness of the buildings is only partially satisfactory, and in some, it is not at all satisfactory. In a majority of the libraries, the physical lay out is not functionally helpful.

Furniture

The findings of the survey indicated that 90% of the libraries have insufficient number of furniture both for stacking and for reading facilities. The seating capacity of the libraries varies from 3 seats in some E and F grade libraries to 100 seats in some A grade libraries.

Other Physical Facilities

Only a little above a quarter of the libraries (27.3%) provide the drinking water facility to the users. It is also observed that in a majority of the libraries, the ventilation, fan, and lighting facility are partially satisfactory. A majority of the libraries

(78.6%) have no toilet room facility to the users. The findings of the survey revealed that physical facilities of the public libraries under study are not satisfactory. Scarcity of sufficient funds is found to be the major reason for this condition.

Equipment

The data available in the survey show that more than half of the libraries (50.27%) have televisions which are mainly used for watching cinemas, sports and listening to news and are rarely used for other informational or educational purpose. More than one third of the libraries (34.22%) have radios which are mainly used for recreational purposes. A small percentage of the libraries (8.56%) have tape recorders, and 3.74% have other equipments like the public addressing system and the video set.

VISITORS

Regarding the access to the public library, The IFLA/UNESCO Public Library Manifesto (1998)[14] proclaims that "the services of the public library are provided on the basis of equality of access for all, regardless of age, race, sex, religion, nationality, language, or social status." From this statement, it is clear that users of the public libraries belong to all sections of the community. They are heterogeneous in nature and belong to different socio-economic status. The users include both registered members and others who visit the library for reading newspapers and magazines, watching TV, and attending library programmes. The data regarding the visitors of the public libraries, grade wise, district wise and location wise during 1999-2000 to 2003-04 are furnished in Tables 41, 42, and 43 respectively. Average visitors per year in a library are a usage indicator and it can be used as a key performance indicator to measure the quality of services and facilities in a library.

From Table 41 it is found that on an average, the number of visitors is the highest in A grade libraries (Mean 27033.62 with SD 21616.76) followed by the libraries under other governing bodies (Mean 25950.00 with SD 12798.63) during 1999-2000. The lowest is in F grade libraries (Mean 10162.17

Table 41
Visitors of the Public Libraries from 1999-2000 to 2003-04 (Grade-wise)

	1999-2000		*2000-01*		*2001-02*		*2002-03*		*2003-04*	
Grade	*Mean*	*SD*	*Mean*	*SD*	*Mean*	*SD*	*Mean*	*SD*	*Mean*	*SD*
A	27033.62	21616.76	27565.90	21882.52	27592.90	22099.76	29537.57	23196.98	28909.05	22767.50
B	22907.40	15326.98	20431.73	13174.09	25098.07	17060.21	26048.53	18194.70	27364.00	19908.67
C	13729.00	8982.50	14140.00	8992.80	14950.43	9544.72	15510.71	9508.52	16445.79	9855.11
D	15882.00	10867.37	16482.36	10378.08	17010.00	10577.76	16942.73	10016.92	17929.91	10510.84
E	14230.10	11622.02	13913.60	9748.76	15542.40	12910.44	15414.50	13667.58	13962.40	5297.43
F	10162.17	3823.73	11007.83	3863.09	10475.14	5692.57	11151.86	6412.68	12910.29	8119.87
Other	25950.00	12798.63	26427.00	13538.27	27799.50	13860.00	28061.00	14338.71	18450.00	636.40
Total	19410.11	15679.77	19274.22	15177.01	20458.59	16314.56	21142.63	17123.31	21398.95	16763.78

Table 42

Visitors of the Public Libraries from 1999-2000 to 2003-04 (District-wise)

	1999-2000		*2000-01*		*2001-02*		*2002-03*		*2003-04*	
District	*Mean*	*SD*	*Mean*	*SD*	*Mean*	*SD*	*Mean*	*SD*	*Mean*	*SD*
Kasaragod	11670.86	5830.96	12085.00	5938.03	12539.29	6023.14	13421.57	6378.53	13886.43	6128.47
Kannur	21627.27	14200.28	20235.12	13007.25	23504.15	15542.52	23096.33	16660.21	24904.54	17325.84
Kozhikode	24063.28	22384.23	24043.28	21967.49	23217.11	22544.88	23931.79	23230.65	22586.78	21826.22
Wayanad	22140.67	21479.99	24371.33	21979.96	25223.67	22904.95	25669.57	22205.84	27808.00	24227.41
Malappuram	12358.67	5753.50	12862.80	5984.20	13527.87	6321.91	14209.80	6235.16	14837.13	6047.14
Palakkad	19718.71	12349.98	20000.86	11785.37	20345.57	11231.71	24086.57	15700.39	20488.29	10484.08
Total	19410.11	15679.77	19274.22	15177.01	20458.59	16314.56	21142.63	17123.31	21398.95	16763.78

Table 43
Visitors of the Public Libraries from 1999-2000 to 2003-04, (Location-wise)

	1999-2000		*2000-01*		*2001-02*		*2002-03*		*2003-04*	
Location	*Mean*	*SD*	*Mean*	*SD*	*Mean*	*SD*	*Mean*	*SD*	*Mean*	*SD*
Rural	18068.91	13999.55	17517.79	13036.21	18832.02	14656.13	19647.54	15816.02	20030.36	14896.26
Urban	23114.38	19510.16	24125.29	19502.30	25028.48	19967.27	25485.52	20259.07	25244.05	21106.65
Total	1941011	15679.77	19274.22	15177.01	20458.59	16314.56	21142.63	17123.31	21398.95	16763.78

with SD 3823.73) during this period. It is also found that there is a steady decrease in the number of users from A to F grades. There is a slight increase in the use of the libraries from 1999-2000 to 2003-04 except in the year 2000-01. The rate of use of the library is positively correlated to the facilities provided by the libraries. It is concluded that the limited use of the libraries by the community may be due to the poor resources and services available in the libraries.

From Table 42, it can be seen that Wayanad is in the fore-front in the use of the public libraries except in the year 1999-2000. During 1999-2000 Kozhikode is in the fore-front. It is also noted that Kasaragod and Malappuram lagged behind in the use of the public libraries and it may be due to the socio-economic backwardness of these two districts. There is a small increase in the number of visitors of the public libraries in the districts of Kasaragod, Wayanad, Malappuram from 1999-2000 to 2003-04, whereas in Kozhikode, Kannur, and Palakkad there is a fluctuation in the number of people who visit the public libraries during these periods.

Table 43 shows that users are more from the urban community and less from the rural community. This may be due to the higher socio-economic standard in the urban area than in the rural area. It can be seen that an average of 19, 410 users made use of the library facilities in 1999-2000. The corresponding figures for the succeeding four years are 19274, 20459, 21143 and 21399 respectively.

From the above analysis, it can be inferred that there is only a marginal increase in the number of users from 1999-2000 to 2003-04. It can also be inferred that the public library authorities have not developed strategies to convert the non-users, who are a major portion of the community into the users of the libraries.

MEMBERS

Members of the public libraries are a subset of the community, so that community characteristics reflect in members. Education, unemployment, occupation, and age are highly correlated. The number of members is considered to be a significant index of the library consciousness in the community. The different categories of members, grade-wise, district-wise, and location-wise are given in Tables 44, 45 and 46 and in Figures 15, 16, and 17 respectively.

Table 44
Different Categories of Members of the Public Libraries (Grade-wise)

	Men		*Women*		*Children*		*Total*	
Grade	*Mean*	*SD*	*Mean*	*SD*	*Mean*	*SD*	*Mean*	*SD*
A	710.80	540.07	241.84	202.18	227.39	231.34	1084.56	818.76
B	314.88	323.77	122.70	202.61	64.08	67.22	471.37	352.81
C	281.91	352.29	91.88	146.56	74.46	123.19	417.21	497.74
D	235.03	254.88	54.74	68.37	52.61	72.65	334.19	309.14
E	164.17	124.72	41.00	37.78	43.53	55.12	242.37	160.23
F	154.65	205.12	62.12	121.10	23.63	35.49	234.54	351.78
Other	1452.00	1930.57	399.67	577.14	309.67	282.62	1709.50	2436.28
Total	316.59	437.50	101.87	166.59	81.57	134.69	478.45	635.41

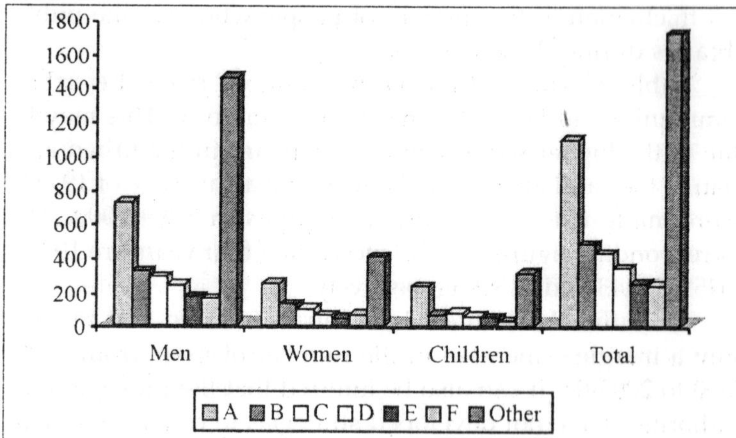

FIGURE 15: Different Categories of Members of the Public Libraries, Grade-wise

The data presented in Table 44 and in Figure 15 indicate that the special characteristic of membership in the public libraries is that the males dominate the females. It also indicates that the average number of children who enrolled as the members of the public libraries is less than female members in all grades except D and E grades where its dominance is negligible. Considering the total membership in the public libraries, the libraries under other governing bodies have the highest average number of members (Mean1709.50 with SD 2436.28), ranging between a minimum of 160 members and a maximum of 5,324 members. Among the grant-in-aid libraries, the average number of members is the highest in A grade libraries (Mean 1084.56 with SD 818.76), ranging between a minimum of 50 members and a maximum of 2, 918 members, and the lowest in F grade libraries (Mean 234.54 with SD 351.78), ranging between a minimum of 30 members and a maximum of 1,865 members. This shows that the libraries under other governing bodies and A grade libraries provide more facilities to the members. The number of members who utilise the libraries is positively correlated to the collection and services provided by the libraries.

Table 45
Different Categories of Members of the Public Libraries (District-wise)

	Men		*Women*		*Children*		*Total*	
District	*Mean*	*SD*	*Mean*	*SD*	*Mean*	*SD*	*Mean*	*SD*
Kasaragod	288.10	427.67	93.43	172.79	68.40	98.43	427.48	590.75
Kannur	314.18	378.43	96.04	138.49	51.55	78.97	454.89	544.38
Kozhikode	394.03	652.64	140.00	207.31	123.74	170.92	619.45	934.76
Wayanad	365.81	435.70	93.38	140.78	76.07	71.44	511.29	534.29
Malappuram	267.33	294.68	58.59	96.82	92.35	205.56	408.93	563.36
Palakkad	233.38	210.52	116.23	223.01	74.75	92.77	393.48	330.83
Total	316.59	437.50	101.87	166.59	81.57	134.69	478.45	635.41

District-wise analysis indicates that in all districts the males dominate the females in the membership. The average number of children who took membership in the public libraries is less than females in all districts except Malappuram. The average number of total members is the highest in Kozhikode (Mean 619.45 with SD 934.76), ranging between a minimum of 57 members and a maximum of 2, 918 members, followed by Wayanad (511.29 with SD 534.29), ranging between a minimum of 95 members and a maximum of 1730 members and the

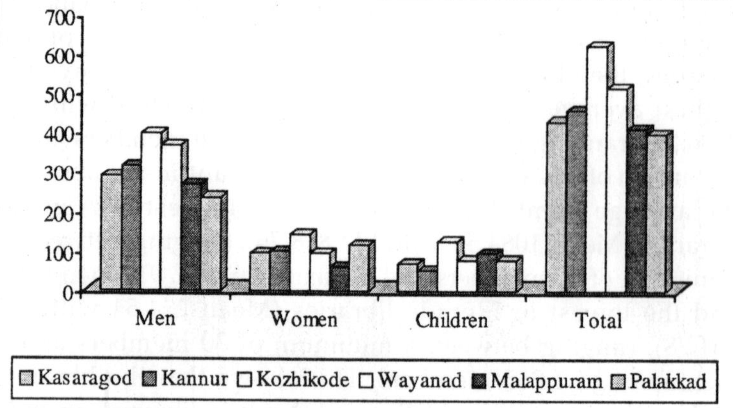

FIGURE 16: Different Categories of Members of the Public Libraries, District-wise

lowest in Palakkad (Mean 393.48 with SD 330.83), ranging between a minimum of 30 members and a maximum of 1, 074 members.

Table 46
Different Categories of Members of the Public Libraries (Location-wise)

	Men		*Women*		*Children*		*Total*	
Location	*Mean*	*SD*	*Mean*	*SD*	*Mean*	*SD*	*Mean*	*SD*
Rural	266.77	305.17	84.66	127.14	76.43	130.86	409.28	444.83
Urban	529.03	754.07	175.76	269.39	104.20	150.72	760.92	1082.55
Total	316.59	437.50	101.87	166.59	81.57	134.69	478.45	635.41

Location-wise analysis shows that both in the urban and the rural community the males dominate the females in the membership and the membership of children is lesser than females. The average number of members of the libraries is more in the urban area (Mean 760.92 with SD 1082.55) than in the rural area (Mean 409.28 with SD 444.83). The variations in the socio-economic status of these two areas are reflected in the membership of the libraries.

The analysis shows that in total, on an average, 317 men, 102 women and 82 children took membership in the public

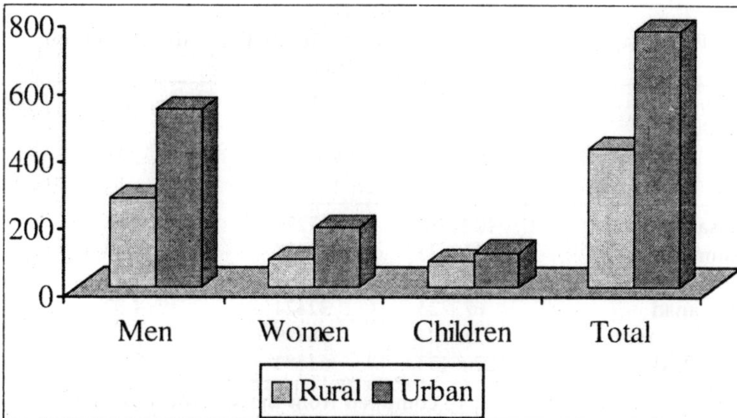

FIGURE 17: **Different Categories of Members of the Public Libraries, Location-wise**

libraries. From this finding it is clear that the males dominate the females in the library utilisation and the average number of children who took membership in the libraries is lesser than the females. This is not a satisfactory trend. The females dominate the males in the population and the State literacy rate of women is 87.7%. This dominance is not reflected in the library membership due to the less involvement of women in social activities and their low reading interests. The IFLA/UNESCO Guidelines (2001)[15] state that "public library has a special responsibility to support the process of learning to read, and to promote books and other media for children." The *IFLA/UNESCO Public Library Manifesto* (1998)[16] states one of the key missions, which should be at the core of public library service. It is "creating and strengthening reading habits in children from an early stage." From the analyses it can be concluded that the library authorities have not taken serious steps to create and strengthen reading habits in the children and in the women.

The percentage of members in the total literate population is a performance indicator which can be used to evaluate and monitor the achievements of the objectives of libraries. The district-wise details are furnished in the Table 47.

Table 47
Percentage of Members in the Total Literate Population and their Rankings (District-wise)

District	*Total Literate Population (census 2001)*	*Total No. of Members*	*Percentage*	*Rank*
Kasaragod	1024886	37229	3.63	4
Kannur	2238675	186518	8.33	1
Kozhikode	2661171	126462	4.75	3
Wayanad	672723	32424	4.82	2
Malappuram	3216224	68499	2.13	6
Palakkad	2206453	61184	2.77	5

Note: Total members were compiled from the statistical data collected by the State Library Council.

The data presented in Table 47 revealed that the percentage of members in the total literate population in six districts appears insignificant; the highest being in Kannur, where 8.33% of its literate population is members of the public libraries; followed by Wayanad, where only 4.82% of the literate population are members. The investigator has observed during visits to some of the libraries that in Wayanad, a majority of libraries both in urban and rural areas are actively involved in different social activities. This may be reflected in the increase in the percentage of library membership, in spite of Wayanad's socio-economic backwardness. The proportion of the number of members to the literate population is less in Malappuram where only 2.13% of the total literate population has registered themselves as library members. The data revealed that people are not aware of the role of public libraries to meet their various informational, cultural, educational, and recreational needs.

Type of Membership

There are two types of membership in the public libraries under study and they are adult membership and child membership. In some of the libraries, adult membership is of more than one type and they are ordinary, life, and patronage. Their membership fee, subscription, and periodicity of the membership are different. The details of different types of membership in the libraries are furnished in Table 48

Table 48
Membership of the Public Libraries

(N =182)

Types of Membership	*No.*	*Percentage*
Ordinary	182	100
Life	76	42
Patronage	7	4
Children	163	90

N = Total number of respondents, based on which the percentage is derived.

Table 48 shows that ordinary membership is issued to its members in all libraries under study, life membership is given in 42% of libraries, and in a small percentage of libraries (4%) patronage is given. Membership to the children is issued in a great majority of the libraries (90%).

Membership Fee

The particulars of membership fee collected from the adults and children are given in Table 49.

Table 49
Membership Fee for Adults and Children in the Public Libraries

Adult Membership			*Children's Membership*		
Fee (in Rs.)	*No. of Membership*	*Percentage*	*Fee (in Rs.)*	*No. of Membership*	*Percentage*
No fees	0	.0	No Fees	82	50.31
1 - 10	111	41.89	1 - 10	64	39.26
11-100	87	32.83	>10	17	10.43
> 100	67	25.28	Total	163	100
Total	265	100.00			

From the data in Table 49, it can be concluded that no library provides free service to adults. This is against the IFLA/UNESCO Public Library Manifesto (1998)[17] which states that "the public library shall in principle be free of charge." Nearly half of the libraries (41.89%) collect Re. 1 to Rs. 10 as membership fee from adults, and this agrees with the National

Policy on Library and Information System recommendation (Barua 1992)[18] and the report of the Working Group on Libraries and Informatics (India. Planning Commission 1986)[19] for the formulation of the 8th Five year Plan that "charging a nominal fee of Re.1 to Rs.10 is desirable for membership to raise funds." Nearly one third of the libraries (32.83%) collect membership fee which varies from Rs. 11 to Rs. 100. A quarter of the libraries (25.28%) collect more than Rs.100/- as membership fee. In life membership, the membership fee varies from Rs.100 to Rs. 2500. In patronage, the membership fee ranges between Rs.1, 000 and Rs.10, 000.

It is also found that half of the libraries (50.31%) do not collect fee from children, and 39% collect a nominal amount of Re.1 to Rs.10. The IFLA/UNESCO Guidelines (2001)[20] state: "Charging users for services and membership should not be used as a source of revenue for public libraries, as it makes the ability to pay a criterion in determining who can use a public library." The finding does not agree with this Guideline.

Subscription

The details of subscription levied from both adult and children who are enrolled as the members of the library are given in Table 50.

Table 50

Annual Subscription for Adults and Children in the Public Libraries

Adult Membership			*Children's Membership*		
Fee (in Rs.)	*No. of Membership*	*Percentage*	*Fee (in Rs.)*	*No. of Membership*	*Percentage*
No fees	87	32.83	No fees	108	66.26
1-10	173	65.28	1 - 10	55	33.74
Above10	5	1.89	Above 10	0	.0
Total	265	100	Total	163	100

The data in the table (Table 50) reveal that only 32.83% of the libraries do not collect subscription from the adults, and more than half of the libraries (65.28%) collect a nominal amount of Re. 1 to Rs.10 in a year. Only 1.89% of the libraries collect above Rs. 10 as the annual subscription from members. More than half of the libraries (66.26%) do not collect subscription from children and the remaining libraries (33.74%) collect a nominal amount of Re. 1 to Rs.10 in a year.

Periodicity

The data regarding the periodicity of membership in different categories are shown in the Table 51.

Table 51

Periodicity of Membership in the Public Libraries

Adults (N_1 = 265)			*Children* (N_2 = 163)		
Periodicity	*No. of Libraries*	*Percentage*	*Periodicity*	*No. of Libraries*	*Percentage*
Below 1 yr.	4	1.51	Up to adult stage	130	80
1 yr.	37	13.96	Below 1 year	3	2
Above 1 yr.	137	51.70	1 Year	28	17
Life	87	32.83	Above 1 year	2	1
Total	265	100.00	Total	163	100

The data in the table (Table 51) indicate that in more than half of the libraries (51.70%), membership is issued to adults for more than 1 year. In 13.96% of the libraries, membership is issued for a year; in 32.83% it is life membership, in which periodicity is 10-12 years or life long. The number of libraries in which membership issued for below 1 year is insignificant (1.51%). In a majority of the libraries (80%) membership is issued to children until they attain adult stage.

ADMINISTRATION

The State Library Council is the administrative authority of the public libraries at the apex level, except in the libraries under other governing bodies. In order to secure proper co-ordination and strategic leadership, the State Library Council delegates some of its powers to district library councils and taluk library unions. The library committee carries out the administrative policy laid down by the administrative authority. In the libraries under other governing bodies, the library committee is the administrative authority.

The survey shows that a vast majority of the libraries (90.91%) are directly under the administrative control of the State Library Council. Only a very few libraries (6.42%) are under the administrative control of panchayaths, and 2.67% of libraries are under the control of other governing bodies.

Library Committee

The library committee is the responsible body which supervises the functioning of the library and manages the library funds properly. It ensures the general efficiency and progress of the library. As per the bye-law of the public libraries prepared by the Kerala State Library Council (1991),[21] "each library should have a separate library committee to manage the functioning of libraries." All the libraries under study report that there is a separate library committee for each library.

Committee Members

As per the bye-law of the public libraries, prepared by the Kerala State Library Council (1991)[22], the committee is made up of not more than 11 members elected by the general body and two nominated members of whom one is a woman and the other is from SC/ST. The constitution of the library committees is given in Table 52.

The analysis of the data in the table (Table 52) indicates that a majority of the libraries (81.8%) have social workers in the library committees. Panchayath/municipal council members are included in the library committees of only 40.12 % of the libraries, 69.5% have political workers, 59.9% have members from the academic field, and 10.2% of the library committees have members from other categories such as government employees, labourers, and students.

The finding does not agree fully with the IFLA/UNESCO Guidelines (2001)[23] which state: "Public libraries should be governed by a properly established body made largely of representatives of the local community including those elected to the local council." The findings of the survey also indicate that in nearly half of the libraries (46%), the librarians are not included as a member of the library committee.

Table 52
Members of the Public Library Committee

Grade	Total Libraries	Social Workers		Members of the Local Councils		Workers		Political		Academicians		Others	
		No.	%	No.	%	No.	%	No.	%	No.	%	No.	%
A	28	21	75.0	9	4.81	16	57.1	17	60.7	5	17.9		
B	27	23	85.2	10	5.35	16	59.3	19	70.4	3	11.1		
C	33	24	75.8	11	5.89	24	72.7	22	66.7	1	3.0		
D	31	28	90.3	16	8.56	23	74.2	18	58.1	3	9.7		
E	35	27	77.1	14	7.49	25	71.4	13	37.1	5	14.3		
F	28	25	92.9	12	6.42	22	78.6	19	67.9	2	7.1		
Other	5	3	60.0	3	1.60	3	80.0	4	80.0	0	.0		
Total	187	153	81.8	75	40.12	130	69.5	112	59.9	19	10.2		

Note: Total percentage comes more than 100 because of multiple co-options.

Committee Meetings

The findings of the survey show that the library committees in a majority of the libraries (87.17%) meet once a month. In a small percentage of libraries (6.42%), committees meet twice a month, 4.81%, bimonthly and 1.6% quarterly. In a great majority of the libraries, this finding agrees with the provision in the bye-law of the public libraries, prepared by the Kerala State Library Council [24] that "each library committee should meet once in a month" and the IFLA/UNESCO Guidelines (2001)[25] that "the library committee should meet on a regular basis."

LIBRARY RECORDS

Libraries throughout their existence have to maintain records and statistics of their working. The registers which are maintained by the libraries under study are the following: Accession register (100%), membership register (100%), periodical register (84.95%), furniture register (91.40%), register for bound volumes (24.19%), issue register (96.23%), visitor register (87.10%), cash book (100%), register for lost books (36.02%), and register for minutes of the meetings (89.25%).

During visits, the investigator has noticed that in most of the public libraries, accession registers are maintained properly and necessary entries were made. It is also noted that in one library under other governing body keeps only the filled up membership form. In a majority of the libraries, the membership register is incomplete and borrowers' records are not accurate and are poorly maintained. The particulars of those library members who cancelled their membership and those who have not renewed the membership for a long time were not deleted from the membership register. The investigator also noticed that visitor registers are not used in most of the libraries.

CONCLUSION

The present status of public libraries in Malabar is not at all at a satisfactory level and is not as proposed in the IFLA/ UNESCO Guidelines. The study reveals that the public libraries are under resourced in terms of reading materials, finance, human resources, technological resources, and physical facilities. A majority of collection in the public libraries are in the categories of non-fiction. The reading materials are not organised scientifically to provide effective service to the members of the library. Only a negligible number of libraries took steps to create computerised databases of books and to provide Internet facility to the members. Only a very small percentage of the community uses public library facilities and takes membership in the libraries. Women and children do not make much use of the public library facilities. The libraries are not able to meet the changing needs of the community. In the era of information explosion, and advanced Information and Communication Technology (ICT), the concept of public libraries has changed drastically. The study reveals that the public libraries have not taken any major steps to change their nature of work and to revamp the contents using the latest trends in information technology.

References

1. IFLA/UNESCO. 2001. *The public library service: IFLA/UNESCO guidelines for development*. Prepared by Philip Gill et al. Munchen: K.G. Saur, sec. 1.12.
2. *Ibid.*, Sec. 4.6.
3. *Ibid.*
4. *Ibid., Sec.* 4.5.1.
5. *Ibid.*, Sec. 2.4.
6. *Ibid.*, Sec. 5.1.
7. *Ibid.*, Sec. 5.5.
8. *Ibid., Sec.* 5.8.
9. *Ibid.*, Sec. 5.8.2.
10. *Ibid.*, Sec. 2.4.5.
11. *Ibid.*, Sec. 3.4.7.
12. *Ibid.*
13. *Ibid.*, 3.10.1.

14. INFLA/UNESCO. 1998. *Public Library Manifesto,* 1994, revised version. *http:// www.ifla.org., para.2.*

15. IFLA/UNESCO, op. cit., 1, sec.3.4.2.

16. INFLA/UNESCO, op. cit., 14, para.3.

17. *Ibid.,* Para.4.

18. Barua, B.P. 1992. *National Policy on Library and Information Systems and Services for India.* Bombay: Popular Prakashan.

19. India. Planning Commission. 1986. Report of the Sub-Group on 'Public Library System' of the Working Group on Libraries and Informatics, convened by D. R. Kalia. *CLIS Observer* 13, No. 1-2 (January-June): 27-34.

20. IFLA/UNESCO, *op. cit.,* 1, *sec.* 2.4.4.

21. Kerala State Library Council. 1991. Bye-law of the public libraries, Sec. 10.

22. *Ibid.*

23. IFLA/UNESCO, *op. cit.,* 1, Sec. 2.5.

24. Kerala State Library Council, *op. cit.,* 21, Sec. 10, No. 9.

25. IFLA/UNESCO, *op. cit.,* 1, Sec. 2.5.

5

UTILISATION OF SERVICES IN THE PUBLIC LIBRARIES–ANALYSIS

INTRODUCTION

The public libraries should provide a range of services, both within the library and in the community, to satisfy their users' needs. The IFLA/UNESCO Guidelines (2001)[1] state: "The public library must provide services based on an analysis of the library and information needs of the local community. In planning services, clear priorities must be established and a strategy be developed for service provision in the medium to long term." This chapter analyses the data on the various services offered by the public libraries under study and also the roles played by them in the society.

LENDING SERVICES

The essential function of a public library which should take precedence over other services is the lending of books and other reading materials to the members. The data regarding the number of books lent per member, loan period, the renewal facility, the fine for overdue books, the action taken to get back the over due books, the method of book circulation, the average books issued per day, total books circulated are furnished below

Number of Books Lent per Member

Analysis of the data available in the survey revealed that nearly half of the libraries (48.1%) lend one book at a time to the members, 39.6% of the libraries lend 2 books at a time, 11.2% lend 3 books, and a very small percentage of libraries (1.1%) lend 5 books at a time to the members.

Loan Period

It is also found that more than half of the libraries (56.1%) lend books for two weeks, whereas 36.4% of the libraries lend books for 7 to 10 days. An insignificant percentage of the libraries (2.7%) lend books for 3 weeks and 4.8% libraries lend books for one month.

Renewal Facility

Analysis of the data also revealed that a majority of the libraries (94.1%) provide the facility to extend the loan period of books.

Fine for Overdue Books

Nearly half of the libraries (44.4%) do not collect any fee from the members for the overdue books. Some of the libraries (20.7%) collect a fine of 10 paisa per day per book, 25.4% of them collect a fine of 25 paisa, and 9.5% of them collect a fine of above 25 paisa per day per book which varies from 50 paisa to Re.1.00. The IFLA/UNESCO Guidelines (2001)[2] states: "Collecting fine for overdue books is sometimes necessary to ensure that items are kept in circulation and not retained for a long time by one user, and it should not be set at a level that would deter any one from using the library".

Action Taken to Recover the Overdue Books

More than half of the librarians (56.45%) reported that they send reminders to the library members asking them to return the overdue books. As many as 34.41% of the libraries inform the person who recommended for the membership, and 22.04% of them collect the overdue books directly from the members.

Circulation Method

The study reveals that a large majority of the libraries (88.2%) adopted ledger system for the circulation of books. In this method, in some libraries, the details of the books issued are recorded in a separate register serially under the date of issue; and in others, a separate page in the ledger is assigned for each member for recording the details of the books borrowed by them. While returning the books, it was marked against the corresponding items.

A small percentage of libraries (7.5%) adopted other methods. In one method, libraries keep a membership card for each member with details of membership, and at the time of issue of books, the details of the books are noted on it and filed according to membership number. In the other method, a book card with details of book is prepared for each book and kept in the books themselves. While issuing the books, the details of the members are noted down on them and filed by the book number. When the books are returned, it is noted on the card and the book card is kept back in the books.

It is found that only in one A grade library, circulation system is computerised using a locally developed software. It is also observed that in 4 out of 5 libraries under other governing bodies (80%) Browne charging system is followed.

Average Books Issued per Day

The data obtained in the survey show that in a small percentage of libraries (10.16%), below 10 books are issued per day; in nearly one third of the libraries (32.62%),10-20 books are issued per day; and in another nearly one third (32.62%), 21-30 books are issued per day; in 10.7% libraries, 31-40 books are issued per day; in 8.02% of libraries, 41-50 books are issued per day and in 5.88% of libraries, 50-100 books are issued per day. This analysis reflects that the use of the libraries by the public is very low.

Lending of Books in Different Categories

The average number of books in different categories such as fiction, non-fiction and children's books issued in 2003-04, grade-wise, district-wise, and location-wise are given in Tables 1, 2 and 3.

Table 1
Lending of Different Categories of Books in the Public Libraries (Grade-wise)

	Fiction		*Non- Fiction*		*Children's Literature*		*Total*	
Grade	*Mean*	*SD*	*Mean*	*SD*	*Mean*	*SD*	*Mean*	*SD*
A	9658.39	3911.56	2018.74	2027.62	2639.04	1649.25	13971.56	4955.69
B	6046.37	3110.27	1374.00	1082.11	1538.89	975.63	8360.95	3580.43
C	3367.11	2462.42	688.79	985.59	1396.68	1587.67	5621.67	2683.21
D	3891.84	2210.50	879.35	1088.74	1200.56	979.55	5511.89	2509.48
E	3107.71	1072.21	403.57	631.78	974.90	1070.84	4327.29	1559.04
F	2597.46	2100.50	270.00	265.16	492.38	455.76	3970.00	3235.02
Total	5034.85	3676.97	1011.60	1345.69	1442.66	1393.25	6592.85	4674.26

Table 2

Lending of Different Categories of Books in the Public Libraries (District-wise)

District	*Fiction*		*Non- Fiction*		*Children's Literature*		*Total*	
	Mean	*SD*	*Mean*	*SD*	*Mean*	*SD*	*Mean*	*SD*
Kasaragod	3567.64	2400.64	872.21	1083.08	1826.07	1713.51	5501.82	3584.53
Kannur	4641.98	3342.97	822.07	862.36	1314.05	1297.49	6789.80	4316.92
Kozhikode	5509.48	4107.90	809.15	937.88	1174.77	1341.18	6976.10	4729.43
Wayanad	3909.89	4377.68	2241.22	3393.43	1566.00	1832.08	6617.92	7403.46
Malappuram	6861.38	3779.92	1153.44	1102.78	1360.69	1117.15	8511.29	4467.87
Palakkad	5910.90	4124.18	1102.11	1060.41	2023.18	1449.45	7164.81	4529.72
Total	5034.85	3676.97	1011.60	1345.69	1442.66	1393.25	6592.85	4674.26

The analysis of the data in Table 1 reveals that the average number of different categories of books lent out during 2003-04 is the highest in A grade libraries, fiction (Mean 9658.39 with SD 3911.56), non-fiction (Mean 2018.74 with SD 2027.62), children's literature (Mean 2639.04 with SD 1649.25) and total books (Mean 13971.56 with SD 4955.69). The number of different categories of books lent out is lowest in the libraries of F grade, fiction (Mean 2597.46 with SD 2100.50), non-fiction (Mean 270.00 with SD 265.16), children's books (Mean 492.38 with SD 455.76) and total books (Mean 3970 with SD 3235.02). It is also found that the number of books lent decreases according to the grades of the libraries from A to F. There is a positive correlation between the number of books lent and the facilities, services, and the total opening hours of the libraries.

District-wise analysis shows that, Malappuram occupies the highest position in the total number of fiction lent in the year 2003-04 (Mean 6861.38 with SD 3779.92) followed by Palakkad (Mean 5910.90 with SD 4124.18) and Kasaragod occupies the last position (Mean 3567.64 with SD 2400.64). Wayanad occupies the first position in the total number of non-fiction lent in the year 2003-04 (Mean 2241.22 with SD 3393.43) followed by Malappuram (Mean 1153.44 with SD 1102.78) and Kozhikode comes last (Mean 809.15 with SD 937.88). Palakkad occupies the first position in the total number of children's books lent in the year 2003-04 (Mean 2023.18 with SD 1449.45) followed by Kasaragod (Mean 1826.07 with SD 1713.51) and Kozhikode occupies the last position (Mean 1174.77 with SD 1341.18). Malappuram occupies the first position with regard to number of the total books lent in the year 2003-04 (Mean 8511.29 with SD 4467.87) followed by Palakkad (Mean 7164.81 with SD 4529.72) and Kasaragod occupies the last position (Mean 5501.82 with SD 3564.53).

Location-wise analysis shows that libraries in the urban area stand first in the average number of different categories of books issued in the year 2003-04, fiction (Mean 5774.54 with SD 3463.91), non-fiction (Mean 1423.41 with SD 2274.80), children's books (Mean 1192.83 with SD 978.57) and total number of books (Mean 8008.55 with SD 5064.31).

Table 3
Lending of Different Categories of Books in the Public Libraries (Location-wise)

	Fiction		*Non- Fiction*		*Children's Literature*		*Total*	
Location	*Mean*	*SD*	*Mean*	*SD*	*Mean*	*SD*	*Mean*	*SD*
Rural	4837.60	3725.36	909.81	987.85	1507.83	1479.97	6693.40	4558.75
Urban	5774.54	3463.91	1423.41	2274.80	1192.83	978.57	8008.55	5064.31
Total	5034.85	3676.97	1011.60	1345.69	1442.66	1393.25	6592.85	4674.26

Growth of Circulation

Growth of average number of books lent out during five years from 1999-2000 to 2003-04, grade-wise, district-wise, and location-wise was analysed and the data are presented in Tables 4, 5 and 6 respectively.

From the data in Table 4, it is clear that in A, B, D, and E grade libraries; there is a fluctuation in the average number of books issued during the period from 1999-2000 to 2003-04, whereas in C and F grade libraries, there is a marginal increase in the average number of books issued during this period. There is no sound reason behind this difference and it may be due to local variations in the reading interests.

The data in Table 5 indicate that there is a fluctuation in the mean number of books lent out in the public libraries in all districts during 1999-2000 to 2003-04.

Location-wise analysis shows that in both rural and urban area there is a fluctuation in the average number of books lent out during the period from 1999-2000 to 2003-04. In the rural area, the circulation of books is the highest in 2003-04 (Mean 6693.40 with SD 4558.75) and the lowest in 1999-2000 (Mean 5999.26 with SD 4650.63). In the urban area, the circulation is the highest in 2000-01(Mean 9636.38 with SD 4265.59) and the lowest in 1999-2000 (Mean 6501.24 with SD 3733.54). It is also clear that the number of books lent out is more in the urban area than in the rural area. The variations in the socio-economic status of these two areas reflect in the difference in total circulation of books in the libraries. It also indicates that there is no steady increase in the number of books lent out during

Table 4
Growth of Book Circulation in the Public Libraries from 1999-2000 to 2003-04 (Grade-wise)

	19999-2000		*2000-01*		*2001-02*		*2002-03*		*2003-04*	
Grade	*Mean*	*SD*	*Mean*	*SD*	*Mean*	*SD*	*Mean*	*SD*	*Mean*	*SD*
A	12683.52	4106.20	14541.28	11219.97	13088.56	4421.09	12962.44	4849.87	13971.56	4955.69
B	8124.40	4137.69	8577.29	3980.67	8698.62	3979.91	8546.90	3939.28	8360.95	580.43
C	4785.25	2070.77	4915.39	2564.91	5212.93	2514.96	5384.41	2611.04	5621.67	683.21
D	4579.04	3556.68	4770.07	3505.74	5148.93	3480.09	5119.63	2771.09	5511.89	2509.48
E	3337.48	1155.29	3919.70	1456.33	4297.96	1628.18	4041.96	1665.33	4327.29	1559.04
F	2821.44	2346.77	3156.06	2847.37	3223.56	2795.46	3351.58	2683.48	3970.00	3235.02
Total	6101.06	4555.11	6686.64	6584.57	6636.55	4606.72	6557.89	4555.90	6952.85	4674.26

Table 5

Growth of Book Circulation in the Public Libraries from 1999-2000 to 2003-04 (District-wise)

District	*19999-2000*		*2000-01*		*2001-02*		*2002-03*		*2003-04*	
	Mean	*SD*	*Mean*	*SD*	*Mean*	*SD*	*Mean*	*SD*	*Mean*	*SD*
Kasaragod	4718.71	4431.82	5065.24	4376.82	5660.53	4271.97	5519.71	4455.30	5501.82	3584.53
Kannur	5600.28	3898.99	6024.48	3976.00	6308.34	4097.69	6334.42	4200.02	5789.80	4316.92
Kozhikode	6403.70	4754.17	6705.57	4894.78	6747.39	4890.40	6592.10	4696.20	6976.10	4729.43
Wayanad	5490.90	5069.29	5791.50	5231.04	5872.50	5366.36	5677.52	6034.86	6617.92	7403.46
Malappuram	7237.95	4912.82	9721.43	13278.20	8064.67	4867.89	7937.14	4440.84	8511.29	4467.87
Palakkad	7527.56	5120.43	6994.00	5156.33	7161.12	5202.38	7143.25	4591.19	7164.81	4529.72
Total	6101.06	4555.11	6686.64	6584.57	6636.55	4606.72	6557.89	4555.90	6952.85	4674.26

Table 6
Growth of Book Circulation in the Public Libraries from 1999-2000 to 2003-04 (Location-wise)

	19999-2000		*2000-01*		*2001-02*		*2002-03*		*2003-04*	
Location	*Mean*	*SD*	*Mean*	*SD*	*Mean*	*SD*	*Mean*	*SD*	*Mean*	*SD*
Rural	5999.26	4750.63	6624.22	7059.75	6516.51	4735.98	6325.16	4482.65	6693.40	4558.75
Urban	6501.24	3733.54	9636.38	4265.59	7120.86	4083.35	7504.86	4807.00	8008.55	5064.31
Total	6101.06	4555.11	6686.64	6584.57	6636.55	4606.72	6557.89	4555.90	6952.85	4674.26

1999-2000 to 2003-04. From this, it can be inferred that there is no significant change in the reading interest of the public during this period.

REFERENCE SERVICE

Reference service is a vital service of a public library. The survey reports show that most of the libraries (60.43%) provide reference service to the members. The investigator has observed that the resources available in the libraries for this service are too meagre and not constitute standard reference books to provide this service satisfactorily. It is also noticed that many of the libraries do not possessed dictionaries or encyclopedias in the reference collection. On rating the frequency of utilisation of reference service by the users of the public library, it is found that, in more than half of these libraries (53.98%), the members make use of reference service "occasionally"; in only 7.96% of libraries, this service is availed "regularly" and in 38.06% of libraries, only "rarely."

Taluk Reference Libraries

One library from each taluk in the State is functioning as taluk reference library. With the financial assistance of Central Government under 11th Financial Commission, this service was started by the Kerala State Library Council in 2002. In the first year, the fund was utilised for the purchase of reference books and educational compact discs. In the consecutive three years, the fund was utilised to install Internet and to purchase books and periodicals. After four years, the libraries themselves should meet the expenditure to provide this service. Approximately 4.5 lakhs of rupees has been received by each taluk reference library. The training programme in computer operation has been offered to the librarians of these libraries.

REFERRAL SERVICE

Referral service is the service in which the user is directed to appropriate information sources such as libraries, agencies, and individuals. For providing this service, the library should have directories, hand books of other institutions, bibliographic sources of other libraries, standard reference tools and such other things. The number of libraries providing referral service is furnished in Table 7.

Table 7
Public Libraries Providing Referral Service (Grade-wise)

Grade	*Total Libraries*	*No.*	*Percentage*
A	28	11	39.29
B	27	9	33.33
C	33	9	27.27
D	31	4	12.90
E	35	9	25.71
F	28	4	14.29
Other	5	2	40.0
Total	187	48	25.67

The data in the table (Table 7) show that only a small percentage of libraries of all grades and those under other governing bodies, A (39.29%), B (33.33%), C (27.27%), D (12.90%), E (25.71%), F (14.29%) and the libraries under other governing bodies (40%) offer referral service to the users.

Table 8
Public Libraries Providing Referral Service(District-wise)

District	*Total Libraries*	*No.*	*Percentage*
Kasaragod	21	5	23.81
Kannur	57	14	24.56
Kozhikode	40	7	17.50
Wayanad	18	7	38.89
Malappuram	28	6	21.43
Palakkad	23	9	39.13
Total	187	48	25.67

District-wise analysis shows that the highest percentage of public libraries in Palakkad (39.13%), followed by Wayanad (38.89%), and the lowest in Kozhikode (17.5%) offer referral service to the users.

Table 9
Public Libraries Providing Referral Service (Location-wise)

Location	*Total Libraries*	*No.*	*Percentage*
Rural	150	39	26.0
Urban	37	9	24.32
Total	187	48	25.67

Almost equal percentage of libraries in the urban (24.32%) and the rural area (26%) provide referral service to their users. The libraries which offer this service provide the addresses of hospitals, government departments, banks, and such other institutions. They also keep handbooks, news letters and such other documents of these institutions. From the analysis it can be seen that the referral service is offered by a small number of libraries and the activities undertaken under this service is only minimal.

EDUCATIONAL ROLE

The *UNESCO Public Library Manifesto* (1994)[3] states that "one of the key missions which should be at the core of public library services is supporting both individual and self conducted education as well as formal education at all levels." The IFLA/UNESCO Guidelines (2001)[4] state: "The public library should provide material in the appropriate media to support formal and informal learning processes." The public library has the following important educational functions to perform: (1) Life long self-education, (2) Formal education, and (3) Distance education.

Service to the Life Long Self-Education of the Neo-Literates

Life long self education is a part of literacy. Those who acquired literacy wish to upgrade their knowledge through life long self-education. Public library is the ideal centre to provide this service effectively to them. The number of libraries, grade-wise, district-wise, and location-wise which support self education of the neo-literates is furnished in Tables 10, 11 and 12 respectively.

Table 10
Public Libraries Offering Service to the Life Long Self-Education of the Neo-Literates (Grade-wise)

Grade	*Total Libraries*	*No.*	*Percentage*
A	28	7	25.0
B	27	11	40.74
C	33	5	15.15
D	31	2	6.45
E	35	4	11.43
F	28	4	14.29
Other	5	1	20.0
Total	187	34	18.18

The data in the table (Table 10) indicate that the number of libraries in all grades and under under other governing bodies which offers service to the neo-literates is small. The respective percentages are: A (25%), B (40.74%), C (15.15%), D (6.45%), E (11.43%), F (14.29%) and the libraries under other governing bodies (20%).

Table 11
Libraries Offering Service to the Life Long Self-Education of the Neo-Literates (District-wise)

District	*Total Libraries*	*No.*	*Percentage*
Kasaragod	21	6	28.57
Kannur	57	8	14.04
Kozhikode	40	5	12.50
Wayanad	18	5	27.78
Malappuram	28	4	14.29
Palakkad	23	6	26.09
Total	187	34	18.18

Among districts, only a small number of libraries in all districts provides services to self-education of the new literates. The respective percentages are: Kasaragod (28.57%), Kannur (14.04%), Kozhikode (12.5%), Wayanad (27.78%), Malappuram (14.29%), and Palakkad (26.09%).

Table 12
Public Libraries Offering Service to the Life Long Self-Education of the Neo-Literates (Location-wise)

Location	*Total Libraries*	*No.*	*Percentage*
Rural	150	29	19.33
Urban	37	5	13.51
Total	187	34	18.18

Location-wise analysis shows that the number of libraries which offer service to the self-education of the neo-literates is more in the rural area (19.33%) than in the urban area (13.51%).

Collection of Books

The findings of the survey indicate that a small percentage of libraries (18.18%) provide service to the self-education of the neo-literates. Out of these libraries, a majority of them (87.27%) have separate collection of books to teach the new literates. The collection of books available for this service grade-wise, district-wise, and location-wise is furnished in Tables 13, 14, and 15 respectively.

Table 13
Collection of Books for Services to the Life Long Self-Education of the Neo-Literates (Grade-wise)

	No. of Books			
Grade	*Mean*	*SD*	*Minimum*	*Maximum*
A	203.33	273.24	32	750
B	100.00	-	100	100
C	147.50	85.78	40	250
D	78.00	-	78	78
E	75.00	35.36	50	100
F	0.00	0.00	0	0
Other	0.00	0.00	0	0
Total	152.71	182.41	32	750

The data in Table 13 indicate that the average number of books acquired for teaching the neo-literates is the highest in A grade libraries (Mean 203.33 with SD 273.24) and the lowest in E grade libraries (Mean 75 with SD 35.36). None of the libraries in F grade and none of the libraries under other governing bodies has a separate collection for this service.

Table 14
Collection of Books for Services to the Life Long Self-Education of the Neo-Literates (District-wise)

	No. of Books			
District	*Mean*	*SD*	*Minimum*	*Maximum*
Kasaragod	100.00	-	100	100
Kannur	50.00	-	50	50
Kozhikode	89.00	15.56	78	100
Wayanad	294.00	396.37	32	750
Malappuram	70.00	42.43	40	100
Palakkad	184.50	47.20	150	250
Total	152.71	182.41	32	750

Among districts, the average collection of books for teaching the neo-literates is more in Wayanad (Mean 294 with SD 396.37), followed by Palakkad (Mean 184.50 with SD 47.20) and least in Malappuram (Mean 70 with SD 42.43).

Table 15
Collection of Books for Services to the Life Long Self-Education of the Neo-Literates (Location-wise)

	Book Collection			
Location	*Mean*	*SD*	*Minimum*	*Maximum*
Rural	156.77	189.20	32	750
Urban	100.00	-	100	100
Total	152.71	182.41	32	750

Location-wise analysis shows that the average number of books collected for service to the self-education of the neo-literates is more in the rural area (Mean 156.77 with SD 189.20) than in the urban area (Mean 100).

The data availed in the survey show that out of the libraries which provide this service, a majority of them (87.27%) collected books including text books needed for different classes, as many as 61.82% of libraries conducted awareness classes on the importance of education and the role of public libraries in their education. A small percentage of these libraries (11.82%) use audio-visual aids to educate them. All libraries which provide this service use black boards to teach the new literates. A majority of the libraries which provide this service (78.1%) have a separate instructor and the remaining libraries (21.9%) managed this service with the librarians or library secretaries. Only two libraries among the libraries under study have received assistance from other institutions for providing this service. One library has received books from panchayaths and the other has received a total of Rs.73, 600/- from Kerala Literacy Mission. Many learners, majority of them women, have appeared for the public examination to qualify the different levels of education such as fourth standard, seventh standard, and tenth standard. From the analyses it is clear that service for self-education of the neo-literates is not provided by a majority of the libraries and thus they fail to fulfil the educational role.

Service to Formal Education

New Education Policy of India stressed the importance of public libraries in education by its statement that instead of laying emphasis on teaching programmes, students should be encouraged to endeavor to learn themselves; and for this there should be free public library services available near the residences of the pupils (India. Ministry of Education 1986).[5]

Service to Students

As a programme of the State Library Council, one academic study centre function in each district which helps the students in their study by providing books they required. The State Library Council allots separate fund of this purpose. Besides these libraries, some of the public libraries also provide separate service to the students.

The survey revealed that only 8.56% of the libraries function as academic study centre. The book collection in this section ranges from 16 books to 3152 books. Out of these libraries, a majority of them (87.5%) consider the suggestions of the students, 62.5% of the libraries collect the list of books from the educational institutions, and 43.75% of the libraries seek help of subject experts for selection of books. The findings also revealed that in total, 15 to 9000 students have made use of this service till the period under consideration. From this analysis, it can be inferred that a vast majority of the public libraries fail to fulfil the educational function by not providing effective and efficient academic service to the student community.

Service to Distance Education

A strong public library system is an important factor for the successful implementation of distance education programmes. The public libraries can act as an intermediary between distance learners and parent institutions and can serve as local information centres in the absence of study centres. The number of libraries which support distance education, grade-wise, district-wise, and location-wise is furnished in Tables 16, 17 and 18 respectively.

Table 16
Public Libraries Providing Service to Distance Education (Grade wise)

Grade	*Total Libraries*	*No.*	*Percentage*
A	28	6	21.43
B	27	7	25.93
C	33	4	12.12
D	31	3	9.68
E	35	0	.0
F	28	0	.0
Other	5	0	.0
Total	187	20	10.7

The data in the table (Table 16) reveal that the number of libraries which provide service to distance learners is less in A to D grade libraries, A (21.43%), B (25.93%), C (12.12%) and D (9.68%), while the libraries in E and F grades and the libraries under other governing bodies do not provide this service. Under this service the libraries are providing a few text books and reference books to the distance learners. No other guidance is given to the learners under this service. Because of the poor facilities, the libraries belonging to E and

F grades and the libraries under other governing bodies provide no such service.

Table 17
Public Libraries Providing Service to Distance Education (District-wise)

District	*Total Libraries*	*No.*	*Percentage*
Kasaragod	21	1	4.76
Kannur	57	4	7.02
Kozhikode	40	2	5.00
Wayanad	18	3	16.67
Malappuram	28	6	21.43
Palakkad	23	4	17.39
Total	187	20	10.70

District-wise analysis shows that Malappuram comes first among the districts, where 21.43% public libraries provide service to distance education and Kasaragod comes last, where only 4.76% of public libraries offer this service.

Table 18
Public Libraries Providing Service to Distance Education (Location-wise)

Location	*Total Libraries*	*No.*	*Percentage*
Rural	132	18	13.64
Urban	35	2	5.71
Total	187	20	10.7

Location-wise analysis shows that the number of libraries which offer service to distant learners is more in the rural area (13.64%) than in the urban area (5.71%). On the whole, only a small percentage of libraries (10.7%) support distance education. From this analysis, it can be inferred that a majority of the public libraries fail to fulfil the educational function of supporting distance learning.

INFORMATIONAL ROLE

Information provision is an important role of the public library. The rapid development of information technology has facilitated to access the vast amount of information through Internet and other electronic media.

Community Information Services (CIS)

Library Association, London (1980)[6] says about community information services: "The services concentrate on the needs of those who are unaware of and who do not have ready access to other sources of assistance and on the most important problems that people have to face, problems to do with their homes, careers, jobs, and their rights." The characteristic feature of the community information sources, which can meet the various community needs, is that they are more of non-book information. The number of libraries offering community information service, grade-wise, district-wise, and location-wise is furnished in Tables 19, 20 and 21 respectively.

Table 19
Public Libraries Offering Community Information Service (Grade-wise)

Grade	*Total Libraries*	*No.*	*Percentage*
A	28	19	67.86
B	27	18	66.67
C	33	18	54.55
D	31	16	51.61
E	35	12	34.29
F	28	14	50.00
Other	5	2	40.00
Total	187	99	52.94

The data in Table 19 reveal that most of the libraries belonging to A to D and F grades provide community information service to the people. The respective percentages are: A (67.86%), B (66.67%), C (54.55%), D (51.61%), F (50%), whereas only 34.29%, of the libraries in E grade and 40% of the libraries under other governing bodies offer this service.

Table 20
Public Libraries Offering Community Information Service (District-wise)

District	*Total Libraries*	*No.*	*Percentage*
Kasaragod	21	11	52.38
Kannur	57	23	40.35
Kozhikode	40	19	47.5
Wayanad	18	16	88.89
Malappuram	28	19	67.86
Palakkad	23	11	47.83
Total	187	99	52.94

District-wise analysis shows that a majority of libraries in Wayanad district (88.89%), followed by 67.86% of libraries in Malappuram and less number of libraries in Kannur (40.35%) offer community information service.

Table 21
Public Libraries Offering Community Information Service (Location-wise)

Location	*Total Libraries*	*No.*	*Percentage*
Rural	150	85	56.67
Urban	37	14	37.84
Total	187	99	52.94

More libraries in the rural area (56.67%) than in the urban area (37.84%) provide community information service to the people. The survey reveals that only 53% of the libraries offer Community Information Service to the people, all of which provide the social or pragmatic information needed for the community such as train and bus timings, and their fares; information about hospitals, doctors, treatment; agricultural information; various government programmes, and health information. Among these libraries, 53.5% of them provide recreational and cultural information about tourist centres, regional history, festivals, and such matters and 64.36% of them provide educational information such as different courses, educational institutions, and examinations. All libraries which offer this service provide minimal professional information. From the analyses it can be concluded that the public libraries under study fail to fulfil the role of disseminator of information at a satisfactory level and they play an insignificant role in the socio- political development of the society.

CHILDREN'S SERVICE

The IFLA/UNESCO Guidelines (2001)[7] state: "By providing a wide range of materials and activities, public libraries should provide an opportunity for children to experience the enjoyment of reading and the excitement of discovering knowledge and works of imagination." The public libraries have a special responsibility to provide this service. All children in a community have a right to access to information through the public libraries. The number of libraries which provide children's service, grade-wise, district-wise, and location-wise is shown in Tables 22, 23, and 24 respectively.

Table 22
Public Libraries Offering Children's Service (Grade-wise)

Grade	*Total Libraries*	*No.*	*Percentage*
A	28	25	89.3
B	27	24	88.9
C	33	28	84.8
D	31	22	71.0
E	35	22	62.9
F	28	21	75.0
Other	5	5	100.0
Total	187	147	78.6

Table 22 shows that a majority of the libraries belong to all grades and all the libraries under other governing bodies offer children's service. The respective percentages are: A (89.3%), B (88.9%), C (84.8%), D (71.1%), E (62.9%), F (75%), and the libraries under other governing bodies (100%).

Table 23
Public Libraries Offering Children's Service (District-wise)

District	*Total Libraries*	*No.*	*Percentage*
Kasaragod	21	16	76.2
Kannur	57	42	73.7
Kozhikode	40	35	87.5
Wayanad	18	17	94.4
Malappuram	28	18	64.3
Palakkad	23	19	82.6
Total	187	147	78.6

District-wise analysis reveals that number of libraries which provide children's service is very high in Wayanad (94.4%), followed by Kozhikode (87.5%). Malappuram district comes last, where only 64.3% of public libraries offer this service.

Table 24
Public Libraries Offering Children's Service (Location-wise)

Location	*Total Libraries*	*No.*	*Percentage*
Rural	150	116	77.3
Urban	37	31	83.8
Total	187	147	78.6

Location-wise analysis shows that the number of libraries which offer children's service is more in the urban area (83.8%) than in the rural area (77.3%).

Utilisation of Children's Services

The survey reveals that an average of below 10 children utilise the children's services per day in 38% libraries, 10 to 15 children (23.5%), 16-20 (11.8%), 21-25 (5.3%) and above 25 children in 4.8% libraries. From the analysis, it is found that the number of children using the public library is very small. It can also be read that the public libraries do not pay proper attention to provide effective children's service and no serious efforts are taken to encourage the children to make use of the libraries.

Children's Collection

The survey reveals the finding that the library collection includes a mean of 586 children's books ranging from 20 volumes to 3,473 volumes. A majority of the libraries (70%) report that the children's collection include books on Social Sciences, History (73.7%), Biography (72.6%), Travellogue (75.6%), and cartoon books and picture stories (75.6%), whereas only less than half of the libraries have science books (45.7%) and a little more than half of the libraries have children's magazines (54.5%) in the library collection. The study reveals that the public libraries do not include more Science books in the children's collection to develop science consciousness in children at an early age.

Language-wise Collection

The data collected in the survey revealed that the children's book section has a collection of (Mean of 577 with SD 244.23) Malayalam books ranging from 16 to 3, 000 Malayalam books, English books (Mean 118.21 with SD 244.23) ranging from 2 to 1, 710 English books, and books in other languages such as Hindi, Tamil and Kannada (Mean 64.89 with SD 103.12) ranging from 4 Hindi books to 487 Kannada books.

Special Collection

From the survey report, it can be seen that a few libraries have special collections such as atlases, toys, and charts for children. A small percentage of them (17%) have charts for educational purposes, 14.97% have toys for nursery kids, 18.18% have atlases and 5.35% have modern formats such as audio-video cassettes, CDs which include jokes and cartoon. The analysis shows that the libraries have poor special collection of atlases, charts, and audio–video cassettes for children.

Children's Programmes

The survey report provides a list of various programmes conducted by the libraries under the children's service. A majority of the libraries which provide children's service (70.07%) have conducted different contests including cultural programmes and sports for the children, 39.45% of them have started reading clubs, 34.69% have provided story hours, 25.85% have conducted picture shows and insignificant percentage of these libraries (3.4%) have conducted other programmes such as puppetry, computer club, and film shows for the children. From the above analyses, it is found that sufficient reading materials for children are not provided in a majority of the libraries and different programmes to children are not conducted at a satisfactory level. The investigator observed personally that book shelves, chairs, tables, and cabinets for children are not suitably designed in the public libraries.

SERVICE TO WOMEN

Women are the most under privileged section in the society. The data available in the survey show that the number of women who use the library is less compared to men (Tables 57, 58, and 59). Their reading interest is limited to light reading. The State Library Council has adopted book circulation programmes for women aimed to raise their reading level and to upgrade their status in the society.

In some of the libraries, special service is provided for women. Under this service, several programmes are conducted to bring them in the main stream of the society. Some of these libraries provide exclusive book collection for them. For this special service, a separate committee consisting of women library members has been constituted in some libraries. The numbers of libraries which provide special service for women, grade-wise, district-wise, and location-wise are furnished in Tables 25, 26, and 27 respectively.

The data in the table (Table 25) reveal that the libraries of all grades provide special services for women with variation in the percentage. It can be seen that the number of libraries which provide special services for women is more in A grade libraries (39.29%), followed by D grade (29.03%), and less in C grade (6.06%). It is interesting to note that no library under other governing bodies offers this special service.

Table 25
Public Libraries Providing Special Services for Women (Grade-wise)

Grade	*Total Libraries*	*No.*	*Percentage*
A	28	11	39.29
B	27	7	25.93
C	33	2	6.06
D	31	9	29.03
E	35	8	22.86
F	28	3	10.71
Other	5	0	.0
Total	187	40	21.39

Table 26
Public Libraries Providing Special Services for Women (District-wise)

District	*Total Libraries*	*No.*	*Percentage*
Kasaragod	21	3	14.29
Kannur	57	11	19.30
Kozhikode	40	6	15.0
Wayanad	18	8	44.44
Malappuram	28	5	17.86
Palakkad	23	7	30.43
Total	187	40	21.39

Among districts, Wayanad occupies the first position in providing special services for women (44.44%), followed by Palakkad (30.43%). Kasaragod stands last in the list where only 14.29% libraries provide this special service for women.

Table 27
Public Libraries Providing Special Services for Women (Location-wise)

Location	*Total Libraries*	*No.*	*Percentage*
Rural	150	35	23.33
Urban	37	5	13.51
Total	187	40	21.39

The data in Table 27 indicate that number of libraries which provide special services for women is more in the rural area (23.33%) than in the urban area (13.51%). On the whole, only

21.39% of the libraries provide special service to women. Out of these libraries, 5 libraries work as women library, where only women enroll as members.

Book Collection in the Women Section

The number of books in women section in the libraries, grade-wise, district-wise, and location-wise is furnished in Tables 28, 29 and 30 respectively.

Table 28

Collection of Books in Women Section in the Public Libraries (Grade-wise)

	No. of Books			
Grade	*Mean*	*SD*	*Minimum*	*Maximum*
A	1531	1847.32	200	5000
B	2636	2863.33	200	5790
C	515	-	515	515
D	313	329.01	40	1028
E	331	546.63	35	1150
F	613	884.42	24	1630
Total	936.36	1479.33	24	5790

The data in the table (Table 28) show that the number of books in the women section is the highest in the libraries of B grade (Mean 2636 with SD 2863.33), followed by A grade (Mean 1531 with SD 1847.32), and the lowest in D grade libraries(Mean 313 with SD 329.01).

Table 29

Collection of Books in Women Section in the Public Libraries (District-wise)

	No. of Books			
District	*Mean*	*SD*	*Minimum*	*Maximum*
Kasaragod	744.33	1017.31	115	1918
Kannur	1133.13	1739.15	35	5000
Kozhikode	703.00	681.44	185	1630
Wayanad	459.20	391.99	40	1028
Malappuram	76.00	73.54	24	128
Palakkad	2242.00	3073.75	386	5790
Total	936.36	1479.33	24	5790

District-wise analysis shows that the number of books collected in the women section is the highest in Palakkad (Mean 2242 with SD 5790) and the least in Malappuram with only (Mean 76 with SD 73.54) books.

Table 30
Collection of Books in Women Section in the Public Libraries (Location-wise)

	No. of Books			
Location	*Mean*	*SD*	*Minimum*	*Maximum*
Rural	583.52	651.60	24	2230
Urban	2757.50	3063.25	40	5790
Total	936.36	1479.33	24	5790

Location-wise analysis shows that the number of books in women section is more in the urban area (Mean 2758 with SD 3063.25), and less in the rural area (Mean 584 with SD 651.60).

Programmes for Women

The survey report shows that the libraries which provide special services for women conduct several programmes for them such as speeches on different socially important topics. They also arrange tours, provide computer classes, form reading forum, initiate debates on current topics, run coaching classes for various career tests, organise seminars, celebrate regional festivals, establish small industrial units, give training for self-employment, conduct study classes, hold meetings of government women-welfare units, provide awareness programmes on important matters, and form Self Help Groups (SHG) as per the programme of Government of India under 9th Five Year Plan (1997-2002) to uplift the rural women.

SERVICE TO COMMUNITIES

The IFLA/UNESCO Guidelines (2001)[8] state: "The public library should be at the centre of the community if it is to play a full part in its activities." The libraries in addition to concentrating on traditional role of collection and circulation of books should play an active social role. The public library should be viewed as an institution which can assist in a positive way in resolving national issues.

Mobile Library Service

Mobile library service is mainly targeted at the disabled people who cannot travel to the library for one or other reasons. The working class does not or hardly make use of the library. The number of women who use the library is less. The librarian will have to go out to these people. If the library does not do this, it will fail to accomplish its aim.

Mobile library service in the area under study is mainly aimed at increasing the reading level of women and to bring them in the main stream of social life. Under this service, a woman librarian circulates books in homes. The State library authority allowed separate librarians' allowance of Rs.500/- per month for this service for 3 years during 2003-04. In 2005-06 the librarians' allowance for this service has been enhanced to Rs.750/- per month. A majority of the libraries do not continue this service due to the non-availability of fund. But in some cases, panchayaths provide librarians' allowance to continue this service. Under this service librarians circulate books by walking. The number of libraries which provide mobile library service, grade-wise, district-wise and location-wise is furnished in Tables 31, 32 and 33 respectively.

Table 31
Public Libraries Offering Mobile Library Service (Grade-wise)

Grade	*Total Libraries*	*No.*	*Percentage*
A	28	11	39.29
B	27	11	40.74
C	33	6	18.18
D	31	7	22.58
E	35	7	20.0
F	28	5	17.86
Other	5	0	.0
Total	187	47	25.13

From the table (Table 31), it is clear that number of libraries which offer mobile library service is the highest in B grade

(40.74%) followed by A grade (39.29%) and the lowest in F grade libraries (17.86%). It is also found that no library under other governing bodies provides this service.

Table 32
Public Libraries Offering Mobile Library Service (District-wise)

District	*Total Libraries*	*No.*	*Percentage*
Kasaragod	21	5	23.81
Kannur	57	14	24.56
Kozhikode	40	12	30.00
Wayanad	18	4	22.22
Malappuram	28	4	14.29
Palakkad	23	8	34.78
Total	187	47	25.13

District-wise analysis shows that the number of libraries which offer mobile library service is the highest in Palakkad (34.78%), followed by Kozhikode (30%) and the lowest in Malappuram (14.29%).

Table 33
Public Libraries Offering Mobile Library Service (Location-wise)

Location	*Total Libraries*	*No.*	*Percentage*
Rural	150	41	27.33
Urban	37	6	16.22
Total	187	47	25.13

The data in the table (Table 33) indicate that the number of libraries which provide mobile library service in the local community is more in the rural area (27.33%) than in the urban area (16.22%). On the whole, only 25.13% of libraries provide mobile library service to the public. All libraries which provide this service keep separate register to record the details of members and the books taken by them. A very few libraries (21.9%) have separate collection of books for this service. 34.6% of libraries which offer this service lend one book at a time, 53.8% of libraries lend 2 books, and 11.5% lend three books.

The investigator has observed during personal visit that in one library under study which is in Palakkad, a brief description of the books read is prepared by each member and it is discussed in the group. More than half of the libraries (57.89%) offer mobile library service once a week, 36.84% libraries offer once a fortnight, and very few libraries (5.27%) offer this service monthly.

Members under Mobile Library Service

In the area under study, the mobile library service is mainly intended for the women, who are reluctant to use the in-house service of the libraries. An average of 70 women ranging between a minimum of 3 women and a maximum of 267 women have taken membership under this service in 2003-04. The corresponding figure for men is 20, ranging between a minimum of 4 men and a maximum of 55 men, and for children, it is 23 ranging between a minimum of 2 children and a maximum of 61 children.

Literacy Activities

The public library should support activities that will enable people to acquire literacy. The aim of this service is to create an educated mind among the adult illiterate. The IFLA/UNESCO Guidelines (2001)[9] state: "The public library should actively support literacy campaigns, as literacy is the key to education and knowledge and to the use of libraries and information services." The number of public libraries which provided literacy activities, grade-wise, district-wise, and location-wise are furnished in Tables 34, 35, and 36 respectively.

The data as figured in the table (Table 34) show that more than 50% of libraries of A, B, and C grade and more than 30 percentages of D, E, and F grade libraries have involved themselves in literacy activities. But no library under other governing bodies has participated in this service. The respective figures are: A (50%), B (59.26%), C (54.55%), D (35.48%), E (31.43%), and F (35.71%).

As a part of endeavour by the Literacy Mission, Kerala; the public libraries in Kerala took part in the literacy activities

Table 34
Public Libraries Provided Literacy Activities (Grade-wise)

Grade	*Total Libraries*	*No.*	*Percentage*
A	28	14	50.00
B	27	16	59.26
C	33	18	54.55
D	31	11	35.48
E	35	11	31.43
F	28	10	35.71
Other	5	0	.0
Total	187	80	42.78

to enhance the literacy rate of people. Now all districts in the area under study have high literacy rate (Table 3.1).

Table 35
Public Libraries Provided Literacy Activities (District-wise)

District	*Total Libraries*	*No.*	*Percentage*
Kasaragod	21	4	19.05
Kannur	57	26	45.61
Kozhikode	40	14	35.00
Wayanad	18	6	33.33
Malappuram	28	14	50.00
Palakkad	23	16	69.57
Total	187	80	42.78

District-wise analysis shows that number of libraries which have been engaged in the literacy activities is the highest in Palakkad (69.57%), followed by Malappuram (50%) and the lowest in Kasaragod (19.05%).

Table 36
Public Libraries Provided Literacy Activities (Location-wise)

Location	*Total Libraries*	*No.*	*Percentage*
Rural	150	71	47.33
Urban	37	9	24.32
Total	187	80	42.78

Location-wise analysis shows that number of libraries that provided literacy service to the illiterate people is more in the rural area (47.33%) than in the urban area (25%). On the whole, only 42.78% of libraries offered literacy service.

Utilisation of Literacy Service

The number of illiterates who utilised the literacy service provided by the public libraries by grade, district, and location is furnished in Tables 37, 38 and 39 respectively.

Table 37
Utilisation of Literacy Service Offered by the Public Libraries (Grade-wise)

	No. of Illiterates			
Grade	*Mean*	*SD*	*Minimum*	*Maximum*
A	99.75	164.34	8	500
B	43.00	46.26	10	160
C	89.50	149.21	10	550
D	51.36	86.71	5	300
E	44.00	59.86	7	154
F	26.63	19.92	5	50
Total	59.35	100.95	5	550

Table 37 illustrates that the number of illiterates who utilised this service is the highest in A grade libraries (Mean 99.75 with SD 164.34), followed by C grade libraries (Mean 89.50 with SD 149.21) and the lowest in F grade libraries (Mean 26.63 with SD 19.92).

Table 38
Utilisation of Literacy Service Offered by the Public Libraries (District-wise)

	No. of Illiterates			
District	*Mean*	*SD*	*Minimum*	*Maximum*
Kasaragod	24.50	17.68	12	37
Kannur	53.74	75.53	6	300
Kozhikode	79.27	146.27	5	500
Wayanad	19.50	20.28	5	60
Malappuram	35.56	15.50	20	65
Palakkad	90.92	143.00	10	550
Total	59.35	100.95	5	550

The number of people who utilised the literacy service is the highest in Palakkad (Mean 90.92 with SD 143.00) followed by Kozhikode (Mean 79.27 with SD 146.27) and the lowest in Wayanad (Mean 19.50 with SD 20.28).

Table 39
Utilisation of Literacy Service Offered by the Public Libraries (Location-wise)

	No. of Illiterates			
Location	*Mean*	*SD*	*Minimum*	*Maximum*
Rural	62.46	107.59	5	550
Urban	39.13	31.83	8	100
Total	59.35	100.95	5	550

The number of illiterates who used this service is more in the rural area (Mean 62.46 with SD 107.59) and less in the urban area (Mean 39.13 with SD 31.83).

Collection of Books for Literacy Activities

The total number of books collected by the libraries for literacy activities, grade-wise, district-wise, and location-wise are given in Tables 40, 41 and 42 respectively.

Table 40
Collection of Books for Literacy Activities in the Public Libraries (Grade-wise)

	No. of Books			
Grade	*Mean*	*SD*	*Minimum*	*Maximum*
A	133.89	74.57	15	250
B	240.44	262.32	10	815
C	76.92	63.18	7	220
D	60.71	44.48	20	140
E	30.83	38.13	5	100
F	34.50	21.25	10	67
Total	101.06	135.31	5	815

The analysis of data in the table (Table 40) shows that the average number of collection of books for literacy activities is the highest in the libraries of B grade (Mean 240.44 with SD 262.32), ranging between a minimum of 10 books and a maximum of 815 books and the lowest in E grade (Mean 30.83 with SD 38.13), ranging between a minimum of 5 books and a maximum of 100 books.

Table 41
Collection of Books for Literacy Activities in the Public Libraries (District-wise)

	No. of Books			
District	*Mean*	*SD*	*Minimum*	*Maximum*
Kasaragod	284.00	265.51	15	815
Kannur	96.88	32.11	5	500
Kozhikode	77.22	21.89	10	182
Wayanad	51.20	17.53	7	100
Malappuram	112.22	28.85	10	250
Palakkad	89.20	21.59	20	220
Total	101.06	135.31	5	815

Among districts, the average number of books stocked for literacy activities is the highest in the libraries in Kasaragod (Mean 284 with SD 265.51) ranging between 15 books and 815 books, followed by Malappuram (Mean 112.22 with SD 28.85) ranging between 10 books and 250 books, and the lowest in Wayanad (Mean 51.20 with SD 17.53) ranging between 7 books and 100 books.

Table 42
Collection of Books for Literacy Activities in the Public Libraries (Location-wise)

	No. of Books			
Location	*Mean*	*SD*	*Minimum*	*Maximum*
Rural	105.73	142.99	5	815
Urban	71.00	66.80	16	200
Total	101.06	135.31	5	815

Location-wise analysis shows that the number of books acquired for literacy activities is more in the rural libraries (Mean 105.73 with SD 142.99) ranging between 5 books and 815 books than in the urban area (Mean 71 books with SD 66.80) ranging between 16 books and 200 books.

The findings of the survey showed that only one library under study has conducted a survey to find out the details of illiterates in its locality to provide the literacy activities. More than half of the libraries (50.6%) which had been involved in this service had a separate instructor to teach the illiterates, and they were given honorarium. In the remaining libraries the library secretaries or librarians engaged the classes.

Service to Disadvantaged

The public library should pay special attention to disadvantaged section such as mentally retarded, elderly disabled and housebound, visually impaired, people in hospitals or prisons, speech and hearing impaired; and should provide specific services and materials suited to them. With regard to the service to disadvantaged, the UNESCO (1994)[10] proposes that "specific services and materials must be provided for those users who cannot for whatever reason use the regular service and materials; for example, linguistic minorities, or people with disabilities or people in hospitals or prison. For this service Braille, cassettes, film shows, medical or health bulletin, picture books, color blocks, record players, and toys have to be collected in public libraries."

The data collected in the survey show that among the surveyed libraries, the librarians of only 8 libraries which are under the State Library Council (4.28%) reported that they have provided some services to the disadvantaged groups. But it is noted that the services provided by them are not mainly information services, but social services to hospitals, orphanages and such places. Two libraries have provided a separate room in the library for old-age persons to sit comfortably for reading and sharing their feelings. Panchayaths have provided assistance by way of finance and furniture to these libraries. The library staff has made arrangements to talk with them to get information about their issues. One library among the surveyed libraries has provided a study centre for the mentally retarded people, but at a minimal level.

Services to Special User Groups

The services for ethnic groups in the community should be developed in consultation with the group concerned. The

IFLA/UNESCO Guidelines (2001)[11] lists the various services to be provided for them, they are:

- The employment of staff from the group in the library,
- Collections including the native literature of the group and reflecting the oral tradition and non-written knowledge of the people, and
- The application of special conditions, developed in conjunction with local people, to culturally sensitive material.

In the area under study, there are places where scheduled tribes are thickly populated. But no separate service is provided to these groups. In Mananthavady (Wayanad) there is a cultural unit named "Kanavu" and as part of it, a public library functions. This library provides mobile library service to the local community.

Other Community Services

The findings of the survey show that a high majority of the libraries (91%) have engaged themselves in various social activities, such as conducting medical camp, cleanliness camp, distributing relief fund for the people in natural disasters, opening pain and palliative care units, providing agricultural support to the people, making different handicrafts, participation in government project of Peoples Planning, formation of blood donation forum, establishing film societies, assistance to poor students, conducting coaching classes for different tests, providing vocational guidance, conducting computer classes, forming science clubs, conducting spoken English classes, and career-information service. From the findings, it can be assessed that a majority of the libraries pay more attention to fulfilling their social role.

CULTURAL ROLE

Public library is a store-house for cultural materials and is an agency of cultural stimulation. The IFLA/UNESCO Guidelines (2001)[12] state: "The public library, by organizing activities and exploiting its resources, should encourage artistic and cultural development in people of all ages."

The findings of the survey show that a significant majority of the libraries (88.77%) have conducted various cultural programmes for the people. As reported by the librarians, the various cultural programmes conducted by the libraries in all grades and the libraries under other governing bodies are the following: celebrating important days and events such as annual day of the libraries, jubilee years of libraries, independence day, republic day, and such days of national importance; celebrating national and regional festivals like onam; celebrating birth and death anniversary of important persons such as Mahatma Gandhi, and Sree Narayana Guru; conducting arts and sports competitions, literary discussions, film shows; conducting a get-together of women and children; performing dramas; conducting quiz competitions; conducting book exhibition; cultural processions, holding literacy camps; celebrating nursery festivals; essay competitions; study tours, picnic; and awarding prizes to the students for the achievements in their studies. As part of some of the libraries, arts and sports clubs also function. Under the auspices of these clubs many cultural programmes are conducted by the libraries. From this analysis, it can be concluded that the public libraries play a remarkable role in the cultural activities of the society.

OTHER ACTIVITIES

User Education

The IFLA/UNESCO Guidelines (2001)[13] state the importance of user education as: "The public library should help its users to develop skills that will enable them to make the most effective use of the library's resources and services. Library staff must act as information navigators to help users of all ages to make the most effective use of information and communication technology, and programmes of user education should be developed." The survey shows that an insignificant number of libraries (2.67%) conducted study classes to the users about the various services including readers' services and community services provided by them.

Personal Assistance Service

According to Sinclair (1965)[14] "to give good personal assistance (advisory service), a staff must read to give good reference and information service, a staff must know its books and how to use them, and the staff must know how to ascertain a reader's tastes and interests." The analysis of the data shows that more than half of the libraries (54.12%) provide personal assistance to the members to find the books, to consult the catalogue, and such other assistance.

Co-operation with Other Organisations

The IFLA/UNESCO Guidelines (2001)[15] state the essentiality of providing co-operation with other organisations as: "Overall service to the community is enhanced when libraries develop links for exchanging information, ideas, services and expertise. Such co-operation results in less duplication of service, a combining of resources for a maximum effect, and an overall improvement in community services. The library should establish formal links with other organisations in the local community, for example, schools, cultural institutions etc. The links should be used to co-ordinate the resources and efforts of each partner and thereby jointly improve services to the community."

Relations with Schools

One of the most important institutional relationships for a public library is with local schools and the education system in the service area. Library service to schools was one of the important responsibilities of the public libraries, as part of their educational role. The IFLA/UNESCO Guidelines (2001)[16] list the different forms of co-operation with the local schools and education system in service area, and they are:

- Sharing resources
- Sharing staff training
- Co-operative collection development
- Co-operative programming
- Class visits to the public library
- Programme of web-awareness for children

The analysis of the data revealed that 26.74% of libraries among the surveyed libraries provide service to schools in the library premise. Out of these libraries, 52% of them lend books to school for the children; 30% give special consideration to the teachers to utilise library resources and services; 20% provide mobile library services to the students; and 12% provide other services to schools, which include free membership to students, involving students in the different contests conducted by the library, conducting quiz competition for the students, and providing text books to the poor students of the schools in the library premise. The libraries do not cater to the academic information requirements of users for want of adequate academic collection.

Resource Sharing

No collection in the libraries can contain all the materials that the members of its public require. Libraries therefore can help their users by providing them with access to the collections of other libraries. The IFLA/UNESCO Guidelines (2001)[17] highlight the need for the resources sharing through the following statement: "Libraries can participate in resource-sharing schemes at any level, local, regional, national, and international. The library should make its collection available for loan to other libraries through participation in a network, for example in a union catalogue or in a local network of information providers, such as schools, colleges and universities."

Among the surveyed libraries, only one other library participated in resource-sharing. This library has lent out 100 books to other libraries for 45 days. Thirty libraries have enjoyed this facility. But this service was discontinued now due to some procedural problems.

Borrowing from Other Libraries

The IFLA/UNECO Guidelines (2001)[18] state the need for and the way of borrowing reading materials from other libraries as follows: "In order to meet the information needs of users, the library should borrow materials from other libraries both within the same organisation and beyond."

Among the surveyed libraries, only one grant-in-aid library enjoys the facility of borrowing books from the book-bank established by the State library Council. As per the programme of the State Library Council one book bank is functioning in each district to loan the books to the public libraries. But it is found that almost all of the libraries do not utilise this service.

Library Awareness

The library awareness can be created among the public through public relation activities. Good public relation is essential for the progress and effective service of the library. This opportunity can also be used for publicizing the library resources and services.

The analysis of the data shows that 66.3% of the libraries use personal contacts, 50.6% of the libraries utilise public meetings including general body meetings, family get-together, and squad works. Only 12% depend on the print media such as circulation of notices, souvenirs, and brochures; and 5.4% use audio-visual media such as radio to make the public aware of the importance of libraries.

Literary Activities

The findings of the survey show that only 16 libraries under study (8.6%) have their own hand written literary works which mainly include poems, short stories, drawings and small articles on recent issues, mostly by the children. The investigator has observed that the works have good layout, with illustrations and drawings. They reflect the creative interests of the children. Some of these are released monthly, others bimonthly, or occasionally.

Evaluation

The IFLA/UNESCO Guidelines (2001)[19] stressed the importance of evaluation of the performance of public libraries through its statement: "All programmes and services should be evaluated by the management on a regular basis to ascertain whether they are:

- Achieving the objectives and declared goals to the library,
- Meeting the needs of the community.

The survey of community needs and user satisfaction and performance indicators are valuable tools in monitoring the achievement of the library. More than half of the librarians (56.7%) reported that they have adopted the method of direct observation for evaluating the various services and activities. They also reported that no library has conducted user survey in monitoring the achievements of the libraries. The district library authorities reported that they do not evaluate the resources, services and programmes of the public libraries in the district.

Incentives

The data collected in the study revealed that among the six districts under study, only Kannur District Library Council gives an award to the best functioning public library in the district in the name of K.C. Madhavan Master, a renowned social worker, from 1998-99 onwards as an incentive. The award consists of books worth Rs. 5000 and a citation.

ACCESS TO SERVICES

The IFLA/UNESCO Guidelines (2001)[20] state the importance of access to service by all as follows: "Physical accessibility is one of the major keys to the successful delivery of public library services. Services of high quality are of no value to those who are unable to access them. Access to services should be structured in a way that maximises convenience to users and potential users."

Opening Hours of the Public Libraries

In almost all libraries under study, there is a practice of providing different opening hours for lending section and periodical section.

Opening Hours of the Lending Section

The opening hours of lending section of the libraries, grade-wise, and location-wise are furnished in Tables 43 and 44 respectively.

Table 43

Opening Hours of Lending Section of the Public Libraries (Grade-wise)

		1–4 Hours		*5–8 Hours*		*9–12 Hours*		*Above 12 Hours*	
Grade	*Total Libraries*	*No.*	*%*	*No.*	*%*	*No.*	*%*	*No.*	*%*
A	28	5	53.6	9	32.1	2	7.1	2	7.1
B	27	20	74.1	4	14.8	1	3.7	2	7.4
C	33	23	69.7	8	24.2	2	6.1	0	.0
D	31	21	67.7	7	22.6	1	3.2	2	6.5
E	35	26	74.3	9	25.7	0	.0	0	.0
F	28	21	75.0	4	14.3	2	7.1	1	3.6
Other	5	2	40.0	2	40.0	0	.0	1	20.0
Total	187	128	68.4	43	23.0	8	4.3	8	4.3

The data in Table 43 clearly show that in a majority of the grant-in-aid libraries, lending section is kept open only for one to four hours a day, mostly in the evening after 4p.m. The respective percentages are: A (53.6%), B (74.1%), C (69.7%), D (67.7%), E (74.3%), and F (75%). It also reveals that 40% of the libraries under other governing bodies keep open the lending section only for 1-4 hours a day. In very few libraries, the lending section is kept open for longer hours extending to more than 9 hours a day. The respective percentages are: A (14.2%), B (11.1%), C (6.1%), D (9.7%), no one in E (.0%), F (10.7%), and the libraries under other governing bodies (20%).

Table 44

Opening Hours of Lending Section of the Public Libraries (Location-wise)

		1–4 Hours		*5–8 Hours*		*9–12 Hours*		*Above 12 Hours*	
Location	*Total Libraries*	*No.*	*%*	*No.*	*%*	*No.*	*%*	*No.*	*%*
Rural	150	112	74.7	29	19.3	3	2.0	6	4.0
Urban	37	16	43.2	14	37.8	5	13.5	2	5.4
Total	187	128	68.4	43	23.0	8	4.3	8	4.3

Location-wise analysis shows that in a majority of the libraries in the rural area (74.7%) and less than half of the libraries in the urban area (43.2%), the lending section is kept open only for one to four hours a day. Only in 19.3% of libraries in the rural area and in more than one third of the libraries in the urban area (37.8%), the lending section is kept open for 5-8 hours. The number of libraries which extend the working hours of the lending section for more than 8 hours is less in both rural (6%) and urban area (7.4%).

Opening Hours of the Periodical Section

The working hours of periodical section of the libraries, grade-wise and location-wise are furnished in Tables 45 and 46 respectively.

Table 45
Opening Hours of Periodical Section of the Public Libraries (Grade-wise)

Grade	*Total Libraries*	*1-4 Hours*		*5-8 Hours*		*9-12 Hours*		*Above 12 Hours*	
		No.	*%*	*No.*	*%*	*No.*	*%*	*No.*	*%*
A	28	4	14.3	7	25.0	8	28.6	9	32.1
B	27	10	37.0	3	11.1	8	29.6	6	22.2
C	33	11	33.3	7	21.2	7	21.2	8	24.2
D	31	7	22.6	5	16.1	6	19.4	13	41.9
E	35	10	28.6	6	17.1	8	22.9	11	31.4
F	28	9	32.1	2	7.1	10	35.7	7	25.0
Other	5	2	40.0	0	.0	2	40.0	1	20.0
Total	187	53	28.3	30	16.0	49	26.2	55	29.4

The data in the table (Table 45) indicate that in a majority of the libraries, periodical section is kept open for longer hours which extended to more than 9 hours a day, the respective percentages are: A (60.7%), B (51.8%), C (45.4%), D (61.3%), E (54.3%), F (60.7%), and the libraries under other governing bodies (60%), whereas the remaining libraries keep open the periodical section only for 1-4 hours or 5-8 hours a day.

Location-wise analysis shows that in majority of the libraries in the rural area (58.7%), the periodical section is kept open for more than 9 hours a day, whereas in the urban area the corresponding percentage is only 43.2%. The number

Table 46
Opening Hours of Periodical Section of the Public Libraries (Location-wise)

		1–4 Hours		*5–8 Hours*		*9–12 Hours*		*Above 12 Hours*	
Location	*Total Libraries*	*No.*	*%*	*No.*	*%*	*No.*	*%*	*No.*	*%*
Rural	150	43	28.7	19	12.7	37	24.7	51	34.0
Urban	37	10	27.0	11	29.7	12	32.4	4	10.8
Total	187	53	28.3	30	16.0	49	26.2	55	29.4

of libraries which keep open the periodical section only for 1-4 hours a day constitute more than one quarter in both locations, rural (28.7%) and urban (27%). The remaining libraries in both locations keep open the periodical section for 5-8 hours a day.

On the whole, in 29.4% of libraries, the periodical section is kept open for more than 12 hours a day; in 26.2% of the libraries, for 9-12 hours; in 16% of the libraries, for 5-8 hours; whereas more than one quarter of the libraries (28.3%) keep open the periodical section only for 1- 4 hours a day. From the data it is clear that in only more than half of the libraries, the periodical section is kept open for longer hours to the public, whereas the number of libraries which keep open the books section to the longer hours to the users is insignificant.

The above findings do not agree with the IFLA/UNESCO Guidelines (2001)[21], which state that: "In order to provide the best possible access to the library service, the library must be open at times of maximum convenience to those who live, work, and study in the community." Since a majority of the libraries are kept open for a few hours in the evening after 4 p.m. many categories of the community like women, children and disabled people cannot use the library services at their convenience.

Working Days

The data regarding the working days of the public libraries in a week, grade-wise, and location-wise are given in Tables 47 and 48 respectively.

Table 47
Working Days of the Public Libraries in a Week (Grade-wise)

		All Days		*6 Days*		*5 Days*		*4 Days*		*Below 4 Days*	
Grade	*Total Libraries*	*No.*	*%*	*No.*	*%*	*No.*	*%*	*No.*	*%*	*No.*	*%*
A	28	13	46.4	15	53.6	0	.0	0	.0	0	.0
B	27	6	22.2	20	74.1	1	3.7	0	.0	0	.0
C	33	10	30.3	23	69.7	0	.0	0	.0	0	.0
D	31	11	35.5	18	58.1	0	.0	1	3.2	1	3.2
E	35	17	48.6	17	48.6	0	.0	0	.0	1	2.9
F	28	8	28.6	13	46.4	3	10.7	1	3.6	3	10.7
Other	5	0	.0	5	100	0	.0	0	.0	0	.0

The analysis of the data in the table (Table 47) reveals that some of the libraries in all grades are kept open on all days in a week except on national holidays. The respective percentages are: A (46.4%), B (22.2%), C (30.3%), D (35.5%), E (48.6%), F (28.6%). It is interesting to note that libraries under other governing bodies are not kept open on all days. The data also revealed that a large number of the libraries declare one holiday in a week. The respective percentages are: A (53.6%), B (74.1%), C (69.7%), D (58.1%), E (48.6%), F (46.4%), and all the libraries under other governing bodies (100%). It is also found that the number of libraries which are kept closed more than one day in a week is insignificant.

Table 48
Working Days of the Public Libraries in a Week (Location-wise)

		All Days		*6 Days*		*5 Days*		*4 Days*		*Below 4 Days*	
Location	*Total Libraries*	*No.*	*%*	*No.*	*%*	*No.*	*%*	*No.*	*%*	*No.*	*%*
Rural	150	53	35.3	88	58.7	4	2.7	2	1.3	3	2
Urban	37	12	32.4	23	62.2	0	.0	0	.0	2	5.4
Total	187	65	34.8	111	59.4	4	2.1	2	1.1	5	2.7

Location-wise analysis shows that as many as 35.3% of the rural libraries and 32.4% of the urban libraries are kept open on all days in a week. A majority of the libraries in both locations declare one holiday, the respective percentages are:

rural (58.7%), and urban (62.2%). On the whole, 34.8% of libraries are kept open on all days in a week and more than half of the libraries (59.4%) are kept open for six days a week. A few libraries work only less than six days a week. The data collected in the survey reveals that the weekly holidays provided by them are not uniform, 35.29% of the libraries are closed on Sundays which cause inconvenience to the local communities. Remaining libraries provide holidays on days other than Sundays.

PROBLEMS OF THE PUBLIC LIBRARIES

The main problems faced by the librarians in the proper functioning of the libraries are furnished in Table 49.

Table 49
Problems Faced by the Librarians of the Public Libraries

(N=187)

Problems	*No. of Responses*	*Percentage*
Inadequate library collection	103	55.08
Non-interest of management	14	7.49
Inadequate staff	22	11.76
Inadequate finance	164	87.70
Non-interest of readers	140	74.86
Inadequate physical facilities	109	58.29
Inadequate services	20	10.70

Note: N = Total number of respondents based on which the percentage is derived.

The analysis of the data in Table 49 shows that a high majority of the librarians in all grades of libraries (87.70%) including those under other governing bodies reported that inadequate finance is the main problem faced in the proper functioning of the libraries. Most of the librarians reported that lack of interest of readers (74.86%) and inadequate physical facilities such as space and furniture (58.29%) are also obstacles to the proper functioning of the libraries. The librarians of 55.08% of the libraries have remarked inadequate reading materials, as an obstacle in the proper utilisation of the libraries. A small percentage of librarians consider lack of interest of management (7.49%) and inadequate services (10.7%) as obstacles to provide effective services.

CONCLUSION

The public libraries, as service units, made least impact on the social change process, this is mainly due to the fact that they concentrate on traditional role of collection and circulation of books and least bothered about other social role of public libraries. Only a few libraries provide some programmes within the community, but it can be seen that they are not in an effective way. Due to the low status of public libraries in the society, the level of utilisation of services provided by them by the reading public is also very low.

References

1. IFLA/UNESCO. Section of Public Libraries. 2001. *The Public Library Service: IFLA/UNESCO Guidelines for Development.* Prepared by Philip Gill et al. Munchen: K.G. Saur, sec. 3.4.
2. *Ibid.*, sec. 2.4.4.
3. UNESCO. 1998. *Public Library Manifesto,* 1994. Revised version. *http:// www.ifla.org.*, para. 3.
4. IFLA/UNESCO, *op. cit.*, 1, sec. 1.3.1.
5. India. Ministry of Education. 1986. *New education policy of India.*
6. Library Association, London. Working Party on Community Information. 1980. *Community Information Service.*
7. IFLA/UNESCO, *op. cit.*, 1, sec. 3.4.2.
8. *Ibid.*, sec.3.4.8.
9. *Ibid.*, sec. 1.3.1.
10. UNESCO, *op. cit.*, 3, para. 2.
11. IFLA/UNESCO., op. cit., 1, sec. 3.4.9.
12. *Ibid.*, sec. 3.4.6.
13. *Ibid.*, sec. 3.6.
14. Sinclair, Dorothy.1965. *Administration of the small public library.* Chicago: American Library Association, 67.
15. IFLA/UNESCO., *op. cit.*, 1, sec. 3.7.
16. *Ibid.*, sec. 3.7.2.

17. *Ibid.*, sec. 3.7.3.
18. *Ibid.*, sec.3.7.5.
19. *Ibid.*, sec. 6.10.2.
20. *Ibid.*, sec. 3.9.
21. *Ibid.*, sec. 3.9.2.

6

USER EVALUATION OF PUBLIC LIBRARIES IN MALABAR

INTRODUCTION

User evaluation of library resources and services has been taken as the measure of library performance. The subjective opinions collected from sample of members in the libraries under study have been used for evaluation. The satisfaction of the library users depends upon ten important parameters namely (1) quality of collections, (2) availability of reading materials, (3) congenial facilities within the library, (4) scientific technical organisation of books, (5) logical arrangement of books, (6) sufficient number of books lent at a time, (7) convenient working hours, (8) adequate working days, (9) various services and programmes and (10) attitudes of library staff. The present study is based on these parameters.

The study is divided into four sections. They are (1) measurement of individual characteristics of library members; (2) measurement of library use; (3) measurement of evaluation of library services; and (4) users' suggestions for the improvements of existing library functions and services.

MEASUREMENT OF INDIVIDUAL CHARACTERISTICS

The members who are the registered users of the libraries belong to different socio-economic status. Five variables were used for describing the individual characteristics of the adult library members. They are age, gender, educational level, economic status, and occupational status. Two variables were used for describing the individual characteristics of children, and they are age and gender. Other individual characteristics related to the library use such as information needs, purpose of visits, benefit of their reading, reading interests of books in different categories and languages, and visits to other libraries are also described in this section.

Age and Gender

Age and gender of adult members, location-wise are presented in Table 1.

Table 1
Age and Gender of the Adult Members (Location-wise)

	Rural	*Urban*	
Variables	*No. of Members*	*No. of Members*	*Total No. of Members*
Age			
15-20	275 (19.5%)	57 (16.6%)	332 (18.9%)
21-30	494 (35.1%)	141 (40.9%)	635 (36.3%)
31-40	302 (21.5%)	59 (17.2%)	361 (20.6%)
41-50	181 (12.9 %)	53 (15.4%)	234 (13.4%)
51-60 Above 60	102 (7.3%)	20 (5.8%)	122 (7.0%)
	53 (3.7%)	14 (4.1%)	67 (3.8%)
Gender			
Male	1136 (80.7%)	250 (72.7%)	1386 (79.2%)
Female	271 (19.3%)	94 (27.3%)	365 (20.8%)
Total	1407 (100%)	344 (100%)	1751 (100%)

The table (Table 1) indicates that the predominant age group among the members of the public libraries is between 21 and 30 representing 35.1% of members in the rural areas and 40.9% of members in the urban areas, followed by the age group 31-40, rural (21.5%) and urban (17.2%), whereas users belonging to above 60 years form the least in number representing only 3.7% of members in the rural areas and 4.1% of members in the urban areas.

The library members constitute 80.7% of males in the rural areas and 72.7% in the urban areas, while the corresponding percentages of females are only 19.3%, and 27.3% respectively.

The analysis indicates in general that youth are the chief component of the members, and women have a poor representation among the members, but also that their representation is a little higher in the urban areas than in the rural areas.

Educational Level

The educational level of adult members is categorised into three groups and they are school educated, graduates, and post-graduates/technically qualified persons. The data are presented location-wise in Table 2.

Table 2
Educational level of the Adult Members (Location-wise)

	Rural	*Urban*	
Educational Level	*No. of Members*	*No. of Members*	*Total No. of Members*
School	940 (66.8%)	171 (49.7%)	1111 (63.4%)
Graduates	374 (26.6%)	127(36.9%)	501 (28.6%)
Post-Graduate/ Technically Qualified	93 (6.6%)	46(13.4%)	139 (8.0%)
Total Members	1407(100%)	344(100%)	1751 (100%)

The data in the table (Table 2) show that the library members comprising 66.8% in the rural areas and 49.7% in the urban areas who have only school education are the largest group among the members; graduates form the next largest group, rural (26.6%), and urban (36.9%). The post- graduates/ technically qualified members comprise only 6.6% in the rural areas and 13.4% in the urban areas which form the smallest group.

Economic Status

An analysis was made to find out the impact of the economic status of the members in relation to the utility of library facilities. The results are presented in Table 3.

The data in Table 3 reveal that the members with middle income constituted the largest user group, rural (72.5%) and urban (76.2%), followed by the low income group, rural

(24.5%), and urban (16.5%). The high income group has a very low representation among the members, rural (3%) and urban (7.3%). A majority of the financially sound people does not show any interest to utilise the public libraries for their information needs.

Table 3
Economic Status of the Adult Members (Location-wise)

	Rural	*Urban*	
Economic Status	*No. of Members*	*No. of Members*	*Total No. of Members*
Low Income	345 (24.5%)	57 (16.5%)	402 (23.0 %)
Middle Income	1020 (72.5%)	262 (76.2 %)	1282 (73.2 %)
High Income	42 (3.0%)	25 (7.3 %)	67 (3.8 %)
Total Members	1407 (100%)	344 (100%)	1751 (100.0%)

Occupational Status

The occupational status of the members, location-wise is presented in Table 4.

Table 4
Occupational Status of the Adult Members (Location-wise)

	Rural	*Urban*	
Economic Status	*No. of Members*	*No. of Members*	*Total No. of Members*
Low Income	345 (24.5%)	57 (16.5%)	402 (23.0%)
Middle Income	1020 (72.5%)	262 (76.2%)	1282 (73.2%)
High Income	42 (3.0%)	25 (7.3%)	67 (3.8%)
Total Members	1407 (100%)	344 (100%)	1751 (100.0%)

Table 4 shows that more than half of the members belong to the employed category, rural (57.4%) and urban (56.4%), which forms a majority group among the library members. Employed category includes those who work in government and private sectors, and self- employed people. They may be interested in developing their personalities, in upgrading their knowledge, and in light reading. The students are the next major group, rural (25.4%) and urban (28.2%). They may use the library for academic purposes and to develop the reading habit. Unemployed and the retired people have small representation among the members, Unemployed, in the rural area (10.4%) and in the urban area (6.7%); and retired, in the rural area (6.8%) and in the urban area (8.7%). The unemployed people may visit the library primarily in search of general news particularly employment news and for passing time. Retired people may primarily use the libraries to spend their leisure time. From the analysis, it can be concluded that the employed people constituted the core users among the members.

Age and Gender of Children

The data collected in the survey indicate that children around 13 years of age are the common users of the public libraries. It also reveals that children of both genders represent almost equal percentages, male (51.6%) and female (48.4%) were registered as members of the public libraries.

Information Needs of the Adult Members

The Public library has a special responsibility to meet the various information needs of its users. A useful categorisation of information needs of public is (1) social or pragmatic needs: information required to cope with day-to-day life, (2) recreational information needs: information satisfying the recreational and cultural interests of an individual, (3) occupational information needs: information required to operate competently within a business or occupational environment, and (4) educational information needs: information required to satisfy the academic requirements of members.

To find out the information needs of the members, they were asked to indicate their information needs from a list of ten needs. The responses are analysed and grouped into four categories and presented in Table 5.

From the Table (Table 5), it can be seen that the information most needed by a majority of the members (87.2%) is related to their day-to-day lives such as welfare, medical, legal and such others. Second most needed information is on education. As many as 73.4% of members felt the need for information on educational activities to improve their educational level. More than half of the members (51.9%) expressed a need for materials which help the improvement of their occupational competence. Only 39.3% of members felt a need of reading for recreational purposes.

Table 5
Information Needs of the Adult Members

(N=1707)

Information Needs	*No. of Responses*
Social needs	1489 (87.2%)
Recreational needs	671 (39.3%)
Occupational needs	886 (51.9%)
Educational needs	1253 (73.4%)

Note: N = Total numbers of respondents, based on which the percentage is derived.
Total percentage is more than 100 because of multiple choices.

The general conclusion of this analysis is that most of the members needed information to solve various problems of their day-to day lives. But the public libraries are not considered as an information source to solve their problems. The tables 5.19, 5.20, and 5.21 reveal that only 52.94% of the public libraries are providing information service to the people at a minimal level.

Adult Members' Purpose of Visit to the Public Libraries

The purpose of visits of the users to the public libraries is varied. To investigate the main purposes for which the members visit the public libraries, the respondents were asked to specify the preferences from a list of six descriptive statements of the purposes. Their responses are presented in Table 6.

The data in the table (Table 6) show that among the many purposes of visit to the public libraries, more than half of the members accounting to 52.4% ranked "to borrow and return books" as their first preference for purpose of visits to the libraries. The second highest percentage of members (39.7%)

Table 6
Adult Members' Purpose of Visit to the Public Libraries and Their Rankings

Purpose	*1st Rank*	*2nd Rank*	*3rd Rank*	*4th Rank*	*5th Rank*	*6th Rank*	*Total No. of Responses*
				No. of Responses			
To borrow and return books	566	213	140	99	48	15	1081
	(52.4%)	(19.7%)	(13.0%)	(9.2%)	(4.4%)	(1.4%)	(100%)
To consult reference books	131	184	165	180	131	30	821
	(16.0%)	(22.4%)	(20.1%)	(21.9%)	(16.0%)	(3.7%)	(100%)
To read daily newspapers	371	251	152	103	45	12	934
	(39.7%)	(26.9%)	(16.3%)	(11.0%)	(4.8%)	(1.3%)	(100%)
To read magazines	62	226	291	21	95	14	90710
	(6.8%)	(24.9%)	(32.1%)	(24.1%)	(10.5%)	(1.5%)	(%)
To attend library programmes	61	96	140	185	304	37	823
	(7.4%)	(11.7%)	(17.0%)	(22.5%)	(36.9%)	(4.5%)	(100%)
Other purposes	1	17	14	33	55	3617	491
	(2.2%)	(3.5%)	(2.9%)	(6.7%)	(11.2%)	(3.5%)	(100%)
Total	1202	987	902	819	678	469	5057
	(23.85)	(19.5%)	(17.8%)	(16.2%)	(13.4%)	(9.3%)	(100%)

ranked "to read daily newspapers" as their first preference. "To consult the reference books in the libraries", "to read magazines", "to attend library programmes" and "other purposes" were ranked as first preference by a small percentage of 16%, 6.8%, 7.4% and 2.2% members respectively.

Children's Motivation to Visit the Public Libraries

The children's motivation to visit the public libraries was examined. For this purpose, the respondents were asked to specify their preference in the descending order of importance. The analysis by gender is presented in Table 7.

Table 7
Children's Motivation to Visit the Public Libraries and their Ranking (by Gender)

Motivation	*Male*	*Female*	*Rank*
To borrow and return books and magazines	56 (72.7%)	59 (80.8%)	1
For the purpose of class project	14 (18.2%)	12 (16.4%)	2
To spend leisure time	5 (6.5%)	1 (1.4%)	3
To attend the library programme	1 (1.3%)	1 (1.4%)	4
Other purposes	1 (1.3%)	0 (.0%)	5
Total	77(100%)	73(100%)	

Chi-square value = 3.795, df = 4, p-value =.434

Table 7 shows that the children visit the libraries more "to borrow and return books and magazines." This secured the highest percentage in both genders, the respective percentages are: boys (72.7%) and girls (80.8%). "For the purpose of class project work" was ranked second by 18.2% boys and 16.4% girls. It is also seen that "to spend leisure time", "to attend the library programmes," and "other purposes" were ranked third, fourth, and fifth respectively by both genders. Since the p-value is .434 (>.05), among the children of both genders there is no significant difference in the motivation to visit the public libraries.

Benefit of Library Use

The purpose for which the library is used by the members was examined. The respondents were asked to indicate the preferences of purposes from a list of six descriptive statements of purposes in the order 1 to 6. The responses are analysed and ranked in Table 8.

As shown in Table 8, visiting the library for "acquisition of knowledge" is the most preferred purpose by nearly half of the members (47.6%). The analysis of the data also revealed that 31.9% of members marked "personality development", 21.5% for "enjoyment", 8.2% for "preparation for examinations", 7.9% for "job improvement", and 2.5% for "other purposes" as the first preference for which the library is used. The analysis reveals that the most significant purposes, for which the library is used are "acquisition of knowledge", followed by "personality development", and "enjoyment". The analysis also shows that library use is not perceived and considered as a means for job competence and education.

Reading Interest of Adult Members

In order to rank the reading materials most used by the members for various purposes, the respondents were asked to specify their preferences in the descending order from a list of seven categories of reading materials. Their responses are analysed and ranked in Table 9.

Table 9 shows that only less than half of the members (44.6%) ranked general books as the most used material in the library. More than one third of the members (36.8%) ranked newspapers as the most used reading materials. The remaining percentages of members ranked following categories of reading materials as the most used; reference books (15.7%), subject periodicals (9.8%), popular magazines (9.8%), text books (3.2%), and others (4.5%).

Members' Interest in Books Written in Different Languages

The members were asked to indicate their preferences of interest in different language books to borrow from the library.

Table 8

Benefit of Library Use to the Adult Members and their Rankings

Purpose	*1st Rank*	*2nd Rank*	*3rd Rank*	*4th Rank*	*5th Rank*	*6th Rank*	*Total No. of Responses*
				No. of Responses			
Enjoyment	208 (21.5%)	140 (14.4%)	266 (27.4%)	210 (21.6%)	137 (14.2%)	9 (0.9%)	970 (100%)
For examination	60 (8.2%)	71 (9.7%	152 (20.9%)	201 (27.5%)	184 (25.2%)	62 (8.5%)	730 (100%)
Job improvement	57 (7.9%)	76 (10.5%)	165 (22.7%)	207 (28.5%)	188 (25.9%)	33 (4.5%)	726 (100%)
Personality development	316 (31.9%)	379 (38.2%)	174 (17.6%)	74 (7.5%)	38 (3.8%)	10 (1.0%)	991 (100%)
Acquisition of knowledge	501 (47.6%)	340 (32.1%)	133 (12.6%)	38 (3.6%)	35 (3.3%)	8 (0.8%)	1058 (100%)
Others	12 (2.5%)	24 (5.0%)	36 (7.5%)	47 (9.8%)	63 (13.2%)	297 (62%)	479 (100%)
Total	1157 (23.4%)	1030 (20.8%)	926 (18.6%)	777 (15.7%)	645 (13.0%)	419 (8.5%)	4954 (100%)

Note: Total number of responses are more than the sample because of multiple choices.

Table 9
Reading Materials Most Used by the Adult Members and their Rankings

Reading Materials	*1st Rank*	*2nd Rank*	*3rd Rank*	*4th Rank*	*5th Rank*	*6th Rank*	*7th Rank*	*Total No. of Responses*
				No. of Responses				
General Books	466 (44.6%)	213 (20.4%)	173 (16.5%)	109 (10.4%)	61 (5.8%)	18 (1.7%)	6 (0.6%)	1046 (100%)
Reference Books	134 (15.7%)	187 (21.9%)	66 (19.4%)	153 (17.9%)	158 (18.5%)	41 (4.8%)	16 (1.9%)	855 (100%)
Subject Periodicals	88 (9.8%)	196 (21.8%)	206 (22.9%)	216 (24.0%)	122 (13.5%)	58 (6.4%)	15 (1.7%)	901 (100%)
Popular Magazines	92 (9.8%)	208 (22.2%)	225 (24.1%)	155 (16.6%)	187 (20%)	55 (5.9%)	13 (1.4%)	935 (100%)
Newspapers	362 (36.8%)	181 (18.4%)	126 (12.8%)	127 (12.9%)	109 (11.1%)	70 (7.1%)	8 (0.8%)	983 (100%)
Text Books	23 (3.2%)	47 (6.6%)	54 (7.6%)	74 (10.4%)	99 (13.9%)	336 (47.3%)	78 (11.0%)	711 (100%)
Others	22 (4.5%)	18 (3.7%)	12 (2.4%)	20 (4.1%)	21 (4.3%)	86 (17.4%)	314 (63.7)	493 (100%)
Total	1187 (20%)	1050 (17.7%)	962 (16.2%)	854 (14.4%)	757 (12.8%)	664 (11.2%)	450 (7.6%)	5924 (100%)

Note: Total numbers of responses are more than the sample because of multiple choices.

The responses, by gender, educational level, and occupational status are presented in tables 6.10, 6.11, and 6.12 respectively.

Tabl e 10
Adult Members' Interest in Books Written in Different Languages (by Gender)

Gender	*Malayalam*	*English*	*Hindi*	*Others*	*Total*
Male	1302 (85.3%)	180 (11.8%)	22 (1.4%)	23 (1.5%)	1527 (100%)
Female	342 (81.2%)	52 (12.4%)	16 (3.8%)	11 (2.6%)	421 (100%)
Total	1644 (84.4%)	232 (11.9%)	38 (2.0%)	34 (1.7%)	1948 (100%)

Note: Total numbers of responses are more than the sample because of multiple choices.

As seen in the table (Table 10), a vast majority of members of both genders, male (85.3%) and female (81.2%) registered high preference for Malayalam books to borrow from the library. Only 11.8% of male members and 12.4% of female members borrowed English books from the library. The percentage of members who preferred Hindi books and other language books is insignificant.

Table 11
Adult Members' Interest in Books Written in Different Languages (by Educational Level)

Educational Level	*Malayalam*	*English*	*Hindi*	*Others*	*Total*
School	1042 (88.3%)	101 (8.6%)	14 (1.2%)	23 (1.9%)	1180 (100%)
Graduate	465 (79.5%)	97 (16.6%)	16 (2.7%)	7 (1.2%)	585 (100%)
Post-Graduate/ Technically Qualified	137 (74.9%)	34 (18.6%)	8 (4.4%)	4 (2.2%)	183 (100%)
Total Members	1644 (84.4%)	232 (11.9%)	38 (2.0%)	34 (1.7%)	1948 (100%)

Note: Total numbers of responses are more than the sample because of multiple choices.

Among the members of different educational levels, a large majority of them, school educated (88.3%), graduates (79.5%), and post-graduates/technically qualified groups (74.9%) expressed a definite preference for Malayalam books. Only

8.6% of the members who have only school education have interest in English books. The corresponding percentages are a little higher in graduates and post-graduates which come 16.6% and 18.6% respectively. Only small percentages of the members like to borrow Hindi and other language books from the library.

Table 12
Adult Members' Interest in Books Written in Different Languages (by Occupational Status)

Occupational Status	*Malayalam*	*English*	*Hindi*	*Others*	*Total*
Student	411	87	9	5	512
	(80.3%)	(17.0%)	(1.8%)	(1.0%)	(100%)
Employed	958	114	18	20	1110
	(86.3%)	(10.3%)	(1.6%)	(1.8%)	(100%)
Unemployed	156	12	5	7	180
	(86.7%)	(6.7%)	(2.8%)	(3.9%)	(100%)
Retired	119	19	6	2	146
	(81.5%)	(13.0%)	(4.1%)	(1.4%)	(100%)
Total Members	1644	232	38	34	1948
	(84.4%)	(11.9%)	(2.0%)	(1.7%)	(100%)

Note: Total number of responses are more than the sample because of multiple choices.

It is observed from Table 12 that Malayalam books were borrowed by a vast majority of members of different occupational groups, students (80.3%), employed (86.3%), unemployed (86.7%), and retired (81.5%). Only 17% of students, 10.3% of employed members, 6.7% of unemployed members, and 13.0% of retired members prefer to borrow English books from the library. The percentages of members who liked borrow and read Hindi and other language books are insignificant.

The general conclusion of the analysis is that most of the members irrespective of genders, education, and occupation prefer to borrow Malayalam books from the public library. This may be mainly for the reasons that Malayalam books accounted for the largest share of the library collections and inadequate availability of English, Hindi, and other language books from the library.

Reading Interests of Children

To find out the children's reading interests in different subjects, they were asked to indicate their interests from a list of seven subjects. The responses were analysed and the results are presented in Table 13.

Table 13
Children's Reading Interests in Different Subjects

(N=156)

Subjects	*No. of Responses*	*Percentage*
Social Science	87	55.8
Science	104	66.5
History	97	62.2
Biographies	100	64.1
Travellogues	95	60.9
Cartoon and comics	98	62.8
Children's magazines	98	62.8

Note: N = Total numbers of respondents, based on which the percentage is derived.

Table 13 reveals that most of the children are interested in reading books in Social science, Science, History, Biographies, Travellogues, cartoons and comics, and magazines for children. The highest percentage of them (66.5%) prefer to read Science books, and lowest percentage of them (55.8%) like to read Social Science books. But the survey shows that only less than half of the libraries (45.7%) have Science books in the children's collections. This finding shows that the children's collections are not based on the needs of the members.

Visits to other Libraries

The reading materials available in the library may not be adequate to satisfy the information needs of its members fully. So they visit other libraries to acquire more knowledge. The data regarding the number of members who visit other libraries to meet their information needs are presented in Table 14.

Table 14 reveals that only a small percentage of members, rural (8.8%) and urban (14.6%) visit other libraries such as academic library or other public library to satisfy their

Table 14
Visits to Other Libraries (Location-wise)

Location	*Not Visited*	*Visited*	*Total*
Rural	1213 (91.2%)	117 (8.8%)	1330 (100%)
Urban	275 (85.4%)	47 (14.6%)	322 (100%)
Total	1488 (90.1%)	164 (9.9%)	1652 (100%)

Chi-square value = 9.750, df = 1, P-value = .002*

information requirements. As the p-value is .002, it can be concluded that the use pattern of members in different locations differ significantly in meeting their reading requirements. Members in the urban areas visit other libraries more frequently than those in the rural areas.

MEASUREMENT OF LIBRARY USE

The following determinants of users' reading behaviour such as frequency of visits, duration of library use and method of location of books from the library are measured.

Frequency of Visits to the Libraries

To determine how frequently the members visit the public library, the members were asked to indicate the frequency of their visits from a list of six intervals ranging from "daily" to "rarely" Their responses; gender wise, by educational level, and by occupational status are furnished in Tables 15, 16, and 17 and in Figures 1, 2, and 3 respectively.

From the table and the figure (Table 15 and Figure 1) it is found that around half of the members of genders, male (51.9%) and female (49.6%) visit the library "more than once a week". It is also revealed that 30.7% of male members and only a small percentage of female members (13.1%) visit the library on a daily basis. It is also seen that 10% of male members and 20% of female members are weekly visitors. As shown in the table and the figure, for other frequencies of visits to the library, the percentages of members in both genders are insignificant which vary from 10.9% to 0.5%.

Since p-value is <.001, it is concluded that there is significant difference in the frequency of visits to the library

Table 15
Frequency of Visits to the Public Libraries by Adult Members (By Gender)

Gender	*Daily*	*More than Once a Week*	*Once a Week*	*Once a Fortnight*	*Once a Month*	*Rarely*	*Total*
Male	421 (30.7%)	711 (51.9%)	136 (10.0%)	73 (5.3%)	22 (1.6%)	7 (0.5%)	1370 (100%)
Female	47 (13.1%)	178 (49.6%)	72 (20.0%)	9 (10.9%)	17 (4.7)	6 (1.7%)	359 (100%)
Total	468 (27.1%)	889 (51.4%)	208 (12.0%)	112 (6.4%)	39 (2.3%)	13 (0.8%)	1729 (100%)

Chi-square value = 88.148, df = 5, p-value = <.001*

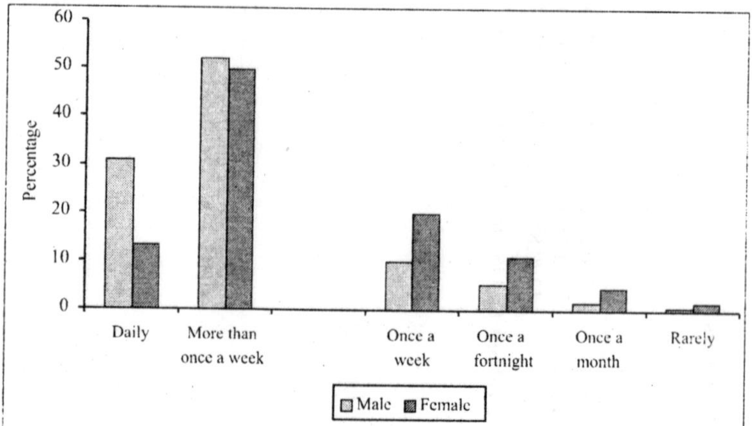

FIGURE 1: Frequency of Visits to the Public Libraries by the Adult Members, by Gender

by the adult members of both genders. Male members visit the library more frequently than female members. This finding shows that female members have low reading interest comparing to that of male members.

By examining the data by educational level of members, it is found that more than half of the members of all categories which form the highest percentage, school educated (50.7%), graduates (52.7%) and post-graduates (52%) visit the library "more than once a week". The next highest percentage of members, school educated (28.6%), graduates (23.5%), and post-graduates (27.9%) visit the library "daily".

A very small percentage of them are the "weekly" visitors, school educated (12.1%), graduates (12.8%), and post-graduates/technically qualified members (8.6%). The remaining percentage of members who visit the library in other frequencies is insignificant.

As the p-value is .252 (>.05) it is concluded that the frequency of visits to the library by members belonging to various education groups are not significantly different. A majority of the members of different educational levels visit the library more frequently.

Table 16
Frequency of Visits to the Public Libraries by Adult Members (by Educational Level)

Educational Level	*Daily*	*More than Once a Week*	*Once a Week*	*Once a Fortnight*	*Once a Month*	*Rarely*	*Total*
School	313 (28.6%)	556 (50.7%)	133 (12.1%)	59 (5.4%)	26 (2.4%)	9 (0.8%)	1096 (100%)
Graduate	116 (23.5%)	260 (52.7%)	63 (12.8%)	41 (8.3%)	9 (1.8%)	4 (0.8%)	493 (100%)
Post-Graduate/ Technically Qualified	39 (27.9%)	73 (52.0%)	12 (8.6%)	12 (8.6%)	4 (2.9%)	0 (.0%)	140 (100%)
Total	468 (27.1%)	889 (51.4%)	208 (12.0%)	112 (6.4%)	9 (2.3)	13 (0.8%)	1729 (100%)

Chi-square value = 12.515, df = 10, P-value = .252

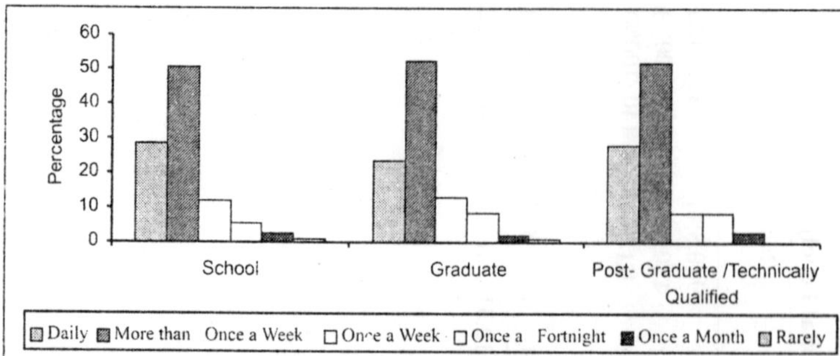

FIGURE 2: Frequency of Visits to the Public Libraries by Adult Members, by Educational Level

By examining the data by occupational status, it is revealed that more than half of the members of different categories; students (53.6%), employed (50.9%), and retired (56.9%) and less than half of the unemployed group (44.8%) visit the library "more than once a week". The next highest percentage of them; students (22.5%), employed (26.5%), unemployed (40%), and retired (30.9%) are "daily" visitors. A negligible percentage of the members visit the library in other frequencies. From the analysis, it is clear that 78.5% of members visit the library regularly.

The p-value (.008<.05) indicates that there is significant difference in the frequency of visits to the library by the members of different occupational status. Unemployed and the retired categories visit library more frequently than the students and the employed groups. The reason may be unemployed and retired categories have sufficient leisure time to visit the library more frequently than other two groups.

Frequency of Library Visits by the Children

The children were asked to indicate the frequency of visits to the library from a list of five intervals. Their responses by gender are analysed and presented in Table 18

The data in Table 18 show that nearly half of the children of both genders, boys (48.7%) and girls (41.3%) visit the library "more than once a week", whereas 24.4% of boys and 13.3%

Table 17

Frequency of Visits to the Public Libraries by Adult Members (by Occupational Status)

Occupational Status	*Daily*	*More than Once a Week*	*Once a Week*	*Once a Fortnight*	*Once a Month*	*Rarely*	*Total*
Student	100 (22.5%)	238 (53.6%)	60 (13.5%)	31 (7.0%)	10 (2.3%)	5 (1.1%)	444 (100%)
Employed	264 (26.5%)	507 (50.9%)	121 (12.1%)	70 (7.0%)	27 (2.7%)	8 (0.8%)	997 (100%)
Unemployed	66 (40%)	74 (44.8%)	15 (9.1%)	8 (4.8%)	2 (1.2%)	0 (.0%)	165 (100%)
Retired	38 (30.9%)	70 (56.9%)	12 (9.8%)	3 (2.4%)	0 (.0%)	0 (.0%)	123 (100%)
Total	468 (27.1%)	889 (51.4%)	208 (12.0%)	112 (6.4%)	39 (2.3%)	13 (0.8%)	1729 (100%)

Chi-square value = 31.397, df = 15, P-value = .008*

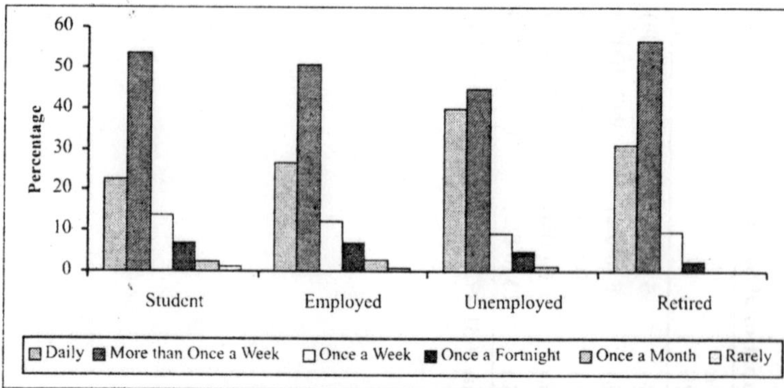

FIGURE 3: Frequency of Visits to the Public Libraries by the Adult Members, by Occupational Status

Table 18
Frequency of Visits to the Public Libraries by the Children (by Gender)

Gender	*Daily*	*More than Once a Week*	*Once a Week*	*Fortnightly*	*Rarely*	*Total*
Male	20	40	16	3	3	82
	(24.4 %)	(48.7 %)	(19.5 %)	(3.7 %)	(3.7 %)	(100 %)
Female	10	31	26	6	2	75
	(13.3 %)	(41.3 %)	(34.7 %)	(8 %)	(2.7 %)	(100 %)
Total	30	71	42	9	5	157
	(19.1%)	(45.2%)	(26.8%)	(5.7%)	(3.2%)	(100%)

Chi-square value 7.758, df = 4, P-value = .101

of girls visit the library "daily"; 19.5% of boys and 34.7% of girls visit the library "once a week"; a very small percentages of them, boys (3.7%) and girls (8%) visit the library "fortnightly"; and 3.7% of boys and 2.7% of girls visit the library "rarely".

Since the p-value is .101 (>.05) no significant difference is observed in the frequency of visits to the public library by the children of both genders. Most of the children of both genders visit the library frequently.

Duration of Library Use

The members were asked to specify the duration of time spent in the public library on an average per day from three alternatives provided. The duration of the library use is one of the factors which determine the users' reading behaviour.

The duration of library use by gender, educational level, and occupational status are figured in Tables 19, 20 and 21 and in Figures 4, 5 and 6 respectively.

Table 19
Duration of Library Use by the Adult Members (by Gender)

Gender	*Less than One Hour*	*1-2 Hours*	*More than 2 Hours*	*Total*
Male	495 (39.8%)	750 (60.2%)	0 (.0%)	1245 (100%)
Female	210 (59.2%)	145 (40.8%)	0 (.0%)	355 (100%)
Total	705 (44.1%)	895 (55.9%)	0 (.0%)	1600 (100%)

Chi-square value = 39.053, df =1, P-value = <.001*

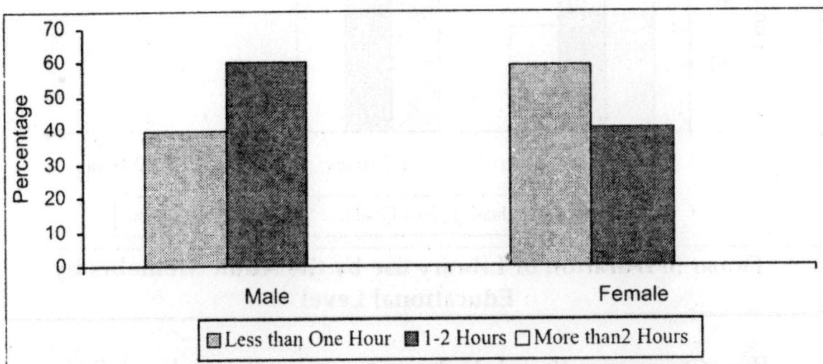

FIGURE 4 : Duration of Library Use by the Adult Members, by Gender

The data in Table 19 and Figure 4 reflect that the highest percentage of male members (60.2%) spend 1-2 hours in the library to make use of the library facilities and services, whereas the highest percentage of female members spend less than one hour in the library (59.2%). No members in both genders spend more than 2 hours a day in the library.

As the p-value is <.001, a significant difference is observed in the duration of library use between men and women. It is concluded that male members spend more time in the library than female members. This finding shows the difference in the reading interest between male and female members.

Table 20
Duration of Library Use by the Adult Members (by Educational Level)

Educational Level	*Less than One Hour*	*1-2 Hours*	*More than 2 Hours*	*Total*
School	484 (47.0%)	544 (53%)	0 (.0%)	028 (100%)
Graduate	185 (40.4%)	273 (59.6%)	0 (.0%)	438 (100%)
Post-Graduate/ Technically Qualified	36 (31.6%)	78 (68.4%)	0 (.0%)	114 (100%)
Total	705(44.1%)	895 (55.9%)	0 (.0%)	1600 (100%)

Chi-square value = 13.512[a], df = 2, P-value = .001*

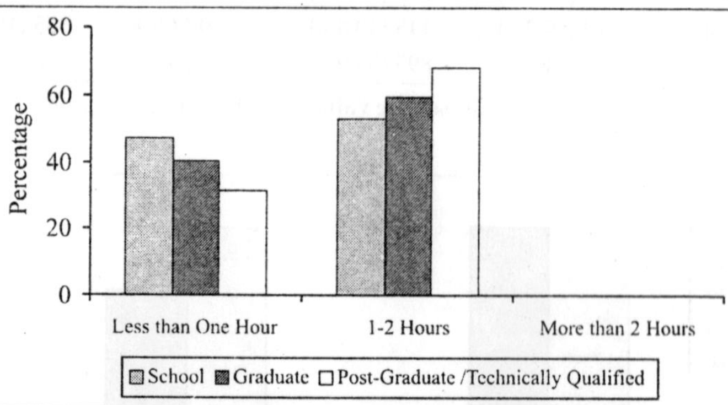

FIGURE 5: **Duration of Library use by the Adult Memebrs by Educational Level**

By examining the data by educational levels, it is found that as many as 53% of school educated members, 59.6% of graduate members and 68.4% of post graduates/technically qualified members spend 1-2 hours in the library. The remaining members in all groups spend less than one hour in the library and no one spend more than 2 hours.

Since the p-value is .001, it can be concluded that the time spent by members of different educational groups is significantly different. The members having a graduate degree and post-graduates/technical qualifications spend more time in the library than members having only school education. From this finding, it can be concluded that the educational level of the members are positively correlated to the use of the public libraries.

Table 21
Duration of Library Use by the Adult Members (by Occupational Status)

Occupational Status	*Less than One Hour*	*1-2 Hours*	*More than 2 Hours*	*Total*
Student	199 (47.7%)	218 (52.3%)	0 (.0%)	417 (100%)
Employed	413 (43.9%)	527 (56.1%)	0 (.0%)	940 (100%)
Unemployed	59 (41.5%)	83 (58.5%)	0 (.0%)	142 (100%)
Retired	34 (33.7%)	67 (66.3%)	0 (.0%)	101 (100%)
Total	705(44.1%)	895 (55.9%)	0 (.0%)	1600 (100%)

Chi-square value =7.067[a], df = 3, P-value = .070

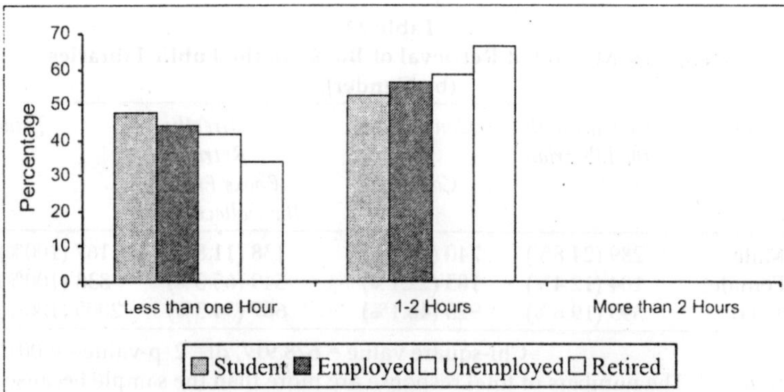

Figure 6: Duration of Library Use by the Adult Members, by Occupational Status

The analysis of time spent in the library by the members of different occupational groups shows that the highest percentage of members of all categories spend 1-2 hours in the libraries, the respective percentages are: students (52.3%), employed (56.1%) unemployed (58.5%), and retired (66.3%). The remaining percentage of members spend less than one hour in the libraries.

Since the p-value is .070, it is clear that the time spent by the members belonging to various occupational statuses is not significantly different. The members of various occupational statuses spend almost equal time in the public libraries. These findings indicate that all members spend a limited time in the libraries and this may be due to the poor reading and sitting facilities in the libraries and also due to poor collection and organisation of reading materials.

Method of Retrieval of Books from the Library

The members were asked to indicate the method they used to retrieve books from the libraries from the three alternatives- "consult with the librarian", "consult the library catalogue", and "directly retrieve the books from the collection". The responses by gender, educational level, and occupational status are summarised in Tables 22, 23 and 24 respectively.

Table 22
Members' Method of Retrieval of Books in the Public Libraries (by Gender)

Gender	*Consult with the Librarian*	*Consult the Library Catalogue*	*Directly Retrieve Books From the Collection*	*Total*
Male	289 (24.8%)	740 (63.4%)	138 (11.8%)	1167 (100%)
Female	104 (12.4%)	185 (22.1%)	549 (65.5%)	838 (100%)
Total	393 (19.6%)	925 (46.1%)	687 (34.3%)	2005 (100%)

Chi-square value = 628.917, df= 2, p-value= <.001*

Note: The numbers of total response are more than the sample because of multiple choices.

The data in Table 22 reflect that only 24.8% male members and 12.4% female members "consult with the librarian" to retrieve the books they wanted from the library collections, whereas 63.4% of male members and 22.1% of female members primarily "consult the library catalogue" for retrieval of books. It is also found that a small number of male members (11.8%) and a majority of female members (65.5%) "directly retrieve books from the collections".

Since the p-value is <.001, we conclude that there is significant difference in the methods adopted by male and female members to locate books in the libraries. A majority of male members consult library catalogue to locate the books, whereas a majority of female members locate books directly from the library collections.

Table 23
Members' Method of Retrieval of Books in the Public Libraries (by Educational Level)

Education Level	*Consult with theLibrarian*	*Consult the Library Catalogue*	*Directly Retrieve Books From the Collection*	*Total*
School	272	562	434	1268
	(21.5%)	(44.3%)	(34.2%)	(100%)
Graduate	91	284	196	571
	(15.9%)	(49.7%)	(34.3%)	(100%)
Post-Graduate/	30	79	57	166
Technically Qualified	(18.1%)	(47.6%)	(34.3%)	(100%)
Total	393	925	687	2005
	(19.6%)	(46.1%)	(34.3%)	(100%)

Chi-square value = 8.910, df = 4, p-value =.063

Note: The numbers of total responses are more than the sample because of multiple choices.

The analysis of the data by the educational level of members shows that a small percentage of members belonging to different educational level "consult with the librarian" for locating books in the library collections. The respective percentages are: school educated (21.5%), graduates (15.9%), and post-graduates/technically qualified (18.1%). Less than half of the members, school educated (44.3%), graduates (49.7%), and post-graduates/technically qualified (47.6%) primarily "consult the library catalogue" for locating documents. More than one third of the different education groups, school educated (34.2%), graduates (34.3%), and post-graduates/technically qualified (34.3%) "directly retrieve books from the collections".

The p-value .063 (>.05) shows that there is no significant difference in the method of location of books in the library collections by the members of various educational levels. Most of the members having only school education, graduate members, and post-graduates/technically qualified members primarily "consult the library catalogue" to locate books in the library collections.

Table 24
Members' Method of Retrieval of Books in the Public Libraries (by Occupational Status)

Occupational Status	*Consult with theLibrarian*	*Consult the Library Catalogue*	*Directly Retrieve Books From the Collection*	*Total*
Students	97 (19.1%)	220 (43.2%)	192 (37.7%)	509 (100%)
Employed	229 (19.8%)	541 (46.8%)	387 (33.4%)	1157 (100%)
Unemployed	39 (21.0%)	89 (47.8%)	58 (31.2%)	186 (100%)
Retired	28 (18.3%)	75 (49%)	50 (32.7%)	153 (100%)
Total	393 (19.6%)	925 (46.1%)	687 (34.3%)	2005 (100%)

Chi-square value = 4.463, df = 6, p-value = .614

Note: The number of total responses are more than the sample because of multiple choices.

Occupational status-wise analysis shows that only 19.1% of student members, 19.8% of employed members, 21% of unemployed members, and 18.3% of retired members "consult with the librarian" for locating the books in the library. Highest percentage of the members, students (43.2%), employed (46.8%), unemployed (47.8%), and retired (49%) "consult the library catalogue" for locating the books in the library. Around one third of members, students (37.7%), employed (33.4%), unemployed (31.2%), and retired (32.7%) "directly retrieve books from the collection".

The p-value .614 (>.05) indicates that there is no significant difference in the methods of location of books in the library collections by the members belonging to various occupational categories. Most of students, employed, unemployed, and retired categories primarily consult the library catalogues to locate books in the library collections. From the analysis, it can be concluded that the most common method to retrieve books from the library collections is by consulting the library catalogues. Absence of open access in many libraries may be the reason that prevents many of the members to locate books directly from the shelves.

MEASUREMENT OF EVALUATION OF PUBLIC LIBRARY SERVICES

The user perceptions and user satisfaction with the library services are the indicators of the public library effectiveness.

Quality of Collections in the Library

The quality of collections including books and periodicals in the library has high impact on the satisfaction of the reading public. To ascertain the user satisfaction on the quality of collections, the members were asked to rate the overall quality of reading materials in the library from five response categories ranging from "very good" to "very poor". The responses by gender, educational level, and occupational status are presented in Tables 25, 26, and 27 respectively.

Table 25
Adult Member's Perceptions on the Quality of Collections in the Public Libraries (by Gender)

Gender	*Very Good*	*Good*	*Partly Good*	*Poor*	*Very Poor*	*Total*
Male	318	693	347	19	4	138
	(23.0%)	(50.2%)	(25.1%)	(1.4%)	(0.3%)	(100%)
Female	118	177	70	2	0	367
	(32.2%)	(48.2%)	(19.1%)	(0.5%)	(.0%)	(100%)
Total	436	870	417	21	4	1748
	(24.9%)	(49.8%)	(23.9%)	(1.2%)	(0.2%)	(100%)

Chi-square value=17.085, df = 4, p-value = .002*

Table 25 shows that around half of the members of both genders, male (50.2%) and female (48.2%) which constitute the highest percentage reported that the quality of collections in the public libraries is "good". Next highest percentage of male members (25.1%) reported that the quality of collections in the public libraries is only "partly good", whereas the next highest percentage of female members (32.2%) remarked as "very good". Only a meagre percentage rated the quality of collections as "poor" or "very poor".

As the p-value is .002 (<.05) it is clear that the opinions of members of both genders regarding the quality of collections in the libraries are significantly different. More percentage of female members (80.4%) and comparatively less percentage of male members (73.2%) have a high opinion regarding the quality of collections in the libraries. This may be due to the fact that female members visit the library mostly for light reading. The existing collection in the library which constitutes primarily novels and general magazines may satisfy their reading interests.

Table 26
Adult Members' Perceptions on the Quality of Collections in the Public Libraries (by Educational Level)

Educational Level	*Very Good*	*Good*	*Partly Good*	*Poor*	*Very Poor*	*Total*
School	299 (27%)	554 (50.0%)	239 (21.6%)	11 (1.2%)	4 (0.4%)	1107 (100%)
Graduate	111 (22.3%)	244 (49%)	136 (27.3%)	7 (1.4%)	0 (.0%)	498 (100%)
Post-Graduate/ Technically Qualified	26 (18.2%)	72 (50.3%)	42 (29.4%)	3 (2.1%)	0 (.0%)	143 (100%)
Total	436 (24.9%)	870 (49.8%)	417 (23.9%)	21 (1.2%)	4 (0.2%)	1748 (100%)

Chi-square value = 16.548, df = 8, P-value = .035*

The analysis of the data in Table 26 revealed that as many as 27% of school educated members, 22.3% of graduate members and 18.2% of post-graduates/technically qualified members rated the collections in the library as "very good". Around half of the members, school educated (50%), graduates (49%), and post-graduates/technically qualified categories (50.3%) reported that the quality of collections in the library is "good". Around a quarter of the members, school educated (21.6%), graduates (27.3%), and post-graduates/technically qualified categories (29.4%) rated the collections as only "partly good". Only a negligible percentage of members rated as "poor" or "very poor".

Since the p-value is .035, there is significant difference in the opinion of members belonging to different educational level regarding the quality of collections in the libraries. A larger percentage of members with only school education have very good opinion regarding the collections than other two groups.

Table 27

Adult Members' Perceptions on the Quality of Collections in the Public Libraries (by Occupational Status)

Occupational Status	*Very Good*	*Good*	*Partly Good*	*Poor*	*Very Poor*	*Total*
Student	114	216	106	9	2	447
	(25.5%)	(48.3%)	(23.8%)	(2.0%)	(0.4%)	(100%)
Employed	255	508	235	11	2	1011
	(25.2%)	(50.2%)	(23.2%)	(1.1%)	(0.3%)	(100%)
Unemployed	38	86	44	0	0	168
	(22.6%)	(51.2%)	(26.2%)	(.0%)	(.0%)	(100%)
Retired	29	60	32	1	0	122
	(23.8%)	(49.2%)	(26.2%)	(0.8%)	(.0%)	(100%)
Total	436	870	417	21	4	1748
	(24.9%)	(49.8%)	(23.9%)	(1.2%)	(0.2%)	(100%)

Chi-square value 8.032, df = 12, P-value =.783

Among the occupational categories of members, around half of them, students (48.3%), employed (50.2%), unemployed (51.2%), and retired (49.2%) who secured the highest percentage reported that the collections are "good". The next highest percentage, students (25.5%) and employed (25.2%) stated that the collections are "very good"; whereas the next highest percentage of unemployed members (26.2%) and retired groups (26.2%) reported that the collections are only "partly good". Only a negligible percentage of the members reported that the collections in the library are "poor" or "very poor".

Since the p-value is .783, the opinion regarding the quality of library collections among the members of different occupational status is not significantly different. A majority of students, employed, unemployed and retired categories have a high opinion regarding the quality of the library collections.

Children's Perceptions on the Quality of Collections for Children

Children were asked to rate the quality of the collections for children in the public libraries from three response categories "good", "partly good" and "poor". Their perceptions by gender are presented in Table 28.

Table 28
Children's Perceptions on the Quality of Collections for Children in the Public Libraries (by Gender)

Gender	*Good*	*Partly Good*	*Poor*	*Total*
Male	49 (60.5%)	30 (37.0%)	2 (2.5%)	81 (100%)
Female	47 (61.0%)	28 (36.4%)	2 (2.6%)	771 (00%)
Total	96 (60.8%)	58 (36.7%)	4 (2.5 %)	158 (100%)

Chi square value = .009,df=2, p-value =.995

Table 28 indicates that a majority of the male child-members (60.5%) and female child-members (61%) are with the perception that the collections for children in the public libraries are "good", whereas more than one third of them, male (37%) and female (36.4%) opined that the collections for the children are only "partly good". Only a small percentage of male child-members (2.5%) and female-child members (2.6%) rated the collections as "poor".

The p-value .995 (>.05) shows that among the children of both genders, the difference is not significant regarding the perception on the quality of collections for children in the public libraries. A majority of child members in both genders have a high opinion regarding the quality of collections for children in the public libraries.

Availability of Reading Materials in the Library

The satisfaction of the members with respect to the services rendered by the public libraries always depends on the availability of adequate quantity of reading materials of various categories and languages. To ascertain the perceptions of members on the availability of reading materials in the libraries, the respondents were asked to rate the level of availability of adequate quantity of reading materials to meet their information requirements from the three response categories of "fully available", "partly available" and "never available". Their views by gender, educational level, and occupational status are presented in Tables 29, 30 and 31 respectively.

Table 29

Adult Members' Perceptions on the Availability of Reading Materials in the Public Libraries (by Gender)

Gender	*Fully Available*	*Partly Available*	*Never Available*	*Total*
Male	266	1065	30	1361
	(19.5%)	(78.3%)	(2.2%)	(100%)
Female	84	274	4	362
	(23.2%)	(75.7%)	(1.1%)	(100%)
Total	350	1339	34	1723
	(20.3%)	(77.7%)	(2.0%)	(100%)

Chi-square value = 3.878, df = 2, P-value = .144

The data in Table 29 show that a majority of the members of both genders, male (78.3%) and female (75.7%) are of the view that reading materials they required are only "partly available" in the library. A smaller percentage of male members (19.5%) and female members (23.2%) opined that the reading materials they wanted are "fully available" in the library. A very small percentage of male members (2.2%) and female members (1.1%) reported that the reading materials they wanted are "never available" in the library.

The p-value (0.144 >.05) indicates that the opinion of members of both genders regarding the adequacy of availability of reading materials in the libraries is not significantly different. A majority of male members and female members have an average opinion regarding the availability of reading materials in the public libraries.

Table 30
Adult Members' Perceptions on the Availability of Reading Materials in the Public Libraries (by Educational Level)

Educational Level	*Fully Available*	*Partly Available*	*Never Available*	*Total*
School	241 (22.2%)	816 (75.1%)	30 (2.7%)	1087 (100%)
Graduate	90 (18.3%)	400 (81.1%)	3 (0.6%)	493 (100%)
Post-Graduates/ Technically Qualified	19 (13.3%)	123 (86%)	1 (0.7%)	143 (100%)
Total	350 (20.3%)	1339 (77.7%)	34 (2.0%)	1723 (100%)

Chi-square value = 18.577, df = 4, P-value = .001*

A majority of the members belonging to different educational levels, school educated (75.1%), graduates (81.1%), and post graduates/technically qualified groups (86%) reported that the reading materials they required are only "partly available" in the libraries, whereas a small percentage of the members, school educated (22.2%), graduates (18.3%), and post graduates/technically qualified categories (13.3%) are of the opinion that the reading materials they required are "fully available", and a small percentage of them reported that reading materials are "never available" in the libraries.

As the p-value is .001, the opinion of members belonging to different education groups regarding the adequacy of availability of reading materials in the libraries is significantly different. It is concluded that higher percentage of graduates as well as post-graduates/technically qualified members, and lower percentage of school educated members have an average opinion regarding the availability of reading materials in the libraries.

A greater percentage of members belonging to different occupational categories, students (77.9%), employed (77%), unemployed (79.2%), and retired (81.1%) reported that the reading materials they required are only "partly available" in the library. A smaller percentage of the members, students (19.6%), employed (21.4%), unemployed (17.7%), and retired (17.2%) reported that the reading materials they required are

Table 31
Adult Members' Perceptions on the Availability of Reading Materials in the Public Libraries (by Occupational Status)

	Perception			
Occupational Status	*Fully Available*	*Partly Available*	*Never Available*	*Total*
Student	87 (19.6%)	346 (77.9%)	11 (2.5%)	444 (100%)
Employed	213 (21.4%)	764 (77%)	16 (1.6%)	993 (100%)
Unemployed	29 (17.7%)	130 (79.2%)	5 (3.1%)	164 (100%)
Retired	21 (17.2%)	99 (81.1%)	2 (1.7%)	122 (100%)
Total	350 (20.3%)	1339 (77.7%)	34 (2.0%)	1723 (100%)

Chi-square value = 4.458, df = 6, P-value = .615

"fully available"; a small percentage of them reported that the reading materials are "never available" in the library.

Since the p-value is .615, there is no significant difference in the opinion of members belonging to different occupational status regarding the adequacy of availability of reading materials in the libraries. A majority of students, employed, unemployed and retired categories have an average opinion regarding the availability of reading materials in the libraries. From the analysis it can be concluded that the public libraries do not provide a wide range of collections in sufficient quantity to the users to meet their various information needs.

Availability of Children's Books in the Library

The availability of children's books in the public libraries was measured by asking the children to rate their perceptions from the three response categories of "fully available", "partly available" and "never available". Gender-wise analysis of the responses is presented in Table 32.

Table 32
Children's Perceptions on the Availability of Books in the Public Libraries (by Gender)

Gender Status	*Fully Available*	*Partly Available*	*Never Available*	*Total*
Male	23 (31.5%)	50 (68.5%)	0 (.0%)	73 (100%)
Female	23 (32.4%)	48 (67.6%)	0 (.0%)	71 (100%)
Total	46 (31.9%)	98 (68.1%)	0 (.0%)	144 (100%)

Chi-square value=.013, df=1, P-value = .909

Table 32 shows that a majority of the child members of both genders, boys (68.5%) and girls (67.6%) opined that the books they required are only "partly available" in the libraries; whereas nearly one third of them, male (31.5%) and female (32.4%) reported that the books they required are "fully available" in the libraries. None of them reported that the books they required are "never available" in the libraries.

The p-value .909 (>.05) reveals that the perception of children of both genders on the availability of children's books in the collection is not significantly different. A majority of children of both genders have an average opinion regarding rate of availability of children's books in the collections. The analysis reveals that children's peculiar needs and interests are not reflected in the collections. It can also be inferred that public libraries do not provide a wide range of children's collection in sufficient quantity to meet their various information needs.

Physical Facilities of the Libraries

The motivation of the reading public always depends upon the congenial physical facilities within the library. To ascertain the perceptions of the members on the physical facilities of the libraries, the respondents were presented with the following statements, descriptive of the physical facilities of the libraries, "convenient location", "is noisy" "is clean and neat", "have enough seats to sit", "satisfactory ventilation and light", "is a pleasant place to visit", "is too crowded". They were asked to indicate their degree of agreement/ disagreement with each of the preceding statements and were provided with four response categories ranging from "strongly agree" to "strongly disagree". The responses are summarised in Table 33.

The data in Table 33 reveal that nearly half of members (49.4%) strongly agree with the statement regarding the physical facilities of the libraries that they are situated in a "convenient location". Other users expressed their opinion in various degrees, "agree" (44.7%), "disagree" (4.6%), and "strongly disagree" (1.3%). Nearly half of the users (48.3%)

Table 33

Adult Members' Perceptions on the Physical Facilities of the Public Libraries

Perceptions	*Strongly Agree*	*Agree*	*Disagree*	*Strongly Disagree*
convenient location	863 (49.4%)	781 (44.7%)	81 (4.6%)	23 (1.3%)
is noisy	191 (10.9%)	481 (27.5%)	844 (48.3%)	232 (13.3%)
is clean and neat	621 (35.5%)	1024 (58.6%)	80 (4.5%)	23 (1.3%)
have enough seats to sit	518 (29.6%)	852 (48.7%)	308 (17.6%)	70 (4%)
satisfactory ventilation and light	448 (25.6%)	841 (48.1%)	339 (19.4%)	120 (6.9%)
is a pleasant place to visit	682 (39%)	944 (54.0%)	108 (6.2%)	14 (0.8%)
is too crowded	129(7.4%)	415 (23.7%)	1003 d(57.4%)	201 (11.5%)

disagree with the statement "the library is "noisy", whereas 27.5% of users agree with this statement. A small percentage of users (10.9%) strongly agree with this statement and 13.3% of users strongly disagree with this statement. The highest percentage of users (58.6%) agrees with the statement "the library is clean and neat", next highest percentage (35.5%) strongly agrees with this statement, a small percentage (4.5%) disagrees and 1.3% strongly disagrees with the statement.

Nearly half of the users (48.7%) agree with the statement that the libraries have "enough seats to sit" to read or refer the reading materials and 29.6% of them strongly agree with this statement, while a small percentage (17.6%) disagrees and 4% strongly disagrees with this statement. Nearly half of the users (48.1%) agree with the statement that the "libraries have satisfactory ventilation and lighting facilities" and 25.6% of them strongly agree with this statement. Small percentages of them (19.4%) disagree and 6.9% strongly disagree with this statement.

Above half of the users (54%) agree with the statement that the library "is a pleasant place to visit", and 39% of them strongly agree with this statement. Small percentage (6.2%) disagrees and 0.8% strongly disagrees with this statement. More than half of the users (57.4%) disagree with the statement that "the library is too crowded", whereas nearly one quarter of the users (23.7%) agree with this statement. A small percentage of them (7.4%) strongly agrees and 11.5% of them strongly disagrees with this statement. From the analyses it can be concluded that a majority of the library members are satisfied with the various physical facilities available in the public libraries.

Perceptions on the Technical Organisation of Books

The best utilisation of reading materials by the members is possible only when the books and other reading materials in the libraries are classified and catalogued in a scientific manner. To ascertain the user evaluation on the technical organisation of reading materials of the libraries, the users were asked to report whether the classification and cataloguing systems followed in the public libraries are "helpful", or "partly helpful" or "not helpful" to locate the books easily. Their responses by gender, educational level and occupational status are summarised in Tables 34, 35, and 36 respectively.

Table 34
Adult Members' Perceptions on the Technical Organisation of Books in the Public Libraries (by Gender)

Gender	*Helpful*	*Partly Helpful*	*Not Helpful*	*Total*
Male	840 (61.7%)	447 (32.8%)	74 (5.4%)	1361 (100%)
Female	250 (68.9%)	102 (28.1%)	11 (3.0%)	363 (100%)
Total	1090 (63.3%)	549 (31.8%)	85 (4.9%)	1724 (100%)

Chi-square value = 7.711, df =2, P-value =0.021*

Table 34 shows that a large percentage of male members (61.7%) and female members (68.9%) find that the existing classification and cataloguing system in the libraries are "helpful" to locate the books easily. Around 30% of them find that it is only "partly helpful", the respective percentages being: male (32.8%) and female (28.1%). A small percentage of male members (5.4%) and female members (3%) find that it is "not helpful" to locate the books easily.

As the p-value is .021 (<.05), there is significant difference between the perception of members of both genders regarding the helpfulness of classification and cataloguing systems followed in the libraries. It is found that female members have a more favourable opinion regarding the helpfulness of classification and cataloguing system followed in the public libraries.

Table 35
Adult Members' Perceptions on the Technical Organisation of Books in the Public Libraries (by Educational Level)

Educational Level	*Helpful*	*Partly Helpful*	*Not Helpful*	*Total*
School	673 (62.0%)	358 (33.0%)	55 (5.1%)	1086 (100%)
Graduate	323 (65.3%)	152 (30.7%)	20 (4.0%)	495 (100%)
Post-Graduates/ Technically Qualified	94 (65.7%)	39 (27.2%)	10 (7.1%)	143 (100%)
Total	1090 (63.3%)	549 (31.8%)	85 (4.9%)	1724 (100%)

Chi-square value = 4.371, df = 4, p-value = 0.358

The analysis of data by the educational level of members shows that most of the members in different educational status find that the existing classification and cataloguing system in the libraries are "helpful" to locate books easily; the respective percentages are: school educated (62%), graduates (65.3%), and post-graduate/technically qualified groups (65.7%). Around 30% of them find that it is only "partly helpful", school educated (33.2%), graduates (30.7%), and post-graduates/technically qualified (27.2%). A small percentage of them, school educated (5%), graduates (4%) and post graduates/technically qualified categories (7.1%) find that it is "not helpful".

The p-value (.358>.05) indicates that there is no significant difference in the perception of members belonging to different educational levels regarding the helpfulness of classification and cataloguing system followed in the libraries. It is seen that most of the members of different educational groups of school educated, graduate, and post-graduates/technically qualified have a high opinion regarding the helpfulness of the classification and cataloguing system followed in the libraries.

Table 36
Adult Members' Perceptions on the Technical Organisation of Books in the Public Libraries (Occupational Status)

Occupational Status	*Helpful*	*Partly Helpful*	*Not Helpful*	*Total*
Student	273 (61.7%)	140 (31.7%)	29 (6.6%)	442 (100%)
Employed	641 (64.6%)	309 (31.1%)	43 (4.3%)	993 (100%)
Unemployed	102 (61.5%)	55 (33.1%)	9 (5.4%)	166 (100%)
Retired	74 (60.2%)	45 (36.5%)	4 (3.3%)	123 (100%)
Total	1090 (63.3%)	549 (31.8%)	85 (4.9%)	1724 (100%)

Chi-square value = 5.708,df= 6, p-value = 0.457

A greater percentage of members belonging to different occupational categories find that the existing classification and cataloguing system followed in the libraries are "helpful" to locate books easily, the respective percentages are: students (61.7%), employed (64.6%), unemployed (61.5%), and retired (60.2%). Around 30% of the members of different occupational categories find that it is only "partly helpful", the respective percentages are: students (31.7%), employed (31.1%), unemployed (33.1%), and retired (36.5%). A small percentage of them reported that the existing cataloguing and classification systems are "not helpful" in locating books easily, students (6.6%), employed (4.3%), unemployed (5.4%), and retired (3.3%).

Since the p-value is .457 (>.05) the members of different occupational categories show no significant difference in their opinion regarding the helpfulness of the classification and cataloguing system followed in the libraries. A majority of members of different occupational status have a high opinion regarding the helpfulness of the classification and cataloguing system followed in the public libraries.

Perceptions on Arrangement of Books in the Public Libraries

The optimum utilization of books in the libraries is effective only when the books are arranged scientifically. The members were asked to express their opinion from the three response categories, "easy to locate books", "moderately easy" and "not easy". The responses by gender, educational level and occupational status are presented in Tables 37, 38 and 39 respectively.

Table 37
Adult Members' Perceptions on Arrangement of Books in the Public Libraries (by Gender)

Gender	*Easy*	*Moderately Easy*	*Not Easy*	*Total*
Male	729 (55.3%)	500 (37.9%)	90 (6.8%)	1319 (100%)
Female	220 (61.8%)	118 (33.1%)	18 (5.1%)	356 (100%)
Total	949 (56.7%)	618 (36.9%)	108 (6.4%)	1675 (100%)

Chi-square value = 5.189, df = 2, P-value = 0.075

The analysis of the data in the table (Table 37) revealed that 55.3% of male members and 61.8% of female members which secured the highest percentage felt that the arrangement of books in the library is "easy" to locate the books they required. More than one third of the members, male (37.9%) and female (33.1%) felt that the arrangement of books is "moderately easy" to locate. A small percentage of male members (6.8%) and female members (5.1%) find that the arrangement of books is "not easy" to locate, which resulted in not finding of the required available books.

The p-value (.075 > .05) shows that the opinion of members of both genders regarding the helpfulness of the arrangement of books in the shelves is not significantly different. A majority of the members of both genders have a high opinion about the helpfulness of the arrangement of books in the shelves.

Table 38
Adult Members' Perceptions on Arrangement of Books in the Public Libraries (by Educational Level)

Educational Level	*Easy*	*Moderately Easy*	*Not Easy*	*Total*
School	604 (57.1%)	383 (36.2%)	71 (6.7%)	1058 (100%)
Graduate	269 (56.4%)	181 (37.9%)	27 (5.7%)	477 (100%)
Post-Graduates/ Technically Qualified	76 (54.3%)	54 (38.6%)	10 (7.1%)	140 (100%)
Total	949 (56.7%)	618 (36.9%)	108 (6.4%)	1675 (100%)

Chi-square Value = 1.244, df = 4, P-value = 0.871

More than half of the members belonging to different educational status, school educated (57.1%), graduates (56.4%), and post-graduates/technically qualified (54.3%) find the arrangement of books in the library as "easy" to secure the required available materials, whereas around 35% of them find it as "moderately easy" to retrieve the books they required, the respective percentages are: students (36.2%) graduates (37.9%), and post graduates/technically qualified (38.6%). A small percentage of school educated members (6.7%), graduate members (5.7%) and post-graduates/technically qualified members (7.1%) reported that the method of arrangement of books in the library is "not easy" to retrieve the books they required.

As the p-value is .871 (>.05), there is no significant difference in the opinion of members of various education categories regarding the helpfulness of arrangement of books in the shelves. It is concluded that most of the school educated members, graduates and post-graduates/technically qualified members have a high opinion regarding the arrangement of books in the shelves.

Table 39

Adult Members' Perceptions on Arrangement of Books in the Public Libraries (by Occupational Status)

Occupational Status	*Easy*	*Moderately Easy*	*Not Easy*	*Total*
Student	232 (53.5%)	169 (38.9%)	33 (7.6%)	434 (100%)
Employed	561 (58.8%)	34 3(36%)	50 (5.2%)	954 (100%)
Unemployed	89 (54.6%)	60 (36.8%)	14 (8.6%)	163 (100%)
Retired	67 (54.0%)	46 (37.1%)	11 (8.9%)	124 (100%)
Total	949 (56.7%)	618 (36.9%)	108 (6.4%)	1675 (100%)

Chi-square value = 7.899, df = 6, p-value = 0.246

Above half of the members in different occupational categories, students (53.5%), employed (58.8%), unemployed, (54.6%) and retired (54%) expressed their view that the arrangement of books in the library is "easy" to locate the required books, around 35% of students (38.9%), employed (36%), unemployed (36.8%) and retired (37.1%) reported that the method of arrangement was "moderately easy". A small percentage of the members find it "not easy" to locate the required books.

Since the p-value is .246 (>.05) there is no significant difference in the opinion of members of various occupation groups regarding the arrangement of books in the libraries. A majority of the students, employed, unemployed and retired categories of members have a good opinion regarding the helpfulness of arrangement of books in the libraries.

Adult Members' Satisfaction with the Number of Books Lent at a Time

The satisfaction of members with the library services is correlated to the adequate number of books lent to them to meet their information needs. Members' satisfaction in this regard is measured by asking them to indicate their opinion from three alternatives of "sufficient", "partly sufficient" and "not sufficient". The summary of the responses by gender, educational level and occupational status is presented in Tables 40, 41 and 42 respectively.

Table 40
Adult Members' Satisfaction with the Number of Books Lent at a Time (by Gender)

Gender	*Sufficient*	*Partly Sufficient*	*Insufficient*	*Total*
Male	902 (67.6%)	353 (26.5%)	79 (5.9%)	1334 (100%)
Female	246 (68.5%)	102 (28.4%)	11 (3.1%)	359 (100%)
Total	1148 (67.8%)	455 (26.9%)	90 (5.3%)	1693 (100%)

Chi-square value = 4.781, df = 2, p-value = .092

The data in Table 40 indicate that a large percentage of members of both genders, male (67.6%) and female (68.5%) expressed that the number of books lent at a time for home reading is "sufficient". The number of books lent at a time is only "partly sufficient" to 26.5% of male members and 28.4% of female members and it is "insufficient" to 5.9% of males and 3.1% of females.

The p-value (.092>.05) shows that there is no significant difference in the perception of members of both genders regarding the adequacy of number of books lent at a time. A majority of members of both genders have a high opinion regarding the sufficiency of books issued at a time.

Table 41
Adult Members' Satisfaction with the Number of Books Lent at a Time (by Educational Level)

Educational Level	*Sufficient*	*Partly Sufficient*	*Insufficient*	*Total*
School	741 (69.4%)	279 (26.1%)	48(4.5%)	1068 (100%)
Graduate	330 (68.0%)	126 (26%)	29 (6.0%)	485 (100%)
Post-Graduates/ Technically Qualified	77 (55%)	50 (35.7%)	13 (9.3%)	140 (100%)
Total	1148 (67.8%)	455 (26.9%)	90 (5.3%)	1693 (100%)

Chi-square value = 14.128, df = 4, p-value = 0.007*

The data in Table 41 show that a majority of the members belonging to different educational level, school educated

(69.4%), graduates (68.0%), and post graduates/technically qualified (55%) reported that the number of books lent at a time for home reading is "sufficient". As many as 26.1% of the members with only school education, 26% of graduates, and 35.7% of post graduates/technically qualified stated that the number of books lent at a time is only "partly sufficient' for their reading requirements. A small percentages of the members, school educated (4.5%), graduates (6.0%), and post-graduates/technically qualified (9.3%) stated that the number of books lent at a time is "insufficient" for their reading requirements.

Since the P-value is .007 (<.05), there is a significant difference in the perception among the members of various education groups regarding the adequacy of books issued at a time. A greater percentage of members having only school education and graduate members have a high opinion regarding adequacy of number of books issued at a time than post-graduates/technically qualified members.

Table 42
Adult Members' Satisfaction with the Number of Books Lent at a Time (by Occupational Status)

Occupational Status	*Sufficient*	*Partly Sufficient*	*Insufficient*	*Total*
Student	271 (62%)	139 (31.8%)	27 (6.2%)	437 (100%)
Employed	682 (70.2%)	236 (24.3%)	53 (5%)	971 (100%)
Unemployed	111 (69.4%)	43 (26.8%)	6 (3.8%)	160 (100%)
Retired	84 (67.2%)	37 (29.6%)	4(3.2%)	125 (100%)
Total	1148 (67.8%)	455 (26.9%)	90(5.3%)	1693 (100%)

Chi-square value = 12.201, df = 6, p-value = 0.058

The data in table (Table 42) show that the members of different occupational groups constitute 62% of students, 70.2% of employed, 69.4% of unemployed, and 67.2 % of retired find that the number of books lent at a time is "sufficient" for their reading requirements. As many as 31.8% of students, 24.3% of employed, 26.8% of unemployed, and 29.6% of retired categories felt that the number of books lent at a time is only "partly sufficient". A small percentage of the members comprised of only 6.2% of students, 5% of employed, 3.8% of unemployed, and 3.2% of retired stated that the number of books lent at a time is "insufficient" for their requirements.

As the p-value is .058, there is no significant difference in the opinion of members of different occupational groups regarding the adequacy of number of books lent at a time. A majority of students, employed, unemployed, and retired categories have a high opinion regarding the adequacy of number of books issued at a time.

Convenience of Working Hours

Convenient working hours of the public libraries will have a high impact on the satisfaction of the public. To ascertain the members' perception on the working hours of the public libraries, the respondents were asked to report whether the working hours of the public library are convenient or not. Their perceptions are analysed and presented in Table 43.

Table 43
Perceptions of Adult Members on the Convenience of Working Hours of the Public Libraries (by Gender)

Gender	*Convenient*	*Not Convenient*	*Total*
Male	1295 (94.0%)	82(6.0%)	1377 (100%)
Female	353 (95.4%)	17 (4.6%)	370 (100%)
Total	1648 (94.3%)	99 (5.7%)	1747 (100%)

Chi-square value =1.010, df =1, p-value = .315

It can be seen from Table 43 that a vast majority of members of both genders, male (94%) and female (95.4%) find that the working hours of the library are convenient. Since the p-value is .315, there is no significant difference in the opinion of both genders regarding the conveniences of working hours of the public libraries. A vast majority of both male and female members have a favourable opinion about the working hours of the public libraries.

Analysis of the data by the educational level of members reveals that a great majority of members of different categories, school educated (95.4%), graduates (92.4%), and post-

Table 44
Perceptions of Adult Members on the Convenience of Working Hours of the Public Libraries (by Educational Level)

Educational Level	*Convenient*	*Not Convenient*	*Total*
School	1054 (95.4%)	51 (4.6%)	1105 (100%)
Graduate	459 (92.4%)	38 (7.6%)	497 (100%)
Post-Graduate/ Technically Qualified	135 (93.1%)	10 (6.9%)	145 (100%)
Total	1648 (94.3%)	99 (5.7%)	1747 (100%)

graduates/technically qualified members (93.1%) felt that the working hours of the library are convenient.

Table 45
Perceptions of Adult Members on the Convenience of Working Hours of the Public Libraries (by Occupational Status)

Occupational Status	*Convenient*	*Not Convenient*	*Total*
Student	410(93.2%)	30 (6.8%)	440(100%)
Employed	947 (94.0%)	60 (6.0%)	1007(100%)
Unemployed	164 (96.0%)	7 (4.0%)	171(100%)
Retired	127 (98.4%)	2 (1.6%)	129(100%)
Total	1648 (94.3%)	99 (5.7%)	1747(100%)

Chi-square value = 6.132[a] , df = 3, p-value = .105

Among occupational categories of members, a vast majority of students (93.2%) employed (94.0%), unemployed (96%) and retired categories (98.4%) reported that the working hours of the library are convenient.

The p-value (.105>.05) reveals that the opinions of members belonging to various occupational status regarding the convenience of working hours of the public libraries are not significantly different. A majority of students, employed, unemployed and retired categories have a favourable opinion regarding the convenience of working hours of the public libraries. From the analysis it can be concluded that a vast majority of the members irrespective of sex, education, and occupation are satisfied with the existing working hours of the library. A majority of the libraries are working in the evening. So there is a coincidence of leisure time of a majority of members with the working hours of the libraries.

Children's Perceptions on the Convenience of Working Hours

To measure the children's perceptions on the convenience of working hours of the public libraries, they were asked to report whether the working hours are convenient or not. Their responses by gender are analysed and presented in Table 46.

Table 46
Children's Perceptions on the Convenience of Working Hours of the Public Libraries (by Gender)

Gender	*Convenient*	*Not Convenient*	*Total*
Male	72(87.8%)	10 (12.2%)	82 (100%)
Female	69(92.0%)	6 (8.0%)	75 (100%)
Total	141 (89.8%)	16 (10.2%)	157 (100%)

Chi-square value = .753, df =1, p-value = .385

The Table 46 indicates that a predominant group of children in both genders, male (87.8%) and female (92.0%) are of the opinion that the existing working hours of the library are convenient for them to visit the library, whereas a small percentage (10.2%) reported that existing working time are inconvenient to them.

Since the p-value is .385, no significant difference is observed in the perception of children of both genders regarding the convenience of working hours of the public libraries. A vast majority of children of both genders have a high opinion about the convenience of working hours of the libraries.

Inconvenience of Holidays on the Use of the Library

To analyse users' opinion regarding the holidays of public libraries, the respondents were asked whether the holidays of the library cause any inconvenience to them in the library use. Their responses by gender, educational level, and occupational level are analysed and presented in Tables 47, 48, and 49 respectively.

Table 47
Adult Members' Perceptions on the Holidays of the Public Libraries (by Gender)

Gender	Inconvenient	Not Inconvenient	Total
Male	350 (27.5%)	925 (72.5%)	1275 (100%)
Female	79 (23.1%)	263 (76.9%)	342 (100%)
Total	429 (26.5%)	1188 (73.5%)	1617 (100%)

Chi-square value =2.620, df = 1, p-value = .106

The analysis of the table (Table 47) revealed that to a predominant group of both genders, male members (72.5%) and female members (76.9%), the library holidays do not cause any inconvenience to them.

As the p-value is .106 (>.05) there is no significant difference in the perception of members of both genders regarding the holidays of the public libraries. A majority of both male and female members have high a degree of satisfaction with the total working days of the public libraries.

Table 48
Adult Members' Perceptions on the Holidays of the Public Libraries (by Educational Level)

Educational Level	Inconvenient	Not Inconvenient	Total
School	257 (25.4%)	754 (74.6%)	1011 (100%)
Graduate	123 (26.0%)	350 (74.0%)	473 (100%)
Post-Graduate/ Technically Qualified	49 (36.8%)	84 (63.2%)	133 (100%)
Total	429 (26.5%)	1188 (73.5%)	1617 (100%)

Chi-square value = 7.962, df = 2, p-value=.019*

Table 48 shows that a majority of school educated members (74.6%) and graduate members (74%), and comparatively less percentage of post-graduates/technically qualified members (63.2%) reported that the library holidays do not cause any inconvenience to them.

Since the p-value is .019 (<.05), it is concluded that there is significant difference in the perception of members belonging to various educational levels regarding the holidays of the public libraries. The members with only school education have a high degree of satisfaction with the total working days of the public libraries than graduates and post-graduates/ technically qualified groups.

Table 49
Adult Members' Perceptions on the Holidays of the Public Libraries (by Occupational Status)

Occupational Status	*Inconvenient*	*Not Inconvenient*	*Total*
Student	137 (33.1%)	277 (66.9%)	414 (100%)
Employed	235 (25.3%)	695 (74.7%)	930 (100%)
Unemployed	39 (25.3%)	115 (74.7%)	154 (100%)
Retired	18 (15.1%)	101 (84.9%)	119 (100%)
Total	429 (26.5%)	1188 (73.5%)	1617 (100%)

Chi-square value =17.959[a] , df = 3, p-value = <.001*

Among the members of different occupational status, a majority of students (66.9%), employed (74.7%), unemployed (74.7%) and retired (84.9%) stated that holidays of the library do not cause any inconvenience to their library use.

The p-value (<.001) shows that there is a significant difference in the perception of members of various occupational status regarding the adequacy of total working days of the public libraries. The retired category has a high degree of satisfaction with the number of working days of the public libraries than graduate and post-graduate/technically qualified categories of members.

Awareness of Library Services and Programmes

Members' awareness of library services and programmes is an important factor which accelerates the use of the libraries. The members' knowledge of library services and programmes was studied and the summary of the result by gender, educational level, and occupational status is presented in Tables 50, 51 and 52 respectively.

Table 50 reveals that a majority of male members (70.2%) and female members (65.7%) are aware of the various services and programmes provided by the public libraries. The p-value (.102 > .05) indicates that there is no significant difference in the level of awareness of various services and programmes between the members of both genders. From the table it is clear

Table 50
Adult Members' Awareness of Various Services and Programmes of the Public Libraries (by Gender)

Gender	*Aware*	*Not Aware*	*Total*
Male	944 (70.2%)	400 (29.8%)	1344 (100%)
Female	232 (65.7%)	121 (34.3%)	353 (100%)
Total	1176 (69.3%)	521 (30.7%)	1697 (100%)

Chi-square value =2.680, df = 1, p-value =0.102

that a large percentage of male members and female members have a high level of awareness of library services and programmes of the libraries.

Table 51
Adult Members' Awareness of Various Services and Programmes of the Public Libraries (by Educational Level)

Educational Level	*Aware*	*Not Aware*	*Total*
School	734 (68.7%)	334 (31.3%)	1068 (100%)
Graduate	337 (69.2%)	150 (30.8%)	487 (100%)
Post-Graduates/ Technically Qualified	105 (73.9%)	37 (26.1%)	142 (100%)
Total	1176(69.3%)	521 (30.7%)	1697 (100%)

Chi-square value = 1.607, df = 2, p-value = 0.448

Among the members of different educational levels, as many as 68.7% of members having only school education, 69.2% of graduates and 73.9% post-graduates/technically qualified are familiar with the various library services and programmes.

Since the p-value is .448 there is no significant difference in the level of awareness of the members belonging to different educational level regarding the various services and programmes of the libraries. A majority of members with only school education, graduate members, and post graduates/ technically qualified members have a high level of awareness of various services and programmes of the public libraries.

Analysis of the data in Table 52 indicates that a majority of the members of different occupational status, students (60.6%), employed (72.9%), unemployed (64.8%), and retired

(77%) are "aware" of the various services and programmes offered by the libraries.

Table 52
Adult Members' Awareness of Various Services and Programmes of the Public Libraries (by Occupational Status)

Occupational Status	*Aware*	*Not Aware*	*Total*
Student	263 (60.6%)	171 (39.4%)	434 (100%)
Employed	709 (72.9%)	263 (27.1%)	972 (100%)
Unemployed	107 (64.8%)	58 (35.2%)	165 (100%)
Retired	97 (77%)	29 (23%)	126 (100%)
Total	1176 (69.3%)	521 (30.7%)	1697 (100%)

Chi-square value =26.538, df = 3, P-value = <0.001*

As the p-value is <.001, the members of different occupational groups show significant difference in the level of awareness of the various and programmes of the public libraries. It is seen that the employed and retired categories have higher level of awareness than the other groups regarding the various services and progrmmes of the public libraries. The study reveals that a total of 30.7% of the members are not aware of the various library services and programmes provided in the public libraries. This may be because library authorities do not give adequate publicity to the various services and programmes. of the libraries. This will adversely affect the optimum utilisation of library resources and services.

Evaluation of Library Services and Programmes

The public library is considered effective and efficient only when it is successful in providing all types of information services to different categories of members. The users' satisfaction with the library services was measured by asking the respondents to rate the over all evaluation of library services and programmes by providing five response categories ranging between "highly satisfied" and "highly dissatisfied". The assessment of members' views by gender, educational level, and occupational status are analysed in Tables 53, 54 and 55 respectively.

Table 53
Members' Evaluation of Library Services and Programmes (by Gender)

Gender	*Highly Satisfied*	*Satisfied*	*Partly Satisfied*	*Not Satisfied*	*Highly Dissatisfied*	*Total*
Male	278	768	271	29	2	1348
	(20.6%)	(57%)	(20.1%)	(2.2%)	(0.1%)	(100%)
Female	94	213	36	6	2	351
	(26.8%)	(60.7%)	(10.3%)	(1.7%)	(0.6%)	(100%)
Total	372	981	307	35	4	1699
	(21.9%)	(57.7%)	(18.1%)	(2.1%)	(0.2%)	(100%)

Chi-square value = 22.797, df = 4, P-value = <0.001*

The analysis of the data in Table 53 shows that 57% of male members and 60.7% of female members are satisfied with the various library services and programmes. Only 20.6% of male members and 26.8% of female members are "highly satisfied" with the various library services and programmes. Some of them are only "partly satisfied" with the library services and programmes, male (20.1%) and female (10.3%). A small percentage of members are dissatisfied with the library programmes and services, male (2.3%), female (2.3%).

Since the p-value is <.001, the members of both genders show significant difference in the degree of satisfaction regarding the library services and programmes. Female members have a higher degree of satisfaction than male members regarding the various services and programmes provided by the public libraries.

Table 54 reveals that more than half of the members belonging to different educational levels are found "satisfied" with library services and programmes, school educated (57.4%), graduate (58.1%) and post graduates/technically qualified (59.3%). Around 20% of the members are "highly satisfied" with the library services and programmes; school educated (23.5%), graduates (18.6%), and post-graduates/technically qualified (20.7%); while some of them are only "partly satisfied" with the library services and programmes, school educated (16.5%), graduates (21.2%) and post-graduates/technically qualified (19.3%). The percentages of members who are "not satisfied" with the various library services and programmes are negligible.

Table 54

Members' Evaluation of Library Services and Programmes (by Educational Level)

Educational Level	*Highly Satisfied*	*Satisfied*	*Partly Satisfied*	*Not Satisfied*	*Highly Dissatisfied*	*Total*
School	254 (23.5%)	619 (57.4%)	178 (16.5%)	24 (2.2%)	4 (0.4%)	1079 (100%)
Graduate	90 (18.6%)	282 (58.1%)	103 (21.2%)	10 (2.1%)	0 (.0%)	485 (100%)
Post-Graduates/ Technically Qualified	28 (20.7%)	80 (59.3%)	26 (19.3%)	1 (0.7%)	0 (.0%)	135 (100%)
Total	372 (21.9%)	981 (57.7%)	307 (18.1%)	35 (2.1%)	4 (0.2%)	1699 (100%)

Chi-square value = 11.835, df = 8, p-value = 0.159

As the p-value is .159 (>.05), there is no significant difference in the degree of satisfaction regarding the library services and programmes among the different education groups of the members. It is concluded that a majority of members belonging to different educational levels have a high degree of satisfaction with the various services and programmes of the public libraries.

It is clear from Table 55 that more than half of members in different occupational groups are satisfied with the library services and programmes, the respective percentages are: students (56.8%), employed (57.3%) unemployed (56.4%) and retired (66.4%). Some of them are highly satisfied with the library services and programmes, students (25.1%), employed (20.9%), unemployed (22.1%) and retired (18.9%). A small percentage of them are partly satisfied with the library services and programmes, students (15.1%), employed (19.8%), unemployed (18.4%), and retired (13.9%). A small percentage of the members are not satisfied with the library services and programmes.

The p-value (.311 > .05) indicates that there is no significant difference in the degree of satisfaction with the services and programmes of the public libraries among the members of different occupational categories. A majority of the members of different occupational groups have a high degree of satisfaction with the various services and programmes provided by the public libraries.

Evaluation of Staff

The success or failure of public libraries in providing satisfactory services to the library users depends upon the attitudes of the library staff working in the libraries. To measure the users' evaluation on the attitudes of staff, the users were presented with the following five statements descriptive of the library staff, "is friendly", "helpful", "is too busy to assist me properly", "appears to be competent" and "is very competent". They were asked to indicate their degree of agreement/disagreement with each of the preceding statements and were provided with four response categories

Table 55

Members' Evaluation of Library Services and Programmes (by Occupational Status)

Occupational Status	*Highly Satisfied*	*Satisfied*	*Partly Satisfied*	*Not Satisfied*	*Highly Dissatisfied*	*Total*
Student	108 (25.1%)	245 (56.8%)	65 (15.1%)	11 (2.5%)	2 (0.5%)	431 (100%)
Employed	205 (20.9%)	563 (57.3%)	195 (19.8%)	18 (1.8%)	2 (0.2%)	983 (100%)
Unemployed	36 (22.1%)	92 (56.4%)	30 (18.4%)	5 (3.1%)	0 (.0%)	163 (100%)
Retired	23 (18.9%)	81 (66.4%)	17 (13.9%)	1 (0.8%)	0 (.0%)	122 (100%)
Total	372 (21.9%)	981 (57.7%)	307 (18.1%)	35 (2.1%)	4 (0.2%)	1699 (100%)

Chi-square value = 13.837, df = 12, P-value = 0.311

ranging from "strongly agree" to "strongly disagree". Users' perceptions are summarised in Table 56.

Table 56
User Evaluation of Staff in the Public Libraries

(N=1722)

Perceptions	*Strongly Agree*	*Agree*	*Disagree*	*Strongly Disagree*
Friendly	954 (55.4%)	756 (43.9%)	9 (0.5%)	3 (0.2%)
Helpful	797 (46.0%)	894 (51.9%)	22 (1.3%)	9 (0.5%)
Is to busy to assist me properly	78 (4.5%)	222 (12.9%)	1090 (63.3%)	332 (19.3%)
Appears to be competent	71 (4.15%)	119 (6.9%)	997 (57.9%)	535 (31.1%)
Is very competent	515 (29.9%)	1068 (62%)	117 (6.8%)	22 (1.3%)

Note: N = Total number of the respondents, based on which the percentage is derived.

The Table 56 assesses the users' views on the attitudes of library staff members and it is clear that higher percentage of them (55.4%) strongly agree with the opinion that the staff members in the public libraries are "friendly". More than half of the members (51.9%) agree that the library staff members are "helpful". A majority of them (63.3%) disagree that the staff members are "too busy to assist the members properly", and also for 57.9% of the members, the staff members "appear to be competent", and 62% of them view that staff members are "very competent". From the analysis it can be said that a majority of the users have a positive opinion about the library staff members.

USERS' SUGGESTIONS FOR IMPROVEMENTS

The users' suggestions for the improvements of existing library functions and services are consolidated and presented as follows:

The different suggestions made by the members reveal that nearly 20% of them felt the need for more books in various subjects in the libraries to meet their information requirements.

As many as 14.1% of the members suggested that the libraries have to provide various social services to the community to fulfil the objectives as a social agency. Some of the members (14%) suggested a library building with sufficient space to provide convenient reading and stacking facilities, 10.1% of them felt that the improved physical facilities such as reading tables, chairs, light, and ventilation would increase the utility of the library services. Some of them (9.9%) opined that the libraries should conduct various cultural programmes to enrich the cultural interest of the people. Various other valuable suggestions made by the members such as more children's books; more books in English and Hindi languages; more standard periodicals; adequate funds for the proper functioning of the libraries; improved physical facilities; non-book materials such as CD, DVD, cassettes and such others; Internet facility; scientific organisation of books; more cultural programmes; more working hours; service to schools; library awareness programmes; service to women, old people, and such others; various social services; and computerisation of the libraries also should be considered seriously by the library authorities to improve the effectiveness and efficiency of the public libraries.

CONCLUSION

The present study on the user behaviour and their satisfaction with the library services measured the functional quality of the public libraries in the area under study. It was observed that some of the library users with different educational levels, and occupational statuses are not satisfied with the library collections and their orgnisation, services, and facilities, and they believe that public libraries are not fully effective to meet their various needs. It exposes the other side of this finding that some of them are satisfied with the collections, services and programmes of the public libraries. This may be based on their limited needs and views and they are not aware of the changing concepts of public libraries and their expected roles in the society.

7

CONSPECTUS

INTRODUCTION

The study on the present status of public libraries in Malabar with respect to their organisation, administration, resources, activities and services brought out information to find out their effectiveness and efficiency. In this concluding chapter a summary of the findings of the study, tenability of hypotheses, suggestions for the improvement of functions and operations of the libraries, a blue-print of the future of the public libraries in Kerala, and suggestions of area for further research are presented.

SUMMARY OF THE FINDINGS

The study on the various aspects of the public libraries has revealed many findings, which are grouped under various headings as follows:

General Characteristics of the Public Libraries in Malabar

1. In Malabar, Kannur is in the fore-front of establishing a large number of libraries, followed by Kozhikode. Wayanad registers slowness in this progress.
2. Among the grant-in- aid libraries, the highest number of libraries is in E grade (18.7%), followed by C (17.6%), D (16.6%), A(15%), F (15.0%), B (14.4%), and the libraries under other governing bodies are the lowest in number (2.7%).

3. Only 10.2% of the libraries were established before 1947, more than one third of the libraries (36.9%) were established during the period 1948-67, 27.8% of the libraries were established during 1968-87, and 25.1% of the libraries were established after 1988.
4. The number of libraries is more in the rural area (80.2%) than in the urban area (19.8%).
5. As many as 88.2% of the libraries are working independently and only 11.8% are working as part of parent institutions.
6. A majority of the libraries under study (65.8%) have registered as per Societies Registration Act, and 34.2% of the libraries have not registered as per the Act.

Different Sections in the Libraries

1. All libraries have a separate general books section, 68.4% of them have a reference section, and 92.5% a periodical section.

Resources

Information Resources

1. Only less than half of the libraries (45.5%) have a book selection committee.
2. No library under study adopts a book selection policy.
3. A large majority of the libraries (84.4%) use publishers' catalogues as the main book selection tool.
4. The public libraries in Malabar possess an average book stock of 5425 volumes, 296 reference books, 170 text books, 586 children's books, and 4248 other books.
5. The libraries under other governing bodies have the highest mean of 13677 total book stock, 1107 reference books and 557 text books, whereas A grade libraries have the highest mean of 1196 children's books.
6. The libraries in Palakkad have the highest average number of 6438 books. The libraries in Kozhikode have the highest

average number of 443 reference books. The libraries in Wayanad have the highest average number of 465 text books. The libraries in Kasaragod have the highest average number of 864 children's books.

7. The mean number of different categories of books available in the public libraries is more in the urban area than in the rural area.
8. No district in Malabar agrees with the IFLA/UNESCO Guidelines, 2001 for book stock that "an established book collection should be between 1.5 and 2.5 books per-capita.
9. The average cost of books in the public libraries in all districts is much less, the highest in Kozhikode (Rs. 30.96) and the lowest in Palakkad (Rs. 19.27).
10. The public libraries possess an average of 3571 fiction books and 1557 non-fiction books.
11. A grade libraries have the highest average number of 7743 fiction books, whereas the libraries under other governing bodies have the highest average number of 6743 non-fiction books.
12. Palakkad tops first with the average number of 4502 fiction books and the libraries in Wayanad possess the highest average number of 1899 non-fiction collection.
13. The average number of fiction and non-fiction books acquired by the public libraries is more in the urban areas.
14. Nearly 60% of the fiction collection in the public libraries is of cheap quality, mostly detective novels, and non-fiction collection does not cover all subjects.
15. The public libraries in Malabar stocked an average of 4497 Malayalam books, 572 English books, 114 Hindi books, and 189 other language books such as Tamil, Kannada and Sanskrit.
16. The highest average number of 10564 Malayalam books and 300 Hindi books are stocked in A grade libraries. The highest average number of 6330 English Books is stocked by the libraries under other governing bodies. D grade

libraries have the highest mean of 330 other language books such as Kannada and Tamil.

17. The highest average number of 5217 Malayalam books and 214 Hindi books are stocked by the public libraries in Palakkad, whereas the highest average number of 663 English books are stocked by the public libraries in Kannur. The public libraries in Kasaragod and Palakkad have the highest average number of "other language" books.
18. The highest average number of Malayalam and English books is available in the libraries in the urban areas, whereas more number of Hindi books is available in the libraries in the rural areas.
19. A vast majority of the collection in the public libraries (87.52%) is Malayalam books, while English, Hindi and other languages occupy a very small portion.
20. There is no steady increase in the acquisition of new books in the public libraries during the period from 1999-2000 to 2003-04, the acquisition ranging from an average of 229 books in 2001- 02 to 337 books in 1999-2000.
21. The libraries in Malabar subscribe to an average of 3 children's periodicals, 12 general periodicals and 5 subject periodicals.
22. The highest average number of 6 children's magazines, 33 general magazines, and 38 total periodicals are subscribed to in the libraries under other governing bodies, whereas the highest number of 8 subject periodicals are subscribed to in A grade libraries.
23. Kozhikode occupies the first position in the subscription with an average number of 4 children's periodicals. The highest average number of 14 general magazines are subscribed to by the libraries in Wayanad. The highest average number of 7 subject periodicals is subscribed to by the public libraries in Malappuram. Kozhikode comes first, with a mean of 21 total periodicals.
24. There is only an insignificant variation between the mean number of the children's magazines subscribed to in rural

libraries and urban libraries, whereas the mean number of general magazines, subject periodicals and total number of periodicals are subscribed to by the libraries is higher in the urban area.

25. Only a small percentage of the libraries (25%) keep the bound volumes of some of the important periodicals subscribed to in the library.
26. More than half of the libraries (54.30%) lend periodicals to members.
27. More than half of the libraries (56.1%) subscribe to between 5 and 9 Malayalam news papers, a high percentage of libraries (93.2%) subscribe to 1 or 2 English newspapers and an insignificant percentage of libraries (3.7%) subscribe to between 1 and 3 "other language" newspapers.
28. Only a small percentage of the libraries (11.8%) have a poor collection of non-book materials such as CDs and Floppies.
29. No library has special collection such as manuscripts and rare books.
30. As many as 72.19% the libraries preserve the books by cleaning them regularly, 17.6% of libraries use pesticides, 76.47% bind the worn out books and 10% of the libraries preserve books by covering them using paper.
31. More than half of the libraries (59.6%) weed out out-dated and worn out books from the collection, and keep them separately. This finding agrees with the IFLA/UNESCO Guidelines, 2001 that "the library collection requires a constant inflow of new material and outflow of old material to ensure that it remains relevant to the community and at an accepted level of accuracy."
32. A vast majority of the libraries (95.19%) conduct stock verification regularly.
33. A majority of the libraries (69.24%) do not classify the books, a small percentage of the libraries (4.3%) use Dewey Decimal Classification Scheme (DDC) to classify books, an insignificant percentage of the libraries (1.6%) use modified form of DDC, and 1.1 % adopt a local classification method.

34. A large majority of the libraries (87.06%) use the cataloguing method in which the bibliographic details are furnished in a register or loose sheets subject wise. A small percentage of libraries (4.5%) use "Classified Catalogue Code"(CCC) to catalogue the books, 1.7% of the libraries use "Anglo American Cataloguing Rules"(AACR) to catalogue the books.
35. A majority of the libraries (81.6%) use the ledger as the physical form of catalogue, a small percentage of the libraries use the card catalogue (6.2%) and the sheet catalogue (10.3%). Two libraries under other governing bodies under study, have been replacing traditional library catalogues by machine readable catalogues using locally developed software.
36. In nearly half of the libraries (48.11%), the books are arranged merely on the basis of accession numbers and 44.32% of the libraries adopted subject-wise arrangement of books. In a very few libraries (5.95%) books are arranged scientifically by class numbers.
37. Nearly half of the libraries (45.71%) provide open access system to the members to browse books directly from the stack room.

Finance

1. There is a fluctuation in the total revenue of the public libraries from 1999-2000 to 2003-04, the maximum being in 2002-03 with an average of Rs.63, 078.27 and minimum in 1999-2000 with an average of Rs.39, 414.01.
2. There is no steady increase in the total expenditure of the public libraries during the period from 1999-2000 to 2003-04.
3. A very small amount is spent for different items such as books and periodicals, staff, building, furniture, and miscellaneous by the public libraries.
4. More than half of the grant-in-aid libraries (55.6%) have received the RRRLF grant for different purposes such as purchase of books and furniture, construction and extension of library buildings.

5. The per-capita income of the public libraries is found very low in the districts in Malabar. The per-capita income of the public libraries is the highest in Kannur (Rs.9.10) and the lowest in Malappuram (Rs.2.58).
6. The State government allocated only a very small percentage of its expenditure on education for the public library development during the period from 1999-2000 to 2003-04 which varies from 0.20% to 0.26%.
7. In all districts in Malabar, the per-capita expenditure on reading materials is very meagre. Kannur records the highest per-capita expenditure of Rs.2.71 for reading materials on literate population and Malappuram records the lowest per-capita expenditure of only Rs.1.22 for reading materials.
8. The per-capita expenditure for reading materials on members is too meagre to meet the various informational needs of the community. The libraries in Malappuram have the highest per-capita expenditure of Rs.57.09 on members and Kannur ranks last with the per-capita expenditure of only Rs.32.57.
9. The amount spent for the staff allowance is very meagre. Kannur comes first position with the per-capita expenditure of Rs.1.23 on staff; and Malappuram lags behind with the per-capita expenditure of only Rs.0.45 on staff.

Human Resources

1. Among the library staff, a majority of them (80.1%) are part-time and 19.9% are full time workers.
2. A majority of the librarians (85.03%) are not professionally qualified, whereas 12.30% of the librarians have done certificate course in Library Science, and. 2.67% of the librarians are graduates in Library Science.
3. More than half of the librarians (56.7%) have participated in the conferences or workshops conducted by library authorities. This finding agrees with the IFLA/UNESCO Guidelines, 2001 which stressed the importance of contacts

as follows: "In addition to in-service training staff should be given opportunities to attend conferences and work shops, relevant to their ability to carry out their work."

4. The number of librarians who has basic computer operating skill constitutes only a small percentage (20.3%).
5. No separate fund is allocated for training the librarians by the public libraries under study. This finding does not agree with the IFLA/UNESCO Guidelines, 2001 which state that "0.5% to 1% of the total budget should be earmarked for training purpose."
6. An amount of Rs.6, 000 was given to the librarians of A to D grade libraries and Rs. 3, 600 was given to the librarians of E and F grade libraries annually during 2003-04. The former LLA libraries, panchayath/municipality libraries, and libraries formerly under Scheduled Caste Developing Corporation give monthly salaries to the library staff in the State government scale. The salary fixed by the library management is given to the staff in the libraries under other governing bodies.

Technological Resources

1. Only a small percentage of libraries (12.83%) possess computers.
2. Only 4.8% of the libraries provide Internet facility to the members, where on an average of 15 to 20 members utilise this facility every day.
3. An amount varying from Rs.5 to Rs. 30 per hour is colleted as Internet usage charges from the users.

Physical Resources

1. A majority of the libraries (73.8%) have their own buildings and sites with an average plinth area of 939.03 sq. ft. The average size of the library building is the largest in the libraries under other governing bodies (Mean 3166.67 sq.ft.) and the smallest in F grade libraries (Mean 450.51 sq.ft.).

2. The public libraries in Kannur own the largest sized library buildings (Mean 1036.06 sq.ft.) compared to the libraries in other districts and the libraries in Palakkad own the smallest sized (Mean 644.53 sq.ft.) library buildings.
3. The average size of the library building is larger in the urban area than in the rural area.
4. The size of the library buildings does not agree with the IFLA/UNESCO Guidelines, 2001 which state that "the library should have adequate space to implement the full range of services."
5. More than half of the libraries (50.27%) have television, 34.22% of the libraries have radios, 8.56% of the libraries have tape-recorders, 3.74% of the libraries have other equipments such as public addressing system, and video set.
6. A majority of the libraries have insufficient furniture both for stacking and for reading facilities.
7. In majority of the libraries, the ventilation, fan, and lighting facility are only partly satisfactory. Only 27.3% of the libraries provide drinking water facility to the users.

Visitors

1. There is only a marginal increase in the number of visitors in the public libraries during the period from 1999-2000 to 2003-04.
2. The total average number of visitors of the public libraries per year ranges between 21732 and 30794.
3. The average number of visitors is the highest in A grade libraries (mean 27034) and the lowest in F grade libraries (mean 10162).
4. Wayanad is in the fore-front in the use of the public libraries by the community except in the year 1999-2000. During 1999-2000 Kozhikode is in the fore-front. The libraries in Kasaragod and Malappuram lagged behind in the use of the public libraries.
5. Users are more from the urban community and less from the rural community.

Members

1. On an average of 317 men, 102 women, and 82 children registered themselves as members of the public libraries at the end of the year 2003-04.
2. The public libraries under other governing bodies have the highest average number of 1710 members. Among the libraries, which are affiliated to the State Library Council, the average number of members is the highest in A grade libraries (Mean1085) and the lowest in F grade (Mean 235).
3. The average number of members is the highest in Kozhikode (Mean 619) and the lowest in Palakkad (Mean 393).
4. The average number of members is more in the urban areas than in the rural areas.
5. A majority of the libraries (90%) provide membership to children.
6. The percentage of members with total literate population in six districts of Malabar appears insignificant. The highest is in Kannur, where 8.33% of its literate population are members of the public libraries; and the lowest in Malappuram, where only 2.13% of the literate population are members.
7. In addition to the ordinary membership provided by all libraries, 42% of the libraries issue life membership, and 4% of the libraries issue patronage.
8. No library provides free service to adults and only half of them (50.3%) provide free service to the children.
9. Nearly one third of the libraries (32.83%) collect membership fee which varies from Rs. 11 to Rs. 100. More than a quarter of the libraries (25.28%) collect above Rs.100/- as membership fee. In the case of life membership, the fee varies from Rs.100 to Rs.2500. In patronage, the membership fee ranges from Rs.1, 000 to Rs.10, 000.
10. The practice of charging users for services and membership does not agree with the IFLA/UNESCO Guidelines, 2001 which state that "charging users for services and

membership should not be used as a source of revenue for public libraries, as it makes the ability to pay a criterion in determining who can use a public library."

Administration

1. A vast majority of the libraries (90.9%) are directly under the control of the State Library Council; 6.4% of the libraries, even though affiliated to the State Library Council, are under the control of local administrative units such as panchayaths/municipalities; and 2.7% are under the administrative control of other governing bodiess.
2. All public libraries have a separate library committee for managing the library activities. A majority of the library committees (81.8%) have included social workers, 69.5% of them have included political workers, 59.9% have academicians, 40.11% have panchayath/municipal council members, and only 10% of them have members from other categories such as government employees, labourers, and students.
3. A majority of the library committees (87.17%) meet once a month, 6.42% of the committees meet twice a month, 4.81% meet bimonthly and 1.6% of the library committees meet once in 3 months.
4. In a majority of the public libraries, the membership registers are incomplete and inaccurate and are poorly maintained. Visitor registers are not maintained in most of the libraries.

Services

1. Nearly half of the libraries (48.1%) lend one book at a time, 39.6% of them lend 2 books at a time, 11.2% of them lend 3 books, and 1.1% of them lend 5 books at a time to the members.
2. More than one third of the libraries (36.4%) lend books for 7 to 10 days, more than half of them (56.1%) lend books for two weeks, a very small percentage of the libraries

(2.7%) lend books for 3 weeks, and 4.8% of the libraries lend books for one month.

3. A majority of the libraries (94.1%) provide the facility to extend the loan period of books.
4. More than half of the librarians (56.45%) have taken action to recover the overdue books from the members.
5. Nearly half of the libraries (48.11%) do not collect any fee from the members for the overdue books.
6. A majority of the libraries (88.2%) adopt the ledger system for the circulation of books.
7. Only in one library under study the circulation system is computerised using a locally developed software.
8. On an average of 4300 fiction, 1184 non-fiction and 1566 children's books were issued during 2003-04.
9. The average number of different categories of books lent out during 2003-04 is high in A grade libraries, fiction (mean 9658), non-fiction (mean 2018), children's literature (Mean 2639) and totalling (mean 13972). The number of different categories of books lent is less in the libraries of F grade, fiction (mean 2597), non-fiction (mean 270), children's books (mean 493) and totally (mean 3970).
10. Malappuram occupies the highest position in the total number of fiction books lent out during the year 2003-04 (Mean 6861) and Kasaragod occupies the last position (mean 3568).
11. Wayanad occupies the first position in the total number of non-fiction books lent in the year 2003-04 (Mean 2241) and Kozhikode comes last (mean 809).
12. Palakkad occupies the first position in the total number of children's books lent in the year 2003-04 (Mean 2023) and Kozhikode occupies the last position (mean 1175).
13. Malappuram occupies the first position with regard to the number of the total books lent in the year 2003-04 (Mean 8511) and Kasaragod occupies the last position (mean 5502).

14. The libraries in the urban areas stand first in the average number of different categories of books issued.
15. There is no steady increase in the number of books lent out during the period from 1999-2000 to 2003-04.
16. A majority of the libraries (60.43%) provide reference service to the members. But the resources available in the libraries for this service are too meagre and not constitute standard reference books to provide this service satisfactorily.
17. Referral service is offered by only a small percentage of libraries (25.67%) and the activities undertaken under this service is only minimal.
18. Only a small percentage of the libraries (29.41%) offer service to the self education of neo-literates and it is at a minimal level.
19. Only a small percentage of the libraries (8.56%) function as academic study centres and their services are not satisfactory.
20. Only a small percentage of the libraries (10.70%) provide service to distance education, but not at a satisfactory level.
21. A majority of the public libraries fail to fulfil the educational function.
22. More than half of the libraries (53%) offer community information service to the public at a minimal level.
23. The public libraries fail to fulfil the role of disseminator of information at a satisfactory level.
24. A majority of the libraries (78.6%) offer children's service.
25. The number of children utilising the public library is very less. Only an average of below 10 children utilise the children's services per day in 38% of the libraries, 10 to 15 children in 23.5% of the libraries, 16-20 in 11.8% of the libraries, 21-25 in 5.3% of the libraries and above 25 children in 4.8% of the libraries.
26. The children's collection includes books on different subjects, but science books are less.

27. The children's book collection has a mean of 577 Malayalam books, 118 English books, and 65 books in other languages such as Hindi, Tamil and Kannada.
28. A majority of the libraries have poor special collections such as atlases, charts, and audio-video cassettes for children.
29. A majority of the libraries which provide children's service (70.07%) conduct different programmes for children.
30. Only less than a quarter of the public libraries (21.39%) provide special services to women. Under this service an average of 931 books were collected especially for the women only.
31. The libraries which provide special services for women conduct several programmes for them.
32. Only a small percentage of the libraries (25.13%) provide mobile library service in the community.
33. An average of 70 women, 20 men, and 23 children have taken membership under mobile library service in 2003-04.
34. Only less than half of the libraries (43%) have participated in literacy activities.
35. An average of 59 illiterates have utilised literacy service provided by the public libraries.
36. Only an insignificant number of libraries (4.28%) provide some social services to the disadvantaged groups such as old-age persons, patients in hospitals, and orphanages.
37. Only one library among the surveyed libraries provides service to ethnic groups.
38. A significant majority of the libraries (88.77%) conduct various cultural programmes for the people.
39. Only a small number of libraries (8.6%) have been engaged in literary activities through their hand written magazines.
40. A very small percentage of the libraries (2.67%) provide user education programme.

41. More than half of the libraries (54.12%) provide personal assistance to the members to locate the books, to consult the catalogue and such other assistance.
42. Only one fourth of the libraries (26.74%) provide service to schools and it is at a minimal level.
43. Only one library under other governing bodies participated in resource-sharing.
44. Among the surveyed libraries, only one grant-in-aid library enjoys the facility of borrowing books from the book-bank established by the State library Council.
45. Most of the public libraries make the public aware of the importance of libraries.
46. More than half of the librarians (56.7%) have adopted direct observation for evaluating the various services and activities of the libraries.
47. Public libraries have contributed more in fulfilling the recreational and cultural roles rather than informational or educational roles in the society.
48. The role of public libraries has not been realized much in the rural areas as compared to the urban areas.

Access to Service

1. A majority of the libraries (68.4%) keep their lending sections open only for one to four hours a day, whereas more than half of the libraries (55.6%) keep their periodical sections open for more than 9 hours a day.
2. More than one third of the libraries (34.8%) are kept open all days in a week, more than half of the libraries (59.4%) are kept open six days in a week and 5.8% of the libraries are kept open 3to 5 days in a week.

Problems of the Public Libraries

1. The district library authorities of Kasaragod, Kannur, Kozhikode, Wayanad, Malappuram, and Palakkad and a majority of the librarians (87.70%) find inadequate finance as the main problem in the proper functioning of the libraries.

Measurement of User Evaluation

Individual Characteristics

1. There is an active participation of youth in using the public library. Employed people, the school educated, and the middle income group constituted the core users among the members, but the hard fact is that women have a poor representation among the members.
2. Children around 13 years of age are the common users of the public libraries. Children of both genders represent almost equal percentages, boys (51.6%) and girls (48.4%) in library membership.
3. A large majority of the members (87.2%) required information to solve various problems of their day-to day lives.
4. The adult members visit the public libraries more to borrow and return books than for other purposes.
5. Among the child members there is no significant difference in the motivation to visit the public libraries. A majority of children (76.7%) give highest preference to borrow and return magazines and books.
6. The members are interested more in general books than in other categories of books in the public libraries.
7. The members visit the public libraries more for the benefit of acquisition of knowledge than for other motivations.
8. Among the members, there is no significant difference in the preference to books in different languages. A majority of members (84.4%) prefer to borrow more Malayalam books from the libraries than books in other languages.
9. A vast majority of the members (90.1%) do not visit other libraries to meet their information requirement.
10. The use pattern of members in different locations differs significantly to meet their reading requirements. Members in urban areas visit other libraries more frequently than those in rural areas.

Measurement of Library Use

1. There is significant difference in the frequency of visits to the library by the adult members. As many as 51.4% of members visit the public libraries more than once a week, whereas 27.1% of members are daily visitors. The frequency of visits to the library by the remaining members are low, the percentage of which varies from 12% to 0.8%.
2. There is significant difference in the frequency of visits to the library by the adult members of both genders. Male members visit the library more frequently than female members.
3. The frequency of visits to the library by the members belonging to various education groups is not significantly different. A majority of the members of different educational levels visit the library frequently.
4. There is significant difference in the frequency of visits to the public library made by the members of different occupational status. Unemployed and retired categories visit library more frequently than the students and employed groups.
5. 5. No significant difference is observed in the frequency of visits to the public library by the children of both genders. Most of them visit the library frequently.
6. More than half of the library members (55.9%) spend 1-2 hours in the public libraries, whereas the remaining members spend less than 1 hour in the public libraries.
7. Significant difference is observed in the duration of library use between men and women. Male members spend more time in the library than female members.
8. The time spent by members of different education groups is significantly different. The members having a graduate degree and post graduate/technical qualifications spend more time in the library than members having only school education.
9. The time spent by the members belonging to various occupational groups is not significantly different. Members

of various occupational levels spend almost equal time in the public library.

10. There is significant difference in the method adopted by male members and female members to locate books in the library. A majority of male members (63.4%) consult library catalogue to locate the books, whereas a majority of female members (65.5%) locate books directly from the library collection.
11. There is no significant difference in the methods of location of books in the library collection by the members of various educational levels and occupational status. A majority of the members of different education groups and occupational categories primarily consult the library catalogue to locate books in the library collection.

Evaluation of Services

1. On the whole, less than half of the adult members (49.8%) rated the library collection as good, nearly one quarter of the members (24.9%) rated the collection as very good, 23.9% rated as only partly good, and the remaining small percentage of members rated it as poor or very poor.
2. The opinion of members of both genders regarding the quality of collections in the libraries is significantly different. More percentage of female members (80.4%) and comparatively less percentage of male members (73.2%) have a good opinion regarding the quality of collections in the libraries.
3. There is significant difference in the opinion of members belonging to various educational levels regarding the quality of collections in the libraries. A higher percentage of members having only school education and graduate members rated the collections in the libraries as good, whereas a higher percentage of post-graduates/technically qualified members rated the quality of collections in the libraries as only partly good.
4. The opinion regarding the quality of library collections among the members of different occupational status is not

significantly different. A majority of the members of different occupational groups have a good opinion regarding the quality of the collections in the public libraries.

5. Among the children of both genders, the difference is not significant regarding the perception on the quality of children's collections in the libraries. A majority of the child members (60.8%) have a good opinion regarding the quality of collections for children in the public libraries.
6. 6 The opinion of members of both genders regarding the adequacy of availability of books in the libraries is not significantly different. A majority of male members (78.3%) and female members (75.7%) are of the view that the books they required are only partly available in the libraries.
7. The opinion of members belonging to different education groups regarding to the adequacy of availability of books in the libraries is significantly different. The higher percentage of graduate members (81.1%) as well as post-graduates/technically qualified members (86%), and comparatively a lower percentage of school educated members (75.1%) are only partly satisfied with the availability of books in the libraries.
8. There is no significant difference in the opinion of members belonging to different occupational status regarding the adequacy of availability of books in the libraries. A majority of students (77.9%), employed (77%), unemployed (79.2%), and retired categories (81.1%) are only partly satisfied with the availability of books in the libraries.
9. The perception of child-members of both genders on the availability of children's books in the collection is not significantly different. A majority of children of both genders, male (68.5%) and female (67.6%) are of the view that their reading requirements are only partly met by the children's collections.
10. There is no significant difference in the perception of children studying in different classes on the adequacy of availability of books in the children's collection.

11. A majority of the library members are satisfied with the location of the libraries and the various physical facilities available in the libraries.
12. On the whole, a majority of the library members (63.3%) find that the classification and cataloguing system followed in the libraries are helpful to them to locate books easily; whereas for 31.8% of members, it is only partly helpful; and for 4.9% of members, it is not at all helpful.
13. There is significant difference between the perception of members of both genders regarding the helpfulness of classification and cataloguing systems followed in the libraries. The percentage of members who find that the classification and cataloguing system followed in the libraries are helpful to them to locate books easily; are more among female members (68.9%) and comparatively less among male members (61.7%).
14. There is no significant difference in the perception of members belonging to different educational levels regarding the helpfulness of classification and cataloguing system followed in the libraries. For a majority of members of different education groups, school educated (62%), graduates (65.3%), and post-graduates/technically qualified members (65.7%), the classification and cataloguing system followed in the libraries are helpful to them to retrieve the books easily.
15. The members of different occupational categories show no significant difference in their opinion regarding the helpfulness of the classification and cataloguing system followed in the libraries. A majority of members of different occupational status, students (61.7%), employed (64.6%), unemployed (61.5%), and retired (60.2%) are of the view that the classification and cataloguing system followed in the public libraries are helpful them to retrieve the books easily.
16. On the whole, many of the members (36.9%) are not fully satisfied with the method of arrangement of books in the libraries. Only a little more than half of the members

(56.7%) are satisfied with the method of arrangement of books in the libraries, and some of them (6.4%) felt dissatisfied with the unscientific organisation.

17. The opinion of members of both genders, different education levels, and various occupation groups regarding the arrangement of books in the shelves is not significantly different. A majority of the members of both genders, different education groups, and different occupational categories felt that the arrangement of books in the libraries is easy for them to locate the books they required.
18. There is no significant difference in the perception of members of both genders regarding the adequacy of number of books lent at a time. A majority of members of both genders, male (67.6%) and female (68.5%) are satisfied with the number of books issued at a time.
19. Among the members of various education groups, there is a significant difference in the perception regarding the adequacy of books issued at a time. A majority of members with only school education (69.4%), and graduate members (68.0%), whereas only 55% post-graduates/technically qualified members are satisfied with the number of books issued at a time.
20. There is no significant difference in the opinion of members of different occupational groups regarding the adequacy of number of books lent at a time. A majority of students, employed, unemployed, and retired categories are satisfied with the number of books issued at a time.
21. A vast majority of the adult members (94.3%) felt that the existing working hours of the public libraries are convenient.
22. There is no significant difference in the opinion of members of both genders regarding the convenience of working hours of the public libraries. A vast majority of male members (94%) and female members (95.4%) opined that the working hours of the public libraries are convenient.
23. A majority of members belonging to different education groups- school educated (95.4%), graduates (92.4%) and

post-graduates/technically qualified members (93.1%) felt that the working hours of the libraries are convenient.

24. The opinion of members belonging to various occupational categories regarding the convenience of working hours of the public libraries is not significantly different. A vast majority of the students (93.2%) employed (94.0%), unemployed (96%) and retired groups (98.4%) reported that the working hours of the library are convenient.
25. No significant difference is observed in the perception of child members of both genders regarding the convenience of working hours of the public libraries. A vast majority of them opined that the working hours of the public libraries are convenient for them.
26. There is no significant difference in the perception of members of both genders regarding the adequacy of total working days of the public libraries. A majority of both male members (72.5%) and female members (76.9%) are satisfied with the total working days of the public libraries.
27. There is significant difference in the perception of members belonging to various educational levels regarding the adequacy of total working days of the public libraries. The members who acquired only school education (74.6%) and graduate members (74%) are more satisfied with the total working days of the public libraries than post-graduates/ technically qualified members (63.2%).
28. There is a significant difference in the perception of members of various occupational status regarding the adequacy of total working days of the public libraries. The retired category has a high degree of satisfaction with the total working days of the public libraries than students, employed, and unemployed categories.
29. There is no significant difference in the level of awareness of various services and programmes between the members of both genders and among different education categories. A majority of them are aware of the various library services and programmes.

30. The members of different occupational groups show significant difference in the level of awareness of the various services and programmes of the public libraries. A higher percentage of employed (72.9%) and retired categories (77%) are aware of various services and progrmmes of the public libraries than the other groups of students (60.6%) and unemployed (64.8%).
31. The members of both genders show significant difference in the degree of satisfaction regarding the library services and programmes. A larger percentage of female members (87.5%) expressed their satisfaction regarding the various library services and programmes than male members (77.6%).
32. There is no significant difference in the degree of satisfaction regarding the library services and programmes among the different education groups of the members. A majority of members belonging to different educational levels - school (80.9%), graduate (76.7%), and post-graduate/technically qualified (80%) are satisfied with the various services and programmes of the public libraries.
33. There is no significant difference in the degree of satisfaction with the services and programmes of the public libraries among the members of different occupational categories. A large majority of members of different occupational groups-students (81.9%), employed (78.2%), unemployed (78.5%), and retired (85.3%) are satisfied with the various services and programmes provided by the public libraries.
34. A majority of the members have a positive attitude towards the library staff.

THE HYPOTHESES TESTED

The following are the hypotheses tested for the study:

1. The development of public libraries in Malabar is in a slow pace.
2. The existing condition of public libraries in Malabar with respect to library resources including staff, finance, technology, and physical facilities are

inadequate and not satisfactory to meet the various requirements of the users.

3. The library resources of the public libraries are not organised on a scientific way, and fast and efficient retrieval of information has not been provided to the members.
4. The various services provided by the public libraries are not effective and not efficient to meet the various needs of the users.
5. The public libraries have contributed more in fulfilling the recreational or cultural needs rather than the informational or educational requirements of the society.
6. The use of the public library resources and services by the different categories of community is very low.

The analysis of the data discussed in detail in chapter 4, 5, 6, and 7 helped to answer the basic questions raised in the study and test the tenability of each of the hypotheses. The study on the whole, substantiated hypothesis 1. The study of the genesis and development of public libraries in Malabar, as presented in chapter 4 has revealed that the development of public libraries in Malabar is in a slow pace.

The analysis of the data in chapter 5 substantiated hypothesis 2. Examination of the existing condition of the public libraries with respect to their collection, finance, staff, technological resources, and physical facilities has revealed that they are inadequate both in quantity and quality to meet the various requirements of the users.

The analysis of the data in chapter 5 also substantiated hypothesis 3. Examination of the existing methods of organisation of reading materials such as classification, cataloguing, and arrangements reveals that a vast majority of the libraries do not organise them on a scientific way, and fast and efficient retrieval of information has not been provided to the members

The analysis of the data in chapter 6 substantiated hypothesis 4. Examination of the various services provided by the public libraries show that they are not effective and efficient to meet the various needs of the users.

The study also provides ample evidence to substantiate hypothesis 5 that the public libraries under study have contributed more in fulfilling the recreational/cultural role rather than the informational/educational requirement of the society.

The analysis of the data in chapter 5 and 6 also substantiated hypothesis 6. Examination of utilisation of the library resources and various services by the public libraries by different categories of community members are less, especially by women and children.

SUGGESTIONS

The study has revealed that the quality and quantity of resources, services, and facilities in the public libraries are very far from the standards and guidelines proposed by the *IFLA/UNESCO Guidelines for Public Library Development, 2001*. They fail to meet effectively the basic functions of the public libraries for which they are established. The following suggestions have been made for the proper functioning and operations of the public libraries.

Need for a Standard

Raja Rammohun Roy Library Foundation (RRRLF), Kolkatta established by the Government of India for the development of public libraries in India, in collaboration with all the State library authorities and library associations should develop public library standards and guidelines considering all its aspects.

The *IFLA/UNESCO Guidelines for Public Library Development, 2001* can be used as a base for the formulation of the standards.

Role of Governments

The role of governments in the development of public libraries is stressed in the UNESCO Seminar on Public Library Development held in Africa in 1962 at the University of Nigeria. It has recommended that "the government should be asked to include the development of public libraries as an integral part of the general educational development plan of the country."[1] Likewise the Government of India/Kerala should take the following steps:

1. The State and Central governments should recognise public libraries as national assets and should provide adequate funds and facilities for the proper development of them.
2. In Kerala Public Libraries (Granthasala Sanghom) Act, 1989; there is a provision for an amount of not more than 1% of total education budget to be set apart for public libraries. Since this amount is meagre, it is suggested that the State government should raise their grant at least to 5% of the total education budget for the public libraries.
3. The library network should be designed at State level by linking State central library, district central libraries, research and special libraries by the State government.
4. The three tiers of local administrative units should include public libraries in their development priorities and should extend adequate support for their proper development.

Real Leadership

The three tier library authorities at State, district, and taluk level; library committees; and librarians have a prime role in the public library development. The library under real leadership can become an active and effective education centre. The role of the library councils should be extended to the following.

1. The State Library Council as the apex administrative body has a crucial role in the establishment of uniform library procedures within the State.
2. The State Library Council should take steps to develop comprehensive library software suitable for public libraries which can accommodate Malayalam language with the help of government agencies.

3. The State Library Council may take the initiative to prepare a union catalogue of books in the public libraries and this should be updated periodically.
4. The State Library Council should endeavour to establish more libraries in the rural areas.
5. Strategies should be employed by the State Library Council to cultivate a reading habit among rural populace especially in women and children.
6. The State library authority should make a separate allocation in the budget to enable the staff of the public libraries to get training in information and communication technology.
7. The library councils at different levels and librarians themselves should create awareness among the public about the importance of the public library and its services through user education programmes.

Free Public Library Service

1. Public library service should be free to provide access to all irrespective of their economic status, otherwise a nominal fee of not more than Rs.10/- for adults as membership fee can be collected.

District Central Library

1. Each district should have a district central library with a lending division, a good reference and periodical section, and Internet facility. It should be kept open for 12 hours or more and be operated by adequate professionally qualified staff.
2. The collections in the district central library should include special materials such as Braille, tapes, films, slides, CDs, DVDs, and Floppies.

Collection Development

1. The library should provide a wide range of standard reading materials in all formats such as books, pamphlets, newspapers, periodicals, Internet, CDs, DVDs, and films.

2. The books in the non-fiction collection in wide ranges of subjects and fiction of worthy titles should be provided in adequate number to meet the different needs of today's society.
3. It should have up to date reference books on all subjects to satisfy the different queries of people.
4. All libraries should include some scholarly journals covering different subjects especially on current topics to meet the educational needs of the students.
5. Library collection should include information bulletin about the programmes and policies of the executive departments of the government and should act as a liaison agent between the community and government departments.
6. It should serve as a heritage library with documents on arts, history, literature, culture and such others.
7. It should have a special collection for children, women, students, neo-literates, career guidance, and visually and hearing impaired.
8. A book selection committee with language and subject experts as its members should be constituted for selecting standard books.
9. Each public library system should require a written collection management policy, endorsed by the library committee.
10. Weeding out of old and unused materials should be ensured to maintain the collection alive.

Access to the Collection

1. The public library should provide open access so as to ensure optimum utilisation of the library collection.

Library Staff

1. The librarian should understand the objectives and improved work methods of the public libraries so as to provide effective service to community.

2. The librarian should have interactions with user groups in encouraging and guiding the users in the use of libraries and be fully acquainted with the book collection in the library.
3. The librarian should improve their proficiency by acquiring professional qualification and update their knowledge by attending training programmes, seminars, and workshops.
4. The government salary scale should be introduced for the professional and semi professional staff and status, and working conditions should be enhanced to improve the standard of service.

Physical Facilities

1. For effective library service, the library should have a well situated building with sufficient space for reading and for stacking, proper lighting and ventilation facility, clean and congenial atmosphere.
2. It should provide sufficient number of standard furniture for the users, for stacking, and other purposes.

Access to Service

1. It should have sufficient working hours convenient to the users and should be kept open on Sundays, and other holidays except a few national holidays.

Computerisation

1. Computer service should be gradually introduced in the following areas of library operation such as house keeping, acquisition, cataloguing, bibliographical services, circulation, and serial control.
2. Internet facility should be provided to the members to enable them to access the world wide information and it should be free to all citizens.
3. Raja Rammohun Roy Library Foundation and Kerala State Library Council may provide special funds for the computerisation of the public libraries.

Co-operation with Other Organisation

1. The library should take part in the programmes of civic, cultural, and educational organisations.
2. The library should require the co-operation and co-ordination with the government agencies for rendering information and referral services.
3. Co-operation between independent libraries in sharing their services and materials will be extended to meet the full needs of users.

Effective and Efficient Services

1. The library service should be adapted to the different needs of the communities in the rural and the urban areas.
2. The lending service, the technical organisation of reading materials such as classification, cataloguing, and shelf arrangement of books should be based on scientific method to improve the standard of library service.
3. A well-equipped and organised children's library should form an integral part of every public library and different programmes such as story hours, film shows, contests, and puppet shows should be organised for their creative development. Their collection should be on all formats and subjects.
4. The libraries should have an important role both in formal and informal education by providing and improving the different activities and services through adult education, act as academic study centre, supporting distance education, providing text book collection and such other services.
5. Service to schools should include talks in schools and in parent-teacher association meetings, instruction in library use, the loan of material for school projects, provision of special library facilities for teachers, book mobiles to the schools, provision of a public library corner at schools under a student in charge and such others.

6. Mobile library service and rural book deposit centers should be provided especially to the disadvantaged sections of the community.
7. The public libraries should provide çommunity information service to ensure access for citizens to all sorts of community information.
8. Service should be provided to special groups such as in patients of hospitals, prisoners, old people, and other disadvantaged groups such as blind and mentally handicapped people.

Publicity and Extension Activities

1. Publicity and extension activities such as seminars, workshops, lectures, and film shows should be a service for every public library to serve the primary purpose of converting non-users to users and to obtain optimum use of services and collections.
2. Display of newly arrived books at prime location; effective interior and exterior sign posting; circulation of library brochures, annual reports and library publications such as resource lists are important publicity programmes.
3. Inter library loan, an effective extension activity to maximise the use of books should be provided in the libraries.
4. Reader's forums should be formed by each library for the participation in various activities to make the members more active.
5. Day-care centers, nursery schools, tuition centers, short term computer courses, classes for different art forms such as dance, music, painting etc. can be started as extension activities of the library.
6. Since educational and social backwardness of women still persists, the library should concentrate more for the development and empowerment of women.

Cultural Activities

1. The public libraries should support various cultural activities in the community by providing accommodation, giving publicity, and organising cultural and recreational activities for the enhancement of social, physical, and mental development of the public.

Evaluation

1. All programmes and services of the public libraries should be evaluated by the library authorities on a regular basis to ascertain whether they are:
   - Achieving the objectives and declared goals of the library,
   - Able to meet changing needs,
   - In need of improvement, and
   - Adequately resourced.
2. User survey and library survey may be used to evaluate and monitor the achievements of the library's objectives and to improve the quality of service.

SUGGESTIONS OF THE LIBRARIANS

The librarians of public libraries covered in the study were requested to offer suggestions for the improvement of their respective libraries. Their key suggestions are analysed and the results are presented as follows: The highest percentage of librarians (56.9%) have suggested for an enhanced library grant and librarians' allowance, 54% of them for adequate physical facilities including functional library building, furniture and such others, 43.1% of them for more qualitative collection, 32.1% of them for computerisation of the library and provision of internet facility to the users, 19% of them for conducting library awareness programme to the public, 14.6% of them for organising various cultural programmes. A small percentage of them have offered many other useful suggestions such as scientific organisation of books, separate grants for children's section, appointment of full time librarians, provision of modern equipments, a well functioning children's section and women's section, mobile library service, participation in various social activities, function as an information centre, co-operate with schools, more working hours, free library service, user education programmes, and open access for more improved library performance. The suggestions made by the librarians from their personal experience are valuable and deserve special attention. Library authorities of six districts also reported that adequate funds and full time librarians are necessary for the proper development of the libraries.

FUTURE OF THE PUBLIC LIBRARIES IN KERALA

The analysis of the strength and weakness of the resources and the past performances provide meaningful inputs to take better decisions in planning the future of the public libraries. On the basis of the data obtained in the study, and also considering the changing concept of public libraries in the present knowledge based society and technological advancement, the future of the public libraries in Kerala are discussed under six headings. Since socio-economic and cultural status of the people in Kerala is almost the same, the study in Malabar is taken as representative of all areas in Kerala.

Electronic Resources

The books have for centuries been the primary channel for the distribution of knowledge and culture. The use of Information Technology brings changes in the communication of knowledge in the society. The future generation will not depend on books for purposes of academic study or knowledge, or leisure. The future public libraries will include books and electronic resources such as internet, CDs, and DVDs. The new medium has given a scope for more efficient means of storage, maintenance, and quick access from remote places.

Computer Based Value Added Services

In future, the public libraries will become attractive by the introduction of new services based on new technology.

Libraries offering traditional services are likely to face increasing competition from new technology and new media. The computerised library services and operations will enhance the effectiveness and efficiency of library services and can provide value added services to the society.

Public Library Network

The public libraries should provide access to its own resources and to those of other libraries through the participation in an electronic network at the local, State, and national level. Through the network, the public libraries can provide the widest possible access to the vast resources of the public libraries.

New Role of Public Libraries

In the present society, where knowledge and information have a crucial role, technological advancement dominates all services, the public libraries have to play new roles in the society. In future, the public libraries will be key information and learning centres in the community. Information revolution and information technology brought about sweeping change in the character and scope of Community Information Service (Sarada 2000).[2] Digital revolution is an opportunity for the undeveloped countries for bridging the gap in access to information across the world (Ramaiah and Ramachander 2000).[3]

Highly Qualified and Skilled Librarians

In the context of changing concepts of public libraries, librarians should be highly qualified and skilled to handle the application of Information and Communication Technology in the libraries. There will be a change in the role of the librarian in the new technological environment. Librarians can act as an effective interface between users and technology. Gaddagimath and Suresh (2000)[4] listed out the following paradigm shifts that the librarians have to face in an ever-changing society:

- Transition from print to electronic media.
- Passive user to active user.

- Demand for accountability on the part of the librarian.
- Concept of networked environment.
- Individual to team work.

Strategic Planning

In the context of the fast changing society and technology, strategic planning is becoming an important management tool for the successful management of public libraries. In this process, the present position of the libraries are analysed and based on the changing concepts of public libraries, decisions are made for the designed future. Balasubramanian (2006)[5] defined it as "the determination of basic long-term goals and objectives of the enterprise and adoption of courses of action and the allocation of resources necessary for carrying out these goals." At present the administrative authorities or library committees do not make any successful planning to meet their goals and objectives. Strategic planning is important to provide effective and efficient library services.

The fore-going remarks provide perspectives for visualising a public library with new dimensions. The provision of Information and Communication Technology (ICT) in public libraries in Kerala will provide a crucial development in the libraries and they will be placed at the central place of the emerging Cyber Kerala Society.

AREAS FOR FURTHER RESEARCH

1. An evaluative study on the current status of public libraries in terms of resources, services and facilities in other parts of the State can be conducted.
2. A survey of the reading habits of users of public libraries in the State can be carried out to determine the cross-sectional and cross-disciplinary interests.
3. The Historical survey of public libraries in the State shall be an interesting topic of heritage value.
4. A perspective plan for computerisation of the public libraries in the State shall be a useful topic.

5. An in-depth analytical study of the finance of the public libraries in the State can be taken as a research topic.
6. The impact of the library Act on the growth and development of public libraries in the State can be studied.
7. The role of public libraries in national and political movements can be studied.
8. Library services on different rural areas and urban settings can be studied to find out how effective it is to meet the various needs of the community.
9. An examination of the role of the public libraries in education and information can be undertaken to suggest ways and means to improve their services.
10. Public library community service such as adult education service, literacy activities can be studied to find whether they meet the social objectives.
11. The analysis of the reading habits of adult non-users of the public libraries is a useful study to convert them into active members.
12. An in-depth study on the various problems faced by the public libraries in the State to suggest valuable solutions.

CONCLUSION

Public library is a dynamic social institution which has many important roles in upgrading the status of people in the society. A well developed public library can fulfil the objectives of prosperity and the development of society.

The historical survey carried out to explore the genesis and development of public librairies in Malabar shows that the special characteristic feature of the public library movement in Malabar is that it is a mass movement. The library association which came to be known as Kerala Granthasala Sanghom has an important role in the growth of public libraries in Malabar. Under the control and management of Kerala State Library Council formed under the Kerala Public Libraries Act, there is alertness in the public library functions and services. The study undertaken on the existing condition of the public libraries revealed that their functions and operations are not satisfactory and cannot meet the changing needs of the community. Malabar is predominantly rural in character. But the role of public libraries has not been realized much in the rural areas as compared to the urban areas.

A vast majority of public libraries in Malabar are under resourced in terms of collection, finance, staff, and physical facilities. So they cannot provide effective and efficient services to their users. A lion's share of the collection is in print-media and books are mainly fiction. Most of the collection is not in a satisfactory standard. The reading materials are not organised scientifically. No libraries spend optimum on reading materials and staff. A majority of the staff in the libraries are not professional or semi-professional. A majority of the library buildings are not functionally useful. The physical facilities are also not satisfactory and cannot provide even adequate seating arrangements for their users. A negligible number of libraries are computerised and provide internet facility to the users. Even though the literacy rate of Malabar is very high, there is a low library consciousness among the public.

The educational, informational, and social functions of the libraries have been completely neglected. They are mainly acting as a recreational centre and have failed to make a significant impact in the national development process. The peculiar needs of the public were not reflected in the library collections and services of the libraries. Therefore the impact of the public libraries on the society was marginal. The public libraries do not cope with the changing needs of the society and with the advancement of information technology. Thus it can be concluded that the present scenario of public libraries in Malabar does not give an encouraging picture.

The current state of decline of public libraries is not merely due to various socio-economic factors, but due to the lack of awareness among the public about the importance of public libraries in the society and the non-inclusion of libraries in the government's development priorities. The public library development is the collective responsibility of the central, State, local governments, and voluntary organisations. The government should include public libraries in their development priorities and this will help the emergence of new strategies and provision of adequate support for the establishment of a well developed public library system in the State.

References

1. UNESCO (1962), Proceedings of the Seminar on Public Library Development, at University of Nigeria, Africa.
2. Sarada, K. (2000), Community Information Services and Internet. In *Vision of Future Library and Information Systems*. Ed. Ashok Babu et al., 26- 29. New Delhi: Viva Books, 28.
3. Ramaiah, L. S. and Ramachander, M. (2000), The Information Divide: Need for Internet Kiosks in Indian Villages for Building the Gap. In *Vision of Future Library and Information Systems*. Ed. Ashok Babu *et al.*, 50-58. New Delhi: Viva Books, 51.
4. Gaddagimath, R. B. and Suresh Jange (2000), Changing Librarians: Competencies and Challenges for University Librarians. In *Vision of Future Library and Information Systems*. Ed. Ashok Babu *et al.*, 14-18. New Delhi: Viva Books, 14.
5. Balasubramanian, P. *et al.* (2006), "Strategic Planning: A Tool for Future Libraries." *SRELS Journal of Information Management*, 43, No. 3 (September): 219-224.
6. Kerala (2001), Information and Communication Technology: Draft IT policy, *http://itforum.kerala.gov.in/site/modules/content/?id/=1*, accessed on March 1, 2007.
7. IFLA/UNESCO (2001), *The Public Library Service: IFLA/UNESCO Guidelines for Development*. Prepared Philip Gill *et al.* Munchen: K. G. Saur, Sec. 3. 8.

BIBLIOGRAPHY

(Based on The Chicago Manual of Style, 15th Ed.)

Allred, John R. "The Purpose of the Public Library: The Historical View." In *Public Library Purpose: A Reader*, edited by Barry Totterdell, 25-31. London: Clive Bingley, 1978.

American Library Association. Public Library Division. Co-ordinating Committee on Revision of Public Library Standards. Public Library Service: A Guide to Evaluation with Minimum Standards. Chicago: ALA, 1956.

American Library Association. *Public Library Service*. Chicago: ALA, 1956.

Amudhavalli, A. and B. P. Sanjay. "Community Information and Public Libraries in the Indian Context." In *Education through Public Libraries: A Practical Approach*. Proceedings of the national seminar on Public Library Movement, Madras, April 19-21, 1991, edited by C. Palanivelu and K. S. Raghavan, 216-223. Madras: Government of Tamil Nadu. Directorate of Public Libraries, 1991.

Anis Khurshid. "City Public Library System for Karachi Metropolis." *Library Herald* 36, No.3 (October- December 1998): 135-151.

Aslam, M. "Rural Libraries in India: As Community Information Centres." *Granthana* 5, Nos.1 & 2 (July 1998): 139-146.

Astbury, Raymond. "The Public Library of the Twenty First Century: The Key Information and Learning Centre in the Community." *Libri* 44, No.2 (1994): 131.

Asundi, A. Y. "Public Library as Community Information Centre: A New Perspective on Renewal of its Role." In *Education through Public Libraries: A Practical Approach*. Proceedings of the national seminar on Public Library Movement, Madras, April 19-21, 1991, edited by C. Palanivelu and K. S. Raghavan, 381-387. Madras: Government of Tamil Nadu, Directorate of Public Libraries, 1991.

Augustine, C. A. and G. Devarajan, ed. *Public Library System in India.* New Delhi: Ess Ess Publications, 1990.

Balakrishnan, A. *Kesariyude Mukhaprasangangal* (Malayalam). Kottayam: D.C. Books, 1989.

Balasubramanian, P. et al. "Strategic Planning: A Tool for Future Libraries." *SRELS Journal of Information Management* 43, No. 3 (September 2006): 219-224.

Balan, C. ed. *Reflections on Malabar: Society, Institutions, and Culture.* Kanhangad: The Post Graduate Department of History, 2000.

Bandy, Alan. "Essential Connections: School and Public Libraries for Lifelong Learning." *Australian Library Journal* 51, No.1 (February 2002), *http://alia.org. au/ publishing/alj/51.1/full text/essential* connections.html.

Barber, Elsa et al. "Information Society and Information Technology: The Situation at the Public Libraries in Buenos Aires City and Surrounding Areas, Argentina." *International Information and Library Review* 38, No.1 (March 2000): 1-14.

Barry, Totterdell: "Public Libraries in a Changing Society." In *Public Library Policy,* edited by K. C. Harrison, 37-42. New York: K.G. Saur, 1981.

Barua, B. P. *National Policy on Library and Information Systems and Services for India.* Bombay: Popular Prakashan, 1992.

Bhaskara Panicker, P.T. "Granthasala Sanghavum Saksharatha Padhathiyum." In *Keralathile Granthasala Prasthanam* (Malayalam), edited by P. N. Panicker, 235-240. Trivandram: Steps, 1982.

Bhatt, R. K. *History and Development of Libraries in India.* New Delhi: Mittal Publications, 1995.

Bhatt, S. C. *The Encyclopaedic District Gazetteers of India.*Vol.2. New Delhi: Gyan Publishing House, 1998.

Bhatt, S.C. and Gopal K.Bhargava. Land and People of Indian States and Union Territories: Kerala. Vol. 14. Delhi: Kalpaz, 2005.

Bouri, Elizebeth N. "Public Libraries Development Reconsidered: The Case of Egypt." *International Information and Library Review* 26 (1994): 151-168.

Brooks, Terrence A. "Naive vs. Sophisticated Methods of Forecasting Public Library Circulation." *Library and Information Science Research* 6 (1984): 205-214.

Brown, Anita. "Reference Services for Children: Information Needs and Wants in the Public Library." *Australian Library Journal* 53, No. 3 (August 2004), *http://alia.org.au/ publishing /alj/53.3/full.text/ brown.html.*

Carnovsky, Leon, ed. *The Public Library in the Urban Setting*. Chicago: The University of Chicago Press, 1968.

Chandraiah, I. "Circulation Libraries: A Study." *Granthana* 4, No. 1&2 (January & July 1993): 37- 40.

Cherian, P. J. *Perspectives on Kerala History: The Second Millennium, Kerala State Gazetteer*. Trivandrum: Government of Kerala, Kerala Gazetteers, 1999.

Childers, Thomas and Nancy A.Van House. *The Public Library Effectiveness*. Washington, D.C: Department of Education, 1989.

Coleman, Pat. "Past to Future. The Public Library's Changing Role." In *Information Communities*, edited by Margaret Kinnel. New Castle, U.K.: Community Service Group of the Library Association, 1992.

Cole, Natalie. "The Influence of Attitudes on Public Library Stock Management Practice." *Libri* 50, No. 1 (March 2000): 37-47, *http:/ /lirijournal.org/2000-1 toc.html.*

D'Elia, George. "The Development and Testing of a Conceptual Model of Public Library User Behavior." *Library Quarterly* 50, No. 4 (1980): 410-430.

D'Elia, George and Sandra Walsh. "Patron's Uses and Evaluations of Library Services: A Comparison across Five Public Libraries." *Library and Information Science Research* 7 (1985): 3-30.

Damanpour, Fariborz. "The Adoption of Innovations in Public Libraries." *Library and Information Science Research* 7 (1985): 231-246.

Danish Public Libraries Act, 1964.

Das, I. V. "Kerala State Library Council, Kerala Granthasala Sanghom" (Malayalam). In *Seminar Report of Kerala State Library Council, Palakkad, 1997.*

Deshpande, K. S. "Public Libraries: Community Fountain of Information, Education, and Culture." *SRELS Journal of Information Management* 37, No. 3 (September 2000): 165-182.

Deshpande, K. S. and B. B. Hungund. "RRRLF and its Role in Galvanising the Public Library Movement in India." *Herald of Library Science* 40, No. 1-2 (2001): 46-57.

Devendra Thakur. *Research Methodology in Social Sciences*. New Delhi: Deep and Deep, 1998.

Diarmid, Errett W. John Mc. *The Administration of the American Public Library*. New York: ALA and University of Illinois Press, 1943.

Dilip M. Menon. *Caste, Nationalism, and Communism in South India: Malabar, 1900-1948*. New Delhi: Foundation Books, 1994.

Doll, Carol A. "A Study of Overlap and Duplication among Children's Collections in Selected Public and Elementary School Libraries." *Library Quarterly* 54, No. 3 (1984): 277 - 289.

Dutch, Martin and Dave Muddiman. "The Public Library, Social Exclusion, and the Information Society in United Kingdom." *Libri* 51(2001): 183-194, *http://librijournal.org* / 2001-4 toc.html.

EK. "Nirakshraraya Krishikkar" (Malayalam). *Prabhatham*, January 11, 1939.

Ekbote, Gopal Rao. *Public Libraries System*. Hyderabad: Ekbote Brothers, 1987.

Ellis, Alec. "Public Library Services for Children in England and Wales." Journal of Librarianship 2, No. 2 (April 1970): 99-105.

Eve, Juliet and Peter Brophy. "Vital Issues: The Perception, and Use of ICT Services in UK Public Libraries." *LIBRES (Library and Information Science Research Electronic Journal)* 10, No. 2 (September 2000), *http://libres.curtin.edu.au/libres10n2 /vital.html.*

Feather, John and Paul Sturges. *International Encyclopedia of Information and Library Science*. London: Routledge, 1997.

Finnish Library Act, 1998. In *Public Library Service: IFLA/UNESCO Guidelines for Development*, 89- 99. Munchen: K.G. Saur, 2001.

Gaddagimath, R. B. and Suresh Jange. "Changing Libraries: Competencies and Challenges for University Librarians." In *Vision of Future and Information Systems*, edited by Ashok Babu et al., 14-18. New Delhi: Viva Books, 2000.

Ganesh K.N. *Keralathinte Innalakal* (Malayalam). Rev.ed. Trivandram: Government of Kerala, Department of Cultural Publications, 1997.

Gans, Herbert J. "Supplier Oriented and User Oriented Planning for the Public Library." In *Public Library Purpose: A Reader*, edited by Barry Totterdell, 71-83. London: Clive Bingley, 1978.

George K. M. "The Malayalis: The People their History and Culture." Vol. 4 of *Malayali Social and Cultural Life*. New Delhi: Cosmo Publications, 2002.

Goldhor, Herbert. "Experimental Effects on the Choice of Books Borrowed by Public Adult Patrons." *Library Quarterly* 51, No. 3 (July 1981): 253-268.

___."The Effect of Prime Display Location of Public Library Circulation of Selected Adult Titles." *Library Quarterly* 42, No. 4 (October 1972): 371-389.

Goswamy, I. M., ed. *Encyclopaedia of Library and Information Science: Development of Library and Information Science*. Vol. 5. New Delhi: Common Wealth Publications, 1997.

Goudy, Frank Wm. "General Revenue Sharing and Public Libraries: An Estimate of Fiscal Impact." *Library Quarterly* 52, No.1 (1982): 1-20.

Granthalokam, editorial 14, No. 1(January 1962).

Griebel, Rosemary. "Partnering Services between Public Libraries and Library Services for the Blind: A Canadian Experience." Proceedings of sixty sixth IFLA council and general conference, Jerusalem, Israel, 13-18 August, 1995. *http://www.ifla.org. (accessed* March 21, 2001).

Groom, Harold A. *Manual of Practical Book Selection for public Libraries*. London: Crafton, 1939.

Guruswamy Naidu, N. *Public Library Finances*. New Delhi: Ess Ess Publications, 1990.

Hamsath, K. 1979. "Public Libraries in Union Territory of Lakshadweep." In Souvenir of twenty fifth all India library conference, Trivandrum, 14-18 May 1979, 141-142.

Hanif Uddin. "The Role of Rural Libraries in the Rural Development of Bangladesh." *IASLIC Bulletin* 45, No. 3 (2000): 97-104.

Hari Sharma, A.D. "Keralathile Pathrapravarthanam: Praramba Kaalam." In *Kerala Granthasala Directory* (Malayalam), 27. Trivandram: Granthasala Sanghom, 1964.

Hennen, Thomas J. "Great American Public Libraries." *American Libraries* (October 2005): 42-48. *http://www.ala.org/al-online* Templatafm?section=october 2005 (accessed January 30, 2006).

IFLA/UNESCO. *Public Library Manifesto, 1994.* The Hague: IFLA. *http://www.unesco. org. (accessed* June 1, 2005).

IFLA/UNESCO. Section of Public Libraries. *Public Library Service: IFLA/UNESCO Guidelines for Development.* Munchen: K.G. Saur, 2001.

Ikoja-Odongo, J. R. "Public Library Politics: The Ugandan Perspective." *Information Development* 20, No. 3 (2004): 169 - 180.

India. Committee on National Policy on Library and Information System (NAPLIS). *Report, 1986.*

India. Ministry of Education and Youth Services. Advisory Committee for Libraries. *Report, 1959.*

India. Planning Commission. Working Group on Libraries and Informatics. "Report of the Sub-Group on Public Library System for the formulation of the 8th Five Year Plan," convened by D. R. Kalia. *CLIS Observer* 13, No. 1-2 (January - June 1986): 27-34.

Innes, C. A. *Madras District Gazetteers.*Vol.1. Madras: Government of Madras, 1951.

Isaac, K.A. "Keralathile Granthasala Prasthanam." In *Kerala Granthasala Sanghom Rajatha Jubilee Souvenir* (Malayalam), 103-111. Trivandrum: Kerala Granthasala Sanghom, 1971.

Jagnayak, S.S. "Public Library Development in India: An Historical Perspective since 1947." In *Fifty Years of Indian Librarianship*, edited by G. Devarajan, 41-74. New Delhi: Ess Ess Publications, 1999.

Job, M. M. "Public Libraries in Ethiopia." *Herald of Library Science* 29, No. 3-4 (July-October 1990): 173-179.

Jogesh Misra. *History of Libraries and Librarianship in Modern India since 1850.* Delhi: Atma Ram, 1979.

John, P. A. and V.K.G. Nair. "Public Library Movement in Kerala." In Proceedings of twenty fifth all India library conference, Trivandrum, 14-18 May 1979, 161-167.

Johnson, Alvin. *The Public Library: A People's University.* New York: American Association for Adults, 1938.

Jones, Arthur. "Criteria for the Evaluation of Public Library Services." *Journal of Librarianship* 2, No. 4 (October 1970): 228-241.

Jones, David J. "Critical Issues in Public Library Planning: The New South Wales Experience." *Australian Library Journal* 53, No. 4 (November 2004), *http://alia.org.au/publishing/alj/53.4/full text/jones.html.*

___. "Public Library Development in New South Wales." *The Australian Library Journal* 54, No. 2 (May 2005), *http://www.alia.org.au/publishing/alj/54.2/full text /jones. html.*

Joseph, P.J. "The Library Movement of Kerala." Vol. 3 of Abstracts of International congress on Kerala Studies, Trivandrum, 27-29 August 1994. Trivandrum: AKG Centre for Research and Studies, 1994.

Kalia, D. R. " A Review of State Public Library System in India" *CLIS Observer* 15, No. 1-2 (1998): 46-51.

Kalia, D.R., et.al. "Guidelines for Public Library Systems and Services." *Granthana* 2, No. 1 (January 1991): 31- 84.

Kannan, R., ed. "*Library Movement in India. After Independence: Problems and Prospects.*" Proceedings of the national seminar, Chennai, Tamil Nadu, 5-6 April 1999. Madras: Directorate of Public Libraries, 1995.

Kannappavar, B.U. and C. R. Bhat. "Integration of Rural Library Services with Adult Education and Illiteracy Eradication." Paper presented at fortieth all India library conference, Goa, January, 5-8, 1995.

Kar P.K. "Users' Reading Habits and Satisfaction in Public Libraries: A Sociological Exploration in Some Select Towns of Orissa." *Indian Journal of Information, Library and Society* 9, No. 3-4 (July–December 1996): 240-245.

Karisiddappa, C. R. "Application of Modern Technology to Public Libraries." *Granthana* 6, Nos. 1-2 (January 1999): 113-123.

Keenan, Stella, Nick Moore, and Anthony Oulton. "On-line Information Services in Public Libraries." *Journal of Librarianship* 13, No. 1 (January 1981): 9-24.

Kelly, Thomas. *Books for the People: An Illustrated History of the British Public Library*. London: Andre Deutsh, 1977.

___. *Early Public Libraries*. London: The Library Association, 1966.

Kerala Gazette, February 15, 1991.

Kerala Granthasala Sanghom. "Granthasala Sanghom: Oru Laghu Charithram" (Malayalam). In *Kerala Granthasala Sanghom Silver Jubilee Souvenir, 1971,* 21-52.

Kerala. Department of Economics and Statistics. *Kerala Economy, 2003.*

Kerala. Directorate of Census Operations. *Census of India 2001, series 33 Kerala.*

Kerala. Gazette, XXX (November 1, 1985).

Kerala. Information and Communication Technology: Draft IT Policy, *http://itforum.kerala. gov.in/site/modules/content/?id/=1.*

Kerala Public Libraries Act, 1989.

Kerala. State Planning Board. *Onpatham Paddhathi Panchayath Vikasana Rekha, 1996, Mattul Panchayath* (Malayalam). Vol.140. Trivandram: State Planning Board, 1997.

___. *Onpatham Paddhathi Panchayath Vikasana Rekha, 1996: Kodiyeri Panchayath* Malayalam). Vol.145. Trivandrum: State Planning Board. 1997.

___. *Onpatham Paddhathi Panchayath Vikasana Rekha, 1996:* Hosdurg (Malayalam). Trivandram: State Planning Board, 1997.

Kesavan, B.S. *Indian National Library*. Calcutta: National Library, 1961.

Khaiser Jahan Begum and Remesh, C. P. "Factors Inhibiting the Public Library Use." In *Education through Public Libraries: A Practical Approach*. Proceedings of the national seminar on Public Library Movement, Madras, April 19-21, 1991, edited by C. Palanivelu and K. S. Raghavan, 332-343. Madras: Directorate of Public Libraries, 1991.

Khan, H. A. "Role of Rural Libraries in the Promotion of Literacy and Adult Education." *Granthana* 2, No. 2 (July 1991): 135-144.

Kodiyeri Public Library, Thalassery Souvenir Committee. "Pinnitta Ara Noottaand: Oru Samkshipta Avalokanam." In *Kodiyeri Public Library Golden Jubilee Souvenir, 1986* (Malayalam), 129-136.

Kothari, C. R. *Research Methodology: Methods and Techniques*. 2nd ed. New Delhi: Wishwa Prakashan, 1990.

Krishna Kurup, Madhuravanam C. "Granthalaya Prasthanam: Innaleyum Naaleyum" (Mal). *Grandhalokam* 12, No. 2 (February 1960.): 71-75.

___. *Keralathile Granthalaya Prasthanam*. Kozhikode: Kerala Granthalaya Sanghom, 1946.

Krishnan, K.V, Secretary, Sree Narayana Guru Library, Achamthuruthi. Interview by Investigator. Achamthuruthi, Kasaragod, 3 April 2001.

Kumaran, T. C. Interview by Investigator. Kakkad, Kannur, 15 August 2001.

Kumbar, Mallinath, and B. S Biradar. "Use of Mass Media and Public Library by the Rural Community: A Study." *Annals of Library Science and Documentation* 44, No. 3 (1997): 86-92.

Kunhan Pillai, Elamkulam. *Studies in Kerala History*. Trivandrum: The Author, 1970.

___. "Nammude Granthasala Prasthanathinte Adigattam." In *Kerala Granthasala Sanghom Rajatha Jubilee Souvenir, 1971*(Malayalam), 44-48, 52.

Kunhiraman Master, Kundanjeri. "Enpathirandu Decemberinthe Adya Saniyazhcha" (Malayalam). Interview by T. Prasad. In *Eranholi Yuvajana Club Library and Reading Room, Thalassery Silver Jubilee Souvenir, 1983.*

Kutty Master, V. P. Interview by Investigator. Vadakara, Thalassery, 22 May 2004.

Larkin-Lieffers, Patricia A. "The Older Adult and Public Library Computer Technology: A Pilot Study in a Canadian Setting." *Libri* 50, No. 4 (December 2000): 225-234, http: / / librijournal.org/pdf/ 2000-4 toc.html.

Laxman Rao, N. and N. Ratna Rao. "Role of Public Libraries in National and Social Movements in Pre-Independent India: A Study with Reference to Andhra Pradesh." Vol.1of *Public Library Systems: Services and Networking*, edited by L.S.Ramaiah, et al. 258-260. New Delhi: Ess Ess Publications, 1997.

Lenin, K.M. "Malabarilekku." In *Keralathile Granthasala Prasthanam* (Malayalam), edited by P. N. Panicker, 139-144. Trivandram: Steps, 1982.

___. "Nineteen Forty Five Muthal Control Board Vare." In *Keralathile Granthasala Prasthanam* (Malayalam), edited by P. N. Panicker, 297-300. Trivandram: Steps, 1982.

___. "Randam Sammelanam." In *Keralathile Granthasala Prasthanam* (Malayalam), edited by P. N. Panicker, 71-78. Trivandram: Steps, 1982.

___. "Sanghathinte Ghadana." In *Keralathile Granthasala Prasthanam* (Malayalam), edited by P. N. Panicker, 171-178. Trivandram: Steps, 1982.

___. "S.P.S.S.mayulla Bandham." In *Keralathile Granthasala Prasthanam* (Malayalam), edited by P. N. Panicker, 132-134. Trivandram: Steps. 1982.

Leong, Ivan Chew Boon and Susan E. Higgins. "Public Library Services for Wheelchair-bound Young People in Singapore." *LIBRES (Library and Information Science Research Electronic Journal)* 12, No. 1 (March 2002.), http://libres.curtin. edu.au/libres12n1.

Library Association (London). Public Libraries Research Group. "Public Library Aims and Objectives." *Library Association Record* 73, No. 12 (December 1971).

Local Library Authority, Cannanore. Minutes Book, 1959-1964.

Local Library Authority, Kozhikode. Minutes Book, 1959.

___. Minutes Book, 1965.

___. Minutes Book, 1973.

___. Minutes Book, 1977.

___. Minutes, May 24, 1959.

Local Library Authority, Malabar. Minutes, August 6, 1950.

___. Minutes Book, 1950.

___. Minutes Book, 1952-1956.

___. Minutes, July 15, 1952.

Logan, William. *Malabar*. Vol.1. New Delhi: Asian Educational Services, 1995.

Lynch, Beverly and Wenxiang Yang. "Evaluation of Public Libraries: The 2001 IFLA Standards and the 2003 Standards for Provincial Libraries in China." *Libri* 54 (2004): 179-189.

Lynch, Mary Jo. "Reference Interviews in Public Libraries." 48, No. 2 (April 1978): 119-142.

Madhava Menon, T., ed. *A Handbook of Kerala*. Vol.1. Trivandrum: International School of Dravidian Languages, 2000.

Madras Public Libraries Act, 1948 (Madras Act XXIV of 1948), and the Rules made there under.

Malabar Gazetteer (Malayalam). Vol. 3. Madras: Government of Madras, 1935.

Malabar Vayanasala Conference: Vayanasalakal Parishkarikkuvan Chila Nirdeshangal (Malayalam). *Mathrubhumi*, June13, 1937, Kozhikode edition.

Malabar Vayanasala Conference (Malayalam). *Mathrubhumi,* April 20, 1937, Kozhikode edition.

Malarvele Ilangovan and Susan E. Higgins. "Library Provision to the Tamil Community in Singapore." *LIBRES (Library and Information Science Research Electronic Journal)* 13, No. 1 (March 2003), *http://libres.curtin.edu.au/libres 13n1.*

Mammad Koya Parappil, P. P. *Kozhikode Muslimngalude Charithram* (Malayalam). Kozhikode: Focus Publications, 1994.

Martin, Lowell A. "Standards for Public Libraries." *Library Trends* (October 1972): 164-176.

Mc Colvin, Lionel R. 'The Purpose and Values of Library Service." In *Public Library Purpose: A Rreader,* edited by Barry Totterdell, 33-37. London: Clive Blingley, 1978.

___. *The Chance to Read.* London: Phoenix House, 1956.

___. "The Purpose and Values of Library Service." In *Public Library Purpose: A Reader,* edited by Barry Totterdell, 33-37. London: Clive Blingley, 1978.

Mcharazo, Alli A.S. "Public Libraries and Distance Education in Tanzania: Issues and Dilemmas." *Libri.* 50, No. 4 (December 2000): 295-301, *http://libri journal.org/ 2000-4 toc.html.*

Meeakshi Sundaram, T. S. "Tamil Nadu Public Library Building." In *Education through Public Libraries: A Practical Approach.* Proceedings of the national seminar on Public Library Movement, Madras, April 19-21, 1991, edited by C. Palanivelu and K. S. Raghavan, 365-369. Madras: Government of Madras, Directorate of Public Libraries, 1991.

Menon, V.K.N. "The Trivandrum Public Library." In *Trivandrum Public Library Platinum Jubilee Souvenir,* edited by Rosscote Krishna Pillai, 14-17. Trivandrum: Government of Kerala. State Librarian, 1974.

Merrifield, Mark. "The Funding of Rural Libraries." *Library Trends* 44, No. 1 (summer 1995): 49-62.

Mithra, C.R. *Sree Narayana Guruvum Samuhya Viplavavum* (Malayalam), translated by C. P. Sivaraj. Kottayam: NBS, 1993.

Mukundan Master, K. Interview by Investigator. Thalassery, Kannur, 10 May 2001.

Murali Kadachira. "Mavilayi Mannile Prakashagopuram" (Malayalam). *Dheshabimani,* April 21, 1993, Kannur edition.

Murali, Pirappankod. "Keralathile Granthasala Prasthanam" (Malayalam). *Grandhalokam*. 49, No. 9 (September 1997): 45-74.

Murison, W. J. *The Public Library: Its Origin, Purpose, and Significance*. 2nd rev. ed. London: George G. Harrap, 1971.

Muthumaster, V. "Granthasalaprasthanam Palakkad Jillayil" (Malayalam). In *Kerala State Library Council Seminar Report, 1997*, 15-18.

Myhill, Christine E. "ICT for Access to Information Services for Disabled People: An Overview of Projects and Services at Gateshead Library Services." *Journal of Management* 36, No. 3 (2002): 176-181. http:// *www.emeraldinsight.com* (accessed June 29, 2005).

Nagar, Murari Lal. *Foundations of Library Movement in India*. Ludhiana: Indian Library Institute and Bibliographical Centre, 1983.

Namboothiripad, E.M.S. "Idu Oru Apoorva Prasthanam" (Malayalam). In *Grandhalokam* 49, No. 9 (September 1997): 27.

___. *How I Became a Communist*, translated by P. K. Nair. Trivandram: Chintha Publications, 1976.

___. *Keralam Malayalikalude Mathrubhumi* (Malayalam). 2nd ed. Trivandram: Kerala Libraries Cooperative Society, 1964.

Nasirudheen, T. P.O. Impact of Kerala Granthasala Sanghom on the Formulation of the Kerala Public Libraries Act, 1989. PhD thesis, University of Calicut, 2004.

Ng'ang'a, S. K. "Delivering Services to the Visually Impaired through Public Libraries: The Kenyan Experience." *Information Development* 20, No. 2 (2004): 130-133.

Nick, Moore. Measuring the Performance of Public Libraries: A Draft Manual. *Granthana* 3, nos. 2 and 3 (July 1992): 160-206.

Nikam, Khaiser and N. Rajashekara. "Reading Habits of Public Library Users: A Survey." *SRELS Journal of Information Management* 40, No. 4 (December 2003): 337-363.

Odini, Cephas. "Planning for Public Library Development in Developing Countries with Special Reference to African Countries." *Libri* 40, No. 1 (March 1990): 33-48.

Ottensmann, John R., Raymond E. Gnat, and Michael E. Gleeson. "Similarities in Circulation Patterns among Public Library Branches Serving Diverse Populations." *Library Quarterly* 65, No. 1 (1995): 89-118.

Padmamma, S., et al. "Public Library Service for Women." *Indian Journal of Information and Library Science* 14, No. 3-4 (July-December 2001): 177-181.

___. "Children's Views on Public Library." *Indian Journal of Information, Library and Society* 14, No. 3-4 (July-December 2001): 167-171.

Palanivelu, C. and K. S. Raghavan. "Education through Public Libraries: A Practical Approach." Proceedings of the national seminar on Public Library Movement, Madras April 19-21, 1991.

Paliwal, P. K. *Compendium of Library Administration*. New Delhi: Ess Ess Publications, 2000.

Panda, B. D. *Handbook of Public Library System*. New Delhi: Anmol, 1993.

Pandey, S. K. Sharma. *Public Libraries in India*. New Delhi: Ess Ess Publications, 1985.

Panicker, P. N. "Library Movement in Kerala." *Herald of Library Science* 13, No. 3-4 (July-October 1974): 253-258.

Papp, Istvan. "The Mutual Influence of Information, Education and Recreation in Public Library Work." In *Public Library Policy*, edited by K. C. Harrison, 49. New York: K.G. Saur, 1981.

Pasilithil, A. "Keralathile Granthasalakalum Amature Nadakavedhiyum" (Malayalam). *Grandhalokam* 45, No. 5-6 (May-June 1993): 31-32, 34.

___. "The Kerala Granthasala Sanghom and its Socio-Cultural Contributions." PhD thesis, University of Kerala, 1992.

Pillai, A.K. *Kongressum Keralavum* (Malayalam). Kottayam: D.C. Books, 1986.

Poduval, A. K. "Vayanasala Prasthanam." In *Keralathile Granthasala Prasthanam* (Mal), edited by P. N. Panicker, 29-30. Trivandram: Steps, 1982.

Prabhatham, March 27, 1939

Priyadharshanan, G. "Malayalathile Aadhyathe Moonnu Pathrangal." In *Kerala Granthasala Sanghom Kannur Jilla Smaranika* (Malayalam), 27-33. Kannur: Granthasala Sanghom Advisory Committee, 1981.

Public Library Association (USA). *Minimum Standards for Public Library Systems, 1966*. Chicago: ALA, 1966.

Pungitore, Verne L. "Dissemination of the Public Library Planning Process among Smaller Libraries." *Library Quarterly* 62, No. 4 (October 1992): 375-407.

Rairappan, K.P.R. Interview by Investigator. Kalliassery, Kannur, 21 February 2001.

Raja Rammohun Roy Library Foundation, Kolkatta. "Eighth Plan Perspective of Public Library Development." All India conference, New Delhi, February 25-25, 1989. *Journal of Library and Information Science* 13, No. 2 (December 1988): 188-190.

___. *Twenty Eighth Annual Report, 1999-2000.*

Raju, A.A.N. "Constraints on the Public Library Services in Andhra Pradesh." *CLIS Observer* 7, Nos. 3-4 (1990): 69-72.

Ramachandra Rao, P. "The Significance of the Library Movement in Andhra, 1900-1948." *Library Herald* 20, No. 2-4 (July-March 1981): 151-158.

Ramachandran Nair, Adoor, K. K., ed. *Kerala District Gazetteers: Trivandram*. Trivandrum: State Editor, Kerala Gazetteers, 1986.

Ramaiah, L.S. "Public Libraries and Public Finances in India." *Herald of Library Science* 32, No. 3-4 (July-October 1993): 171-179.

Ramaiah, L.S. and Ramchander, M. "The information Divide: Need for Internet Kiosks in Indian Villages for Building the Gap." In *Vision of Future and Information Systems*, edited by Ashok Babu et al., 50-56. New Delhi: Viva Books, 2000.

Raman Nair, R. *People's Library Movement*. New Delhi: Concept, 2000.

___, ed. *Public Library Development*. New Delhi: Ess Ess Publications, 1993.

Raman Nair, Vettoor. "Keralathinu Oru Granthasalaniyamam." *Grandhalokam* 19, No. 1: 45-47.

Ramanujan Nair, P. "Strong Library Movement in Kerala." In *Trivandrum Public Library Platinum Jubilee Souvenir, 1974*, 111-115.

___. *Library Movement in Kerala*. Trivandrum: Writers Club, 1974.

Ramaraj Urs, R. "Survey of the Reading Habits of the Clientele of Public Library System of Rural District of Bangalore." *ILA Bulletin* 20, No. 1-2 (April- September 1984): 14-20.

Ramasamy, R. *Status of State Central Libraries in India: An Analytical Study*. Delhi: Gyan Publishing House, 2003.

Ranganathan, S. R. "Keralathile Granthalayaprasthana Vikasanathinu Chila Nirdesangal" (Malayalam). *Grandhalokam* 12, No. 9 (September 1960): 469-470, 504-5.

___. *Library Manual*. 2nd ed. New Delhi: UBSPD, 1988.

___. *Public Library System*. Bangalore: Sarada Ranganathan Endowment for Library Science, 1972.

Ranganathan S. R., et al., ed. *Free Book Service for All: An International Survey*. Bombay: Asia Publishing House, 1968.

Ranjith, K. S. *Rural Libraries of Kerala*. TVM: CDS, 2004.

Ravi, N., ed. "Library Movement in Madras." In *The Hindu Speaks on Libraries*, 3. Madras: Kasthuri and sons, 1992.

Ravinder Kumar Chadha. The Role of Public Libraries in India in this Age of Rapid Growth of Information Technology. *CLIS Observer* 18, No. 3 & 4 (July & December 2001): 84-88.

Ravindran, K. "Public libraries in India." In *Public Library System*, edited by C. A. Augustin and G. Devarajan, 1-7. New Delhi: Ess Ess Publications, 1990.

Rawat, P. P. et al., eds. *Current Development in Library and Information Science*. New Delhi: Reliance, 1998.

Richardson, Selma K. "Children's Services of Public Libraries in the US." *International Library Review* (1987): 15-24.

Rodger, Eleanor Jo et al. "Partnerships and Collaboration among Public Libraries, Public Broadcast Media, and Museums: Current Context and Future Potential." *Library Quarterly* 75, No. 1 (January 2005): 42-66, http.//www.journals. uchicago.edu/ LQ. Journal contents.

Sahib Singh Verma. "A Study of Public Libraries and Literacy Movement in India with Special Reference to Delhi, Haryana, and Rajasthan: A Research Report." *Library Herald* 39, No. 3 (September 2001): 187-190.

Saiful Islam, K. M. "Public Library Systems and Services." *Herald of Library Science* 29, No. 3-4 (1990): 163-171

Salma, Joel H. and Idris Mohammed Yelwa. "A Survey of Students' Attitudes towards Public Library Services: A Case Study of Central Library in Borno State of Nigeria." *International Library Movement*. 26, No. 2 (2004): 61-70.

Sarada, K. *Rural Library Services in India*. New Delhi: Ess Ess Publications, 1986.

___ "Community Information Services and Internet." In *Vision of Future Library and Information Systems*, edited by Ashok Babu et al, 26-29. New Delhi: Viva Books, 2000.

Sarantakos, S. *Social Research*. 2nd ed. London: Macmillan Press, 1998.

Satyanarayana, M. "Use of Public Library: A case of Deposit Holders of Visakhapatnam District Central Library." *Annals of Library Science and Documentation* 43, No. 3 (1996): 118-115.

___. *Public Library and Community Analysis*. New Delhi: Reliance Publishing House, 1997.

Seethapathy, R. K. "Collection Building in Public Libraries in Tamil Nadu: Problems and Prospects." In *Education through Public Libraries: A Practical Approach*. Proceedings of the national seminar on Public Library Movement, Madras, April 19-21, 1991, edited by C. Palanivelu and K. S. Raghavan, 142-150. Madras: Government of Madras, Directorate of Public Libraries, 1991.

Selma K. Richardson. Children's Services of Public Libraries in the United States. *International Library Review* 18 (1987): 15-24.

Serebnick, Judith and Frank Quinn. "Measuring Diversity of Opinion in Public Library Collections." *Library Quarterly* 65, No. 1 (1995): 1- 38.

Sewa Singh. "Public Library Development in Punjab." *Granthana* 2, No. 2 (July 1991), 147-154.

___. "The Crow's Nest: Public Relations in Libraries." International Library Movement. 10, No. 1 (1988): 7-13.

Sewny, Katherine W. "The Popular Image of the Library and the Librarian." *Library Journal* 85 (June 1960): 2089-2091.

Shankaran, Thayat. "Granthasala Prasthanam: Charithravum Sadhyathakalum." In *Vidhyabhyasam Noothandukalilude* (Malayalam), by Thayat Shankaran. Trissur: Kerala Sasthra Sahitya Parishath, 414-427.

___. "Granthasala Prasthanam: Paschathalavum Sadhyathakalum." In *Chintha Maydina Pathip* (Malayalam), 79-81. Trivandram: Chintha Publications, 1976.

Shantaram, G. M. "History of the Public Library Movement in Maharashtra, 1805-1921." *CLIS Observer* 2, No. 3-4 (July - October 1985): 22-24.

Shiva Kanaujia and Rochna Srivasthava. "Public Library Legislation in Changing Information Scenario." *Library Progress (International)* 23, No. 2 (2003): 107-110.

Shores, Louis. "The Future of References in American Society." *Wilson Library Bulletin*, 32, (December 1957): 286 -288.

Sinclair, Dorothy. *Administration of the Small Public Library*. Chicago: American Library Association, 1965.

Singh, R.S.P. "Public Library Movement in Bihar." *Granthana* 2, No. 2 (July1991): 193- 203.

Smith, Ester Gottlieb. "The Literacy Education Gap: The Involvement of Public Libraries in Literacy Education." *Library and Information Science Research* 6 (1984): 75-94.

Sonal Singh and Surendra Singh. "Role of Library in Literacy Mission and Continuing Education." *Indian Journal of Information, Library and Society* 14, No. 3 (July- December 2001): 172-176.

Spiller, David. "The Provision of Fiction for Public Libraries." *Journal of Librarianship* 12, No. 4 (October 1980): 239-264.

Sree Narayana Guru. In *Sree Narayana Guru Swantham Vachanangalilude*, edited by C. R. Keshavan Vaidyar, 124. Kottayam: DC Books, 1990.Orginally published in *Vivekodayam*, Makaram-Meenam (Malayalam months), 1912.

Sreedhara Menon, A. *A Cultural Heritage of Kerala*. 2nd ed. Madras: V. Subramanian, 1996.

___. *A Survey of Kerala History*. Rev. ed. Chennai: Ananda Book Depot, 1996.

___, ed., *Kerala District Gazetteers, Kozhikode*. Trivandrum: State Editor, Kerala Gazetteers, 1962.

Sreenidhi Iyengar, ed. *Organisation, Staffing, and Administration of Public Library*. New Delhi: Anmol, 1996

Stanffer, Suzanne M. "Polygamy and the Public Library: The Establishment of Public Libraries in Utah before 1910." *Library Quarterly* 75, No. 3 (July 2005): 346-70, *http://www.journals.uchicago.edu/LQ/journal/issues/V75n3/750305/ 750 305.html*.

Stevenson, Gordon. "The Public Library in a Communications Setting." *Library Quarterly* 48, No. 4 (October 1978): 401

Sule, Nathaniel N. et al. "The Contributions of Rural Library Services to Literacy Development in Nigeria: A Review of the Past Century and Prospect of the New Millennium." *Library Progress (International)* 23, No. 2 (2003): 133-141.

Sumsion et al. "The Economic Value of Book Borrowing from Public Libraries: An Optimisation Model." *Journal of Documentation* 58, No. 6 (2002), http:// *www.emeraldinsight.com.*

Sunil Kumar. "Rural Library and Community Resource Centers (RLCRCs) in India with Special Reference to States having Library Legislation: Problems and Prospects." *SRELS Journal of Information Management* 42, No. 3 (September 2005): 275-280.

Thomas, V. K. "Computerisation of Public Libraries in India." *CLIS observer* 18, No. 3 (July-December 2001): 92-98.

___. *Public Libraries in India: Development and Finance.* New Delhi: Vikas, 1997.

___. Computerisation of Public Libraries in India." *CLIS observer* 18, No. 3 (July-December 2001): 92-98.

Thozhilali Library and Reading Room, Chovva, Kannur. *Report of fiftieth annual meeting, 1982.*

Toffler, Alvin. *The Third Wave.* New York: William Morris, 1980.

Totterdell, Barry. "Public Libraries in a Changing Society." In *Public Library Policy,* edited by K. C. Harrison, 37- 42. New York: K.G. Saur, 1981.

Turner, Katherine and Margaret Kendall. "Public Use of the Internet at Chester Library, U.K." *Information Research* 5, No. 3 (April 2000), http:// information r.net/ir//5.3/paper 75.html.

United Kingdom. Department of Culture. Media and Sports. Libraries, Information, and Archives Division. *Library Standards. http:// www.culture.gov.uk/NR/rdonlyres/ .../o/ Librarystandard scons.pdf* (accessed May 25, 2004).

___. Board of Education. Public Libraries Committee. *Report on Public Libraries in England and Wales.* London: H. M. Stationery Office, 1927.

Udayabhanu, P. "Prasthanathinte Adiverukal." In *Keralathile Granthasala Prasthanam* Malayalam), edited by P. N. Panicker, 31-32. Trivandram: Steps, 1982.

UNESCO. *Bulletin for Libraries* (December 1966): 289.

___. *Report of the international seminar on Development of Public Libraries in Asia, Delhi, 6-26 October, 1955.*

___. Section of Public Libraries. The Role of Public Libraries in Life Long Learning: A Project. www. Ifla.org.

Uthara Kerala Granthalaya Sammelanam (Malayalam). *Mathrubhumi*, December 4, 1946, Kozhikode edition.

Van House, Nancy A. "Public Library Effectiveness: Theory, Measures, and Determinants." *Library Information Science Research* 8 (1986): 261-283.

Vang, Vang. 'Public Library Services to the Hmong-American Community: Much Room for Improvement." *IFLA Journal* 31, No. 4 (2005): 315-323.

Varalakshmi, R. S. R. "Open Learning and Public Libraries." *ILA Bulletin* XXVIII, Nos. 1& 2 (April - September 1992): 10-15.

Vashisth, C.P., ed. *Libraries as Rural Community Resource Centres*. Delhi: B.R. Publishing Corporation, 1995.

____, ed. "Library Movement and Library Development in India." Proceedings of thirty ninth all India conference, Bangalore, January 7-10, 1994. Delhi: ILA, 1994.

Velam Public Library, Kannur. Administrative Committee. "Velam Pothujana Vayanasala." In *Velam Pothujana Vayanasala Suvarna Jubilee Souvenir, 1984*. (Malayalam), 13-14.

Venkata Ramana, V, and E. A. Vinod Kumar. "Need Based Planning for Public Library Automation." Vol. 2 of *Public Library Systems, Services, and* Net*working*, edited by S. Ramaiah et al. 61-67. New Delhi: Ess Ess Publications, 1997.

Venkateswara Rao, L. "Opening School and College Libraries to Public." In *New Horizons in Library and Information Science*, edited by P. Vashisth et al., 371. Madras: T. R. Publications, 1974.

Verma, L. N. and U. K. Agarwal, ed. *Public Library Services in India*. Udaipur: Himanushu Publications, 1994.

Vijayakumar, M. and Kumar N. "Problems and Prospects of Rural Libraries." *SRELS Journal of Information Management*. 38, No. 2 (June 2001): 165-176.

Vijayan, M. N., ed. *Nammude Saahithyam, Nammude Samooham, 1901-2000* (Mal). Vol.2. Thrissur: Kerala Sahithya Academy, 2000.

Viswanathan, C. G. *Public Library Organisation*. 4th ed. New Delhi: Ess Ess Publications, 1990.

Ward, Benjamin Swain and Peter Eyre Connor. *A Descriptive Memoir of Malabar*. Trivandrum: State Editor, Kerala Gazetteers, 1995.

Wheeler, Joseph L. and Herbert Goldhor. *Practical Administration of Public Libraries*. New York: Harper and Row, 1962.

Wiele, Nic Van De. "Public Libraries." *Journal of Library and Information Science* 16, No. 1 (June 1991): 48-59.

Wigg, Ristina. "Across Towns and Across Times: Library Service to Young People in Rural Libraries." *Library Trends* 44, No.1 (Summer 1995): 88-111.

Williams, Patrick. "Double Fault: A Critique of Planning Process for Public Libraries." *Library Quarterly* 53, No. 4 (October 1983): 450.

Williamson, Kirsty. "Adoption of Outline Databases in Public Libraries: An Australian Case Study." *LIBRES (Library and Information Science Research Electronic Journal)* 13, No. 2 (September 2003), *http://libres.curtin.edu.au/libres 13n2*.

Wisker, Gina. *The Postgraduate Research Handbook*. New York: Palgrave, 2001.

INDEX